THE DIVE SITES OF
THAILAND

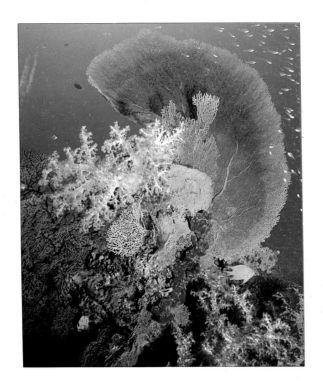

PAUL LEES

Series Consultant: Nick Hanna

Paul Lees is a highly experienced diving instructor who has taught at and managed several of Thailand's best diving schools.

This second edition published in the UK in 1999 by
New Holland Publishers (UK) Ltd
London • Cape Town • Sydney • Singapore

First published in 1995

24 Nutford Place	80 McKenzie Street	3/2 Aquatic Drive
London W1H 6DQ	Cape Town 8001	Frenchs Forest, NSW 2086
UK	South Africa	Australia

ISBN 1 85974 0561

Project development: Charlotte Parry-Crooke
Series editors: Charlotte Fox, Paul Barnett, Pete Duncan
Design concept: Philip Mann, ACE Ltd
Design/cartography: ML Design, William Smuts
Cover design: Peter Bosman
Index: Alex Corrin

Typeset by ML Design, London
Reproduction by Hirt and Carter, South Africa
Printed and bound in Singapore by Tien Wah Press (Pte) Ltd

10 9 8 7 6 5 4 3

Photographic Acknowledgements:
Apinan Buahapakdee 94; Ashley Boyd 1, 16, 19, 33, 55, 67, 79, 89, 91, 102, 111, 112, 119, 131, 137, 141, 145, 147, 149, 153, 155, 161 (2nd), 161 (5th), 162 (2nd), 162 (3rd); Jim Breakall 25; Matthew Burns 22; Gerald Cubitt 9, 12, 15, 72, 140, 150, 157; Abbie Enock 48; John Everingham 8, 47, 84; Footprints 13 (Haydn Jones), 70 (Nick Hanna) 122, 128 (Mark Graham), 132; Paul Lees 27 (top), 27 (bottom), 58, 65, 66, 77, 109, 113; Mongkol Kiatkanjanakul (Panorama Co. Ltd) 77 (bottom); Mark Strickland 2, 17, 23, 28, 33 (left), 34, 35, 37, 39, 40, 43, 45, 49, 51, 52, 57, 59, 63, 67, 71, 73, 75, 79 (top), 80, 81, 83, 85, 95, 101, 103, 107 (top), 107 (bottom), 117 (top), 117 (bottom), 123, 125, 129, 133, 135, 137, 145, 151, 153 (top), 155 (bottom), 159, 161 (1st), 161 (3rd), 161 (4th), 162 (1st), 162 (4th), 162 (5th); Lawson Wood 99.
Front cover: *Lush soft corals and iridescent gorgonians (Mark Strickland).*
Front cover inset: *Koh Samui (John Everingham).*
Spine: *Grouper (Mark Strickland).*
Back cover: *Diver and school of Bigeyes (Mark Strickland).*
Title page: *Reef garden with fan coral (Ashley Boyd).*
Contents page: *A cornucopia of diverse marine life awaits divers and snorkellers (Mark Strickland).*

AUTHOR'S ACKNOWLEDGEMENTS

Not enough thanks and admiration can be relayed to Pee Suphaphun 'Add' Phuangphetch for acting as guide, researcher, translator and trustworthy diving buddy in the Andaman Sea area. I would also like to express my sincere thanks to the following people:

- Adam, Marlene and Graham Frost of South East Asia Liveaboards, Phuket
- Mark Strickland and Suzanne Foreman
- Patrick Cotter of the Dive Inn, Phuket
- Ken Scott for his contributions of encouragement
- Khun Most and Ron 'Ling' Hoffman for their valuable assistance and support
- Heinz Oswald of Moskito Diving, Phi Phi
- Master Instructor Dave Wright for his valuable information on a number of local dive sites in Pattaya
- Chris Smart and Ryan Dowling of Samui International Diving School on Koh Tao
- Cesare Benelli, Lee Bright, Richard 'Jamie' MacLeod, Tamar Le Clue, and Mick and Tik Fay of Samui International Diving School, Koh Samui
- Enormous thanks to Tim Redford of Divelink Thailand, Bangkok, for arranging and co-ordinating virtually all the diving
- Ashley Boyd for his detailed site explanations
- Huw Cuckson of Planet Scuba
- A big thank you for all the support and encouragement from 'Young' Joy Menzies at the Barbican and Bulls Head, Bangkok
- Extra special thanks to Gavin Parsons of Sport Diver Magazine in London
- Michael Willcox and Nick Hanna for their tremendous support
- Alan Burgess, Terri Yamaka, and Mary-Lynn Ballaram, from the Tourism Authority of Thailand in London, for their help with the Regional Directories
- Judy Fellor at Thai International Airways in London for assisting with flights
- Jackie, Claude, Mark, Angela, Daniel and Emma Lees, Stan and Nell West
- Garth Wynn of Hertz UK
- U. Aung Kyi, the best guide in Myanmar
- Del Hunter for his photography tips
- Khun Sumalee Chaitientong at Bangkok Airways
- Novotel Phuket Resort
- Chia Ai Lian at Chanpen Vimolchaichit at Novotel Bangkok on Siam Square

PUBLISHERS' ACKNOWLEDGEMENTS

The publishers gratefully acknowledge the assistance of Nick Hanna for his involvement in developing the series, Dr Elizabeth M. Wood for acting as Marine Biological Consultant and Jim Breakall of Scuba Safaris.

CONTENTS

How to use this Book

THE REGIONS

The dive site areas included in the book are divided between the Andaman Sea and the Gulf of Thailand. Regional introductions describe the key characteristics and features of these areas and provide background information on climate, the environment, points of interest, and advantages and disadvantages of diving in the locality.

THE MAPS

A map is included near the front of each regional or subregional section. The prime purpose of the maps is to identify the location of the dive sites described and to provide other useful information for divers and snorkellers. Though certain reefs are indicated, the maps do not set out to provide detailed nautical information such as exact reef contours or water depths. In general the maps show: the locations of the dive sites, indicated by white numbers in red boxes corresponding to those placed at the start of the individual dive site descriptions; the locations of key access points to the sites (ports, marinas, beach resorts and so on); reefs and wrecks. The site description gives details of how to access the dive site. (Note: the border around the maps is not a scale bar.)

MAP LEGEND

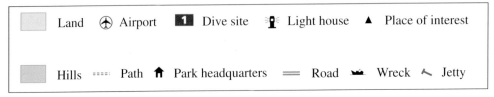

| Land | ⊕ Airport | ▮1 Dive site | ⚑ Light house | ▲ Place of interest |
| Hills | ⋯⋯ Path | ♠ Park headquarters | ═ Road | ⚓ Wreck | ⟍ Jetty |

THE DIVE SITE DESCRIPTIONS

Placed within the geographical sections are the descriptions of each region's premier dive sites. Each site description starts with a number (to enable the site to be located on the relevant map), a star rating (see opposite), and a selection of key symbols (see opposite). Crucial practical details (on location, access, conditions, typical visibility and minimum and maximum depths) precede the description of the site, its marine life and special points of interest. In these entries, 'typical visibility' assumes good conditions.

THE STAR RATING SYSTEM

Each site has been awarded a star rating, with a maximum of five red stars for diving and five blue stars for snorkelling.

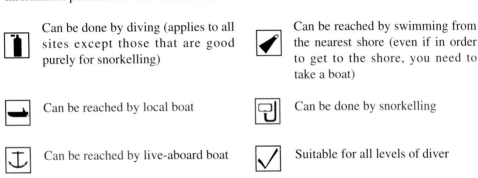

Diving		*Snorkelling*	
★★★★★	**first class**	☆☆☆☆☆	**first class**
★★★★	highly recommended	☆☆☆☆	highly recommended
★★★	good	☆☆☆	good
★★	average	☆☆	average
★	poor	☆	poor

THE SYMBOLS

The symbols placed at the start of each site description provide a quick reference to crucial information pertinent to individual sites.

Can be done by diving (applies to all sites except those that are good purely for snorkelling)

Can be reached by swimming from the nearest shore (even if in order to get to the shore, you need to take a boat)

Can be reached by local boat

Can be done by snorkelling

Can be reached by live-aboard boat

Suitable for all levels of diver

THE REGIONAL DIRECTORIES

A 'regional directory', which will help you plan and make the most of your trip, is included at the end of each regional section. Here you will find, where relevant, practical information on how to get to an area, where to stay and eat and available dive facilities. Local 'non-diving' highlights are also described, with suggestions for sightseeing and excursions.

OTHER FEATURES

At the start of the book you will find practical details and tips about travelling to and in Thailand, as well as a general introduction to the country itself. Also provided is a wealth of information about the general principles and conditions of diving in the area. Throughout the book, features and small fact panels on topics of interest to divers and snorkellers are included. At the end of the book are sections on the marine environment (including coverage of marine life, conservation and codes of practice) and underwater photography and video. Also to be found here is information on health, safety and first aid as well as a guide to marine creatures to look out for when diving in Thailand.

INTRODUCTION
TO THAILAND

At the heart of Southeast Asia, Thailand is an independent kingdom which combines 20th-century sophistication with an ancient culture that has evolved over the past 700 years. Covering just over 500,000 sq km (190,500 sq miles) it is bordered by Malaysia to the south, Myanmar (formerly Burma) to the west, Laos to the north and Kampuchea to the east. It is unique amongst Southeast Asian nations in that it has never been occupied by a foreign colonial power, and has maintained a cohesive sense of national identity and traditional culture.

TOURISM
With over five million annual visitors, Thailand is one of the most popular tourist destinations in Asia. It has an enormous amount to offer, from ancient temples to rainforests and remote islands with palm-fringed beaches - and, of course, coral reefs teeming with life for divers and snorkellers. Tourism is an important part of the service economy. The country's rapid development in recent years has brought with it all the usual problems, such as infrastructure bottlenecks, environmental degradation and increased social pressures. Despite a spectacular economic growth, the majority of the population still earn their living from farming, with rice being the main crop.

BANGKOK AND THE REGIONS OF THAILAND
The population of Thailand is around 60 million, with approximately 10 million people living in the capital, Bangkok. This massive, vibrant, traffic-bound city dominates the country's central region and functions as the cultural, religious, economic and political centre of the country.

Thailand is divided into four distinct regions: the mountainous north, the vast northeast plateau, the central plains, and the narrow Isthmus of Kra to the south, stretching down to the border with Malaysia.

Once covered in teakwood forests, the mountainous northern region appeals to the

Opposite: *One of many glorious beaches of Koh Samui.*
Above: *Thai festivals are traditionally celebrated with the 'Dance of the Long Drum'.*

adventurous traveller, with one of the main attractions being the prospect of trekking through remote - and not so remote - villages inhabited by a diversity of tribal peoples. The main focal point for the region is the growing centre of Chiang Mai, Thailand's 'second' city.

ISAN

Separated from Laos by the Mekong River, the northeast plateau is dominated by agriculture (rice, fruit and vegetables) and is one of the poorest regions in the country. Known as Isan, this region has a distinct culture and dialect (reflecting its proximity to Laos), and although it is the least developed area in Thailand it is an interesting area to visit, with ancient stone temples dating back almost 10 centuries. It is growing in importance as the gateway to the newly reopened destination of Laos.

The central plains are another important rice-growing area, and, although most visitors tend to pass them by on their way further north, there are ancient cities, such as Ayutthaya and Sukhothai, which repay exploration.

IDYLLIC ISLANDS

It is the islands and beaches of southern Thailand which hold the greatest appeal for tourists, and, whether you're looking for solitude or sophisticated nightlife, there is plenty of choice. The Andaman coastline, to the west of the Kra Isthmus, boasts fabulous scenery and dazzling beaches. The largest and best-known of the island destinations here is Koh Phuket, which has been attracting tourists for a number of years and is now in danger of becoming over-developed as high-rise hotels appear inexorably above the palm trees. Further south, the beautiful Koh Phi Phi and Krabi (on the mainland) are still mostly geared to independent travellers, while the more remote Koh Lanta is just beginning to be opened up to tourism.

THE GULF OF THAILAND

In the Gulf of Thailand, on the other side of the Kra Isthmus, the best-known destination is the island of Koh Samui; other islands within the Samui Archipelago, such as Koh Phangan and Koh Tao, are also popular. To the east of Bangkok, the beach resort of Pattaya bears little resemblance to the real Thailand and has a notorious reputation, but further east still there are several virtually untouched islands awaiting the adventurous traveller - Koh Chang, for instance, which is the country's second largest island offers miles of beaches and unexplored forest.

FACT FILE

Area
513,115 sq km (198,446 sq miles)
Population
60 million
Language
Thai (though English is spoken in cities and tourist locations)
Religion
Over 90% Theravada Buddhist, approximately 7% Muslim, 3% others

---

CULTURE AND ETIQUETTE

According to Hindu belief (and as adopted by the Thais), the head is the holiest part of the body and the feet are the least holiest/most unclean. It is very important, therefore, never to touch anyone's head (don't pat children, for example), and it is considered extremely rude to point your feet at anyone, and especially at a sacred image. Always sit cross-legged in temples, and never stretch your feet out towards the Buddha. The worst possible insult is to place your feet higher than anyone's head.

Modest clothing (long trousers and, to cover the arms, a long-sleeved shirt) should be worn when visiting temples. Shoes should always be removed in temples and private homes — they are considered even more unclean than bare feet.

Dress modestly in public places: despite the liberal values of the Thai sex industry, most Thais find bare flesh offensive, and such attire as shorts and singlets should really be worn only in the major resorts. If you show respect by wearing long trousers in places such as Bangkok you are more likely to be treated with respect yourself.

Thais also find topless and nude bathing distasteful - they often bathe fully clothed - and, although topless bathing is the norm at some beach resorts, if you are in any doubt it is safer to wear a swimming costume and avoid causing offence.

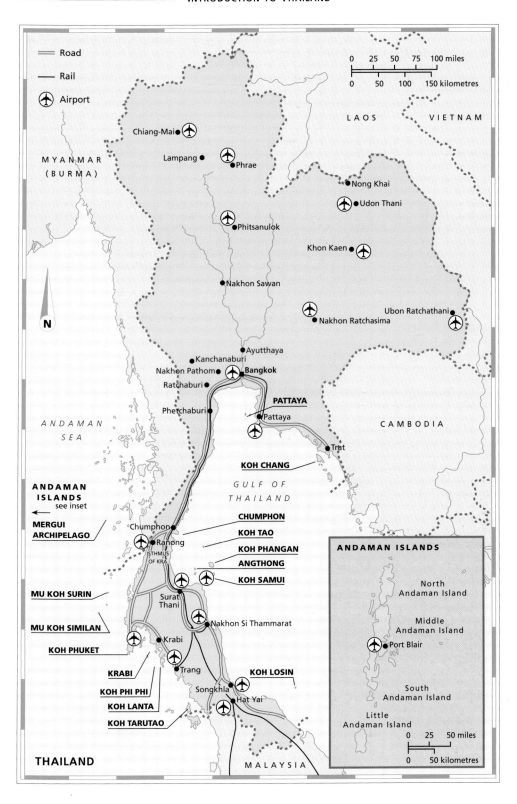

Road
Rail
Airport

100 miles
150 kilometres

LAOS   VIETNAM

Chiang-Mai

MYANMAR
(BURMA)

Lampang
Phrae

Nong Khai
Udon Thani

Phitsanulok

Khon Kaen

N

Nakhon Sawan

Ubon Ratchathani
Nakhon Ratchasima

Ayutthaya
Kanchanaburi
Nakhon Pathom   Bangkok
Ratchaburi

PATTAYA

Phetchaburi   Pattaya

CAMBODIA

ANDAMAN
SEA

Trat

KOH CHANG

ANDAMAN
ISLANDS
see inset

GULF OF
THAILAND

MERGUI
ARCHIPELAGO

CHUMPHON

Chumphon   KOH TAO
Ranong
ISTHMUS
OF KRA   KOH PHANGAN
ANGTHONG

MU KOH SURIN

KOH SAMUI

Surat
Thani

MU KOH SIMILAN

Nakhon Si Thammarat

KOH PHUKET   Krabi

KRABI   Trang   KOH LOSIN

KOH PHI PHI   Songkhla
KOH LANTA   Hat Yai
KOH TARUTAO

THAILAND

MALAYSIA

ANDAMAN ISLANDS

North
Andaman Island

Middle
Andaman Island

Port Blair

South
Andaman Island

Little
Andaman Island

0   25   50 miles

0   50 kilometres

TRAVELLING TO AND AROUND THAILAND

There is little difficulty involved in reaching Thailand: more than 50 international airlines serve the country. Daily direct flights to Bangkok depart from most major cities in Europe, the USA and Australia, and there are also frequent flights from other countries in Southeast Asia. You can drive into Thailand from Malaysia and Laos - the latter journey takes you over the famous Thai-Laos Friendship Bridge across the Mekong, at Nong Khai. Note that you cannot drive into Thailand from Myanmar (Burma).

If you are coming into the country from Singapore or Malaysia - and if you have a great deal of money to spare - you might decide to make the 34hr journey on the luxurious Eastern and Oriental Express, sister to the famous Orient Express.

VISAS

People of most nationalities can obtain free visas on arrival at Bangkok International airport and other entry points; these are valid for 30 days, and will be issued only if you have a current passport and ticket to take you out of the country at the end of your stay. Longer-stay visas are available, for a fee, from Thai embassies and consulates around the world: specify whether you want a transit visa (valid for 30 days), a tourist visa (valid for 60 days) or a non-immigrant visa (valid for 90 days and difficult to obtain). If you have a tourist visa you can, once you are in Thailand, apply for it to be extended by 30 days. If you plan to leave Thailand temporarily during your stay, you must obtain a re-entry visa, available from the Immigration Department in Bangkok.

CUSTOMS

Customs are usually no trouble, unless you happen to be carrying pornography, firearms, very large amounts of cash (over $10,000), or illicit drugs - for possession of which the penalties can be draconian. The allowances for the usual luxury goods - perfume, alcohol and the like - can vary, so check them before departure. Please note that you are required to bring a minimum amount of currency into the country which varies depending on your visa.

Opposite: *Fishing boats are sometimes used as house removal vessels.*
Above: *Squadrons of Songthaews (local taxis) transport tourists to their destinations.*

GETTING AROUND

Thailand has a good rail service: the fares are inexpensive, timetables are usually adhered to, and the trains themselves are comfortable and clean – with four classes – so that you can choose between economy and air-conditioned luxury. One pitfall to avoid is that of not booking early enough: on the trunk routes you should book at least a month in advance. The main railway station serving the southern destinations in Bangkok is Hualampong.

Long-distance buses are a cheaper alternative, but you take your life in your hands if you travel on one of these: the driving is often atrocious. If you decide to risk it, opt for an air-conditioned service: the comparatively small cost difference is worth it. In more remote areas you may be able to go to the opposite extreme - from air-conditioning to just plain air - by travelling on a songthaew. This is essentially a pickup truck with a couple of wooden benches in the back. Songthaews travel on fixed routes, like buses, and are very cheap.

Taxis, tuk tuks (three-wheeled scooters) and pedal-tricycles operate in most parts of Thailand. You use these much as you would use a taxi at home, except that the latter require you to negotiate a price before setting off - and remember to bargain. Do note that in many areas the drivers may not speak English, so, to avoid confusion, get your hotel receptionist to write down your destination in Thai so that you can show it to the driver. Ask at your hotel what a reasonable fare to the destination might be.

For most of the longer distances, however, air travel is the easiest option and not prohibitively expensive. Thai Airways International has an extensive network; Bangkok Airways has a much smaller one but serves some destinations that Thai Airways International does not, notably Koh Samui and Ranong.

MONEY

The unit of currency is the Thai Baht, which comprises 100 satang. All major credit cards are widely accepted. If you prefer travellers' cheques, it is advisable to obtain them in either Sterling or US dollars. Currency exchange can be done either at banks or, in the major tourist areas, at currency exchange counters. Daily exchange rates are published in two newspapers – the Bangkok Post and the Nation. The larger hotels will also change money, but usually give a poor rate of exchange.

KEY FACTS

Electricity
The supply is 220v AC 50Hz. Two-pin plugs with either round or flat pins are used, so you should take an adaptor

Mean temperatures
Air: 30-40°C (86-104°F)
Sea: 27-31°C (81-88°F)

Time zone
GMT + 7hr

Clothing
Lightweight clothes are suitable. Long trousers guard ankles from mosquito bites during the evenings and are strongly recommended. Lightweight waterproofs are a good idea for long dive-boat journeys

Diving agencies
Mainly PADI, but some NAUI and one BSAC and IANTD

Diving gear
Included in the price of diving courses on some dive trips; the larger dive centres all provide a full rental service

---

LOCAL DIALLING CODES

- Bangkok: 02
- Koh Samui: 077
- Koh Phuket: 076
- Krabi: 075
- Pattaya: 038
- Koh Chang: 039
- Chumphon: 077

Most of the smaller islands have mobile phone numbers and are not at present on any of the local direct exchanges.

THE NATIONAL PARKS OF THAILAND

Thailand's National Parks form part of the country's heritage. There are presently 74 of them, evenly distributed throughout the kingdom, covering an area of more than 38,695 sq km (15,115 sq miles). The Parks encompass every type of topography found in Thailand, from mountain scenery in the north to coastal mangroves in the south. They are ideal places for the visitor to enjoy the vast variety of protected Thai flora and fauna: everything from wild orchids and waterfalls to butterflies and tigers.

HEALTH

No particular vaccinations or inoculations are officially required before you enter the country, unless you do so from some area where an infection is rife: check your route with your local consulate or embassy in case there are any necessary innoculations.

However, there are some injections you should certainly have before leaving for Thailand, and you should visit your GP about these well beforehand. Ask to be protected against hepatitis A and B, tetanus, malaria and typhoid.

Once you are in Thailand, do not drink tap water. Venereal diseases - notably AIDS - are extremely prevalent so avoid casual liaisons. Rabies is likewise: if bitten by any animal, seek medical attention immediately. The standard of medical services in Thailand is generally high - certainly in Bangkok and other big cities and in the major tourist centres. **A note of warning**: even if you take anti-malarial tablets before travelling it is still possible to contract malaria so if you feel feverish when you return home contact your GP immediately and have a check-up.

TOURIST OFFICES

The Tourism Authority of Thailand (TAT) maintains 12 regional offices in the country and several in overseas cities. Regional branches are open 08.30-16.30 daily.

Head office
Ratchadamnoen Nok Avenue, Bangkok 10100. Tel 02 282 1143

Australia
12th Floor, Royal Exchange Building, 56 Pitt Street, Sydney 2000.
Tel 02 247 7549

UK
49 Albemarle Street, London W1X 3FE.
Tel 0171 499 7679

USA
5 World Trade Centre, Suite #3443, New York, NY 10048.
Tel 212 432 0435

Tourists arrive at Koh Wuatalab, Ang Thong Marine National Park.

DIVING AND SNORKELLING IN AND AROUND THAILAND

Thailand has much to offer the visiting diver and snorkeller. There is a vast range of exhilarating sites of many different kinds, providing something for everyone, regardless of their qualification levels or experience. With over 2000km (1250 miles) of coastline and hundreds of offshore islands the variety is phenomenal, encompassing everything from extensive fringing reefs to deep dropoffs, dramatic granite walls, caves and tunnels, coral-covered pinnacles, and seamounts in the open ocean. Spectacular hard and soft corals abound, and the marine life is prolific, ranging from minute and colourful reef dwellers to Manta Rays, sharks and pelagic visitors such as Giant Barracuda, tuna, trevally and the mighty Whale Shark.

With the Andaman Sea to the west and the Gulf of Thailand to the east, Thailand is unique in that it borders two distinct oceanic zones, each with their own peculiarities and marine life. Many dive sites all around the coast share common species, but on others the underwater terrain and reef communities show marked differences between the two sides of the peninsula's coastline. Each side has its own distinct diving season.

Extending from Myanmar down past the west coast of Thailand to beyond the Malaysian border, the **Andaman Sea** forms part of the Indian Ocean. Many of the 155 islands in the Andaman Sea are uninhabited (apart from communities of Chao Ley - 'sea gypsies'), and are crowned by lush primary vegetation tumbling down to a shoreline punctuated by idyllic sandy beaches. Most of the diving in this region is organized from the popular holiday destination of **Koh Phuket**, with a wide variety of operators offering training, day trips, and live-aboard options. The best time for diving is between October and May.

In general the Andaman Sea has more extensive coral reefs and better visibility than the Gulf of Thailand, with most of the reefs around the offshore islands occurring on the east sides of the islands, due to the influence of the southwest monsoon; the west coasts tend to have rocky slopes descending to 10-30m (33-100ft) in depth. Towards the northern end of the Thai coastline, a series of granitic outcrops lie in deep, clear water with reefs descending to 25-30m (80-100ft) and beyond in depth. These are the **Similan** and **Surin**

Opposite: *Barrel sponges (Petrosia sp.) are found on the majority of Thai reefs.*
Above: *The Purple flame goby (Nemateleotris decora) is found in Thailand's deeper waters.*

Islands, whose breathtaking underwater scenery and great diversity of marine life have gained them a considerable reputation in the diving community. Given their proximity to Koh Phuket, it is not surprising that these two island groups are among the country's most popular destinations for live-aboard trips.

Further to the north is the recently opened **Mergui Archipelago**, projecting across territorial waters from Myanmar into Thailand, and offering real wilderness diving over unusual underwater terrain, with shark encounters guaranteed. Beyond the watery borderline with Indian territory, the **Andaman Islands** present another frontier for Koh Phuket live-aboards - although current Indian government restrictions on access mean that it cannot be guaranteed that these remote and interesting islands can be dived from Thailand.

The coastline of **Koh Phuket** itself offers little for the experienced diver, although there are dive sites that can be (and are) used for training and which serve as a last resort during the off-season if bad weather prevents boats getting to the better sites. These offshore sites are all to the south, and can be reached by relatively short boat rides of between one and two hours. They are all well worth the journey, but two in particular (Shark Point and Anemone Reef) stand out as being special in terms of the abundance of marine life.

Further south, the coastline at **Krabi** offers shallow fringing reefs around impressive limestone formations (ranging in size from underwater pillars to whole islands). Some of the best snorkelling sites in the country are to be found here. Offshore, the **Phi Phi islands**, with their palm-fringed beaches, have been growing in popularity as a dive base, with good visibility and a good variety of coral and fish; shallow fringing and patch reefs are an added attraction for snorkellers.

The most southerly dive sites in the country are around **Koh Lanta**. They feature pristine corals and spectacular fringing reefs in potentially excellent visibility. Here are some of the finest dive sites in the country, such as Hin Mouang, which features the deepest drop-off in Thailand, with depths in excess of 70m (230ft), and Hin Daeng, one of the few dive sites where schooling Grey Reef Sharks are seen. The coastal waters of Koh Lipong remain one of the very few places where endangered Dugong can be seen in their natural habitat.

Another new dive destination in the Andaman Sea which is currently being surveyed

---

RENTING EQUIPMENT

Faulty or unfamiliar equipment adds to the risks of scuba diving. When you rent equipment, check the following:

Buoyancy Control Device (BCD)
- Select the correct size. The last thing you want is a BCD that restricts your breathing because it is too tight. Conversely, if it is too large, you may feel you are about to slip out of it.
- Select a style or make that you are familiar with and take into consideration belts, buckles and fastenings.
- Check there are no leaks.
- Ensure that the low-pressure inflator connector is securely tightened.
- Ensure that both the deflator and power inflator buttons function correctly and do not stick.

Mask
- Ensure the mask fits correctly and does not leak.
- Check the skirt for damage or tears.
- Check the strap for signs of wear and tear. Bear in mind that if you lose the mask you might be asked to pay for it.
- Don't be afraid to ask for an optical mask if required: some of the larger operators carry a wide selection of prescription lenses.

Regulators
- Check ease of breathing through both regulators.
- Ensure regulator mouthpieces are in good condition and that the bite lobes are okay.
- Purge regulator before putting it in your mouth - in the tropics, you never know what might have crawled inside!
- Check the pressure gauge, and satisfy yourself that it does not stick.

Fins and booties
- Be careful to get the size right: too small can result in cramp, too large and they may fall off.

is **Mu Koh Tarutao Marine National Park** (just north of the Malaysian border), where Dugongs have also been seen.

The **Gulf of Thailand** coast, at 1840km (1150 miles) well over twice as long as the Andaman Sea coastline, follows a great parabola from the border with Malaysia on the south coast around to Kampuchea and the southwest tip of Vietnam. The Gulf itself is a vast, shallow depression - generally less than 60m (200ft) deep and reaching a maximum of 85m (280ft) - which, while incredibly productive, does not have great visibility or extensive corals. This is largely due to the turbid waters from river outlets being trapped in the Gulf by an underwater shelf that stretches across the mouth of the Gulf from Malaysia to Vietnam. True reefs do not occur further north than Chumphon, 480km (300 miles) south of Bangkok.

There are 112 islands in the offshore waters of the Gulf, many with fringing reefs interspersed with rocks and soft seabed. Visibility around their shorelines tends to be better than in the Gulf as a whole, where inshore waters are affected not only by turbidity but by freshwater runoff and urban/industrial pollution. The offshore reefs have a lower diversity than the reefs of the Andaman Sea, but marine life is still reasonably prolific, with Indo-Pacific species predominating.

The closest good diving and snorkelling to Bangkok is in **Chumphon** Province.

Thailand is renowned for its spectacular corals.

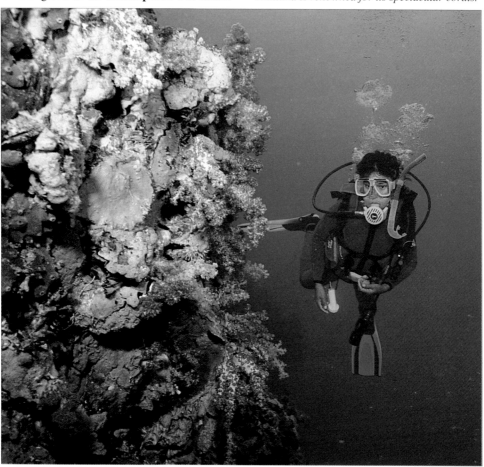

Inshore reefs have been subject to typhoon damage (1988), tourism and anchor damage, but there are plenty of good dive sites on the fringing reefs around rocky outcrops and islets offshore. Divers and snorkellers will find radiant hard and soft corals, colourful schools of reef fish and an exciting selection of visiting pelagics, including Giant Barracuda and Whale Sharks (the latter are regularly sighted around Hin Lak Ngam).

Some of the best dive sites in Thailand can be found in the Gulf of Thailand around **Koh Tao**, 80km (50 miles) from the mainland. Sheer wall dives around submerged pinnacles, tunnels and archways carpeted with iridescent soft corals, pelagics (including sharks), and easy snorkelling from the beaches over impressive coral gardens are just some of the highlights of Koh Tao.

Koh Phangan, 47km (30 miles) to the south of Koh Tao, is a Bohemian paradise. The fringing reefs around the island are limited in their appeal, but two sites to the north - Sail Rock and Samran Pinnacles - are truly world-class, spectacular wall dives which act as a magnet for numerous schools of pelagics.

Koh Samui, adjoining Koh Phangan, has a well developed tourist infrastructure (including several dive operators) and some enjoyable dive sites on its fringing reef - including one of the only beach dives in the country which you can do independently. Visibility on Koh Samui is only slightly better than that around Koh Phangan, and most people use it as a convenient (and fun) base from which to dive sites to the north of Koh Phangan or around Koh Tao. Further to the south, the clear waters around Koh Losin, located above the Malaysian border, are currently opening up for live-aboard excursions.

Working eastwards from Bangkok, **Pattaya** has a well developed dive industry. The better dive sites here are located on the outer islands, where there are also secluded beaches with shallow patch corals for snorkellers. There are also two well known wreck dives. Thailand's easternmost diving and snorkelling area - around **Koh Chang**, in Trat province - is still relatively undived.

DIVING SEASONS

The weather on either side of the Kra Isthmus and diving conditions in the Andaman Sea and the Gulf of Thailand are dominated by two opposing monsoons, the northeast and southwest monsoons. The northeast monsoon sweeps across the Gulf of Thailand between November and April, bringing heavy rain and strong winds - most dive sites become inaccessible, but even those that can be reached are likely to suffer from strong currents and reduced visibility. It is during this period that all the tourists and divers switch, as if by magic, to the west coast. Those foolhardy enough to stay on in the Gulf during the monsoon will find themselves on nearly empty beaches, hoping for a ray of sun to appear from behind the rainclouds. An anomaly is that the easternmost diving regions in Trat province remain sheltered during this period.

The Andaman Sea is sheltered from the worst effects of the northeast monsoon, and diving and snorkelling is at its best from November to April. Underwater visibility ranges from 5m to 30m (16-100ft) or more during this period. From May to October the southwest monsoon strikes this region, bringing in its wake towering seas and strong currents and increased turbidity.

TSCWA

The Thai Society for the Conservation of Wild Animals looks after the upkeep of the country's wildlife, especially those listed as endangered species. Animals such as tigers and bears formerly abused as domestic showpieces have been rescued and nursed back to health. TSCWA deal with marine life issues as well. They hold regular environmental marine awareness days, which are both educational and popular with divers.

TSCWA: 32 Pratum Court, 85/3-8 Soi Rajaprarop, Makkasan, Bangkok 10400, Thailand
tel 02 732 7617, 248 0405
fax 02 248 1490
email: tscwa@ibm.net

Conversely, the dive sites in the Gulf of Thailand are at their best during this season, with only minimal winds and light showers to disturb the tranquillity of the beaches and seas. Visibility can sometimes (though far from always) equal that of the Andaman Sea during this period. There are always dive sites on either side of the Isthmus that are sheltered enough to be dived whatever the weather so, if you find yourself in the wrong place at the wrong time, don't despair!

Water temperatures in Thailand range from 27°C (75°F) to 31°C (88°F). A thin wetsuit or lycra suit is recommended, not simply for protection from exposure but also as a barrier to marine hazards such as stinging cells. Oceanic sites (such as the Similans or the Burma Banks) are subject to sudden cold currents or thermoclines which can chill the water by up to 10C°(18F°) and, although these temperature dips are localized, most divers still prefer to don 3-4mm wetsuits for thermal protection.

DIVE OPERATORS

There are many top-notch dive centres in both the Andaman Sea and the Gulf of Thailand, with a number of PADI Five Star centres in the country. PADI is the main certification agency, closely followed by NAUI; there is one BSAC Premier School and three IANTD centres. Entry-level courses through to instructor programmes and specialities like cave diving and underwater photography are widely available.

Most of the larger and better-established dive operators maintain their equipment to high standards, with a good selection of sizes. BCDs, masks, fins and regulator and pressure consoles are obtainable everywhere, however, wetsuits, diving computers and underwater cameras are not so easy to find.

DIVELINK THAILAND

This is the first diving consultancy service covering the entire country, and it's free. Divelink Thailand's extensive knowledge covers diving services and sites throughout Thailand whilst other operators tend only to provide information on the area in which they are located.

Daily and short duration dive trips as well as live-aboard excursions can all be suggested, with relevant recommendations regarding where and when to dive based on seasons, tides, experience levels, personal choice, budget and available time. Divelink Thailand also act as booking agents for foremost dive operators in Thailand.

For those wishing instruction there is a database of highly experienced instructors capable of teaching the entire range of diving courses in a number of languages, with the choice of completing your course at any diving area in the country. Last but not least, there is an extensive library of marine publications, slides and photographs available.

Divelink Thailand
PO Box 53, Santisuk Post Office,
Bangkok 10113, Thailand
tel/fax 02 392 2267
homepage:
http://www.geocities.com/TheTropics/2315
email: divelinkthailand@hotmail.com

BANGKOK DIVE SHOPS

Divemaster
A good diving shop with an extensive stock for retail.
Divemaster also offers trips on board its own luxurious live-aboard boat.
Diving instruction is available under both the PADI and NAUI systems.

Divemaster, 110/63 Lardprao Soi 18,
Lardprao, Bangkok 10900
tel 02 512 1664; fax 02 512 4889
email: divemstr@ksc9.th.com
http://www.sino.net/divemaster

Planet Scuba/Wild Planet
(PADI 5-star IDC Center)
Planet Scuba's fine retail outlet features established brands such as Mares, Tusa and Coltri-Sub.
The full range of PADI dive courses including Instructor is available in a variety of languages.

Planet Scuba/Wild Planet, 9 Sukhumvit 55 Soi 25, Prakanong, Bangkok 10110
tel 02 712 8407; tel/fax 02 391 2083
email: info@wild-planet.co.th
http://www.wild-planet.co.th

Sport Time
Another diving shop with a good selection for retail.
Sport Time has associated instructors offering courses following the PADI and NAUI systems.

Sport Time
39 Sukhumvit Soi 40, Bangkok 10110
Thailand
tel 02 712 1535-8
fax 02 391 3386

KOH PHUKET

The largest island in Thailand, Koh Phuket is the second most developed (after Pattaya) of the country's tourist destinations. The island is separated from the mainland by a narrow bridged strait.

The island's west and south coastlines are liberally sprinkled with beaches, many of them long, curving arcs of golden sand with mounds of boulders separating them from the neighbouring beaches.

The number of tourists – and the ubiquitous high rise hotels – has shot up on Koh Phuket over the last decade or so, and many parts of the island are a far cry from the palm-fringed paradise portrayed in the travel brochures. On the positive side, there is a huge choice of accommodation ranging from superbly-designed deluxe hotels to moderately-priced guest houses.

With an international airport and good transport links to the rest of Thailand, Phuket also makes a good base for exploring further afield or as the jumping-off point for destinations further south such as Krabi, Koh Phi Phi and Koh Lanta.

DIVING AROUND PHUKET

Koh Phuket is the largest dive centre in Thailand and the main base for live-aboards heading for destinations in the Andaman Sea.

Boats are also kept busy ferrying divers backwards and forwards to the local dive sites around Phuket. There are very few good dive sites around the immediate coastline of Phuket Island itself, since the marine life and visibility have been heavily affected by off-shore tin-dredging operations. However, I have included two sites simply because they can be accessed in just a few minutes directly from the shore, and at least you'll be able to find somewhere to snorkel without getting on a boat.

Conditions improve considerably around the outcrops, islets and islands off the south of Koh Phuket, since the currents here carry away algae and silt and the corals have more chance of flourishing. The reefs are generally in a healthy condition with good hard corals

Opposite: *The coastline of Koh Phuket is endowed with superb beaches.*
Above: *This filter feeding crinoid (Oxycomanthus bennetti) frequents areas of perpetual current.*

as well as colourful soft corals. Marine life is plentiful, with visits from large pelagics sometimes adding spice to the diving. Some sites are quite deep with ripping currents often present, but there are plenty of other locations suitable for all levels of diver.

1 MERIDIAN REEF

★★

Location: A shallow reef following the shoreline north from the Meridian Hotel Beach, between Patong and Karon Beaches.

Access: Enter from the beach and simply follow the headland north, or go by Longtail (about 5min).

Conditions: Visibility is poor, averaging 6m (20ft); at its best it reaches 12m (40ft). Currents are weak to moderate.

Average depth: 7m (23ft)

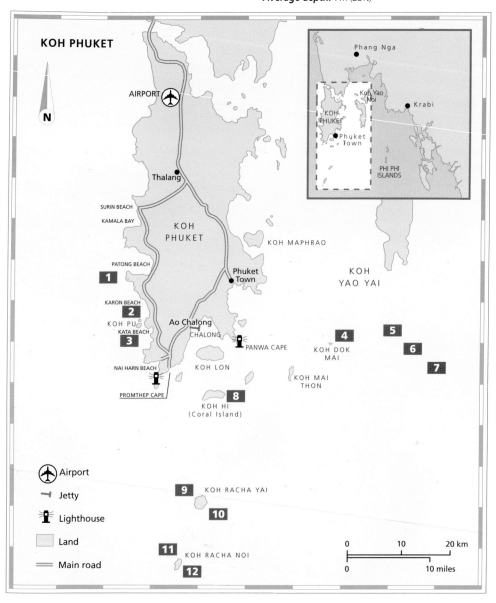

Maximum depth: 18m (86ft)

This site has comparatively few hard and soft corals and fish-life is only sporadically present – although you might discover a Blue-spotted Ribbontail Ray beneath one of the rocks, and very occasionally you might encounter a small Whitetip Reef Shark. Snorkellers can have more fun, following the fringing reef and seeing whatever there is to see. However, all these disadvantages make the site a very good one for training or for introducing new divers to scuba: students can concentrate on learning to dive, without their attention being distracted by deep waters, strong currents or too many fish!

2 KATA HOUSE REEF

★★

Location: Around the headland at the western end of Kata Beach and through the narrow strait between Koh Phuket and Koh Pu.

Access: Enter the water from the beach or take a 5min trip in a Longtail.

Conditions: Visibility is poor, averaging 6m (20ft); at its best it reaches 12m (40ft). Currents are weak to moderate.

Average depth: 5m (16ft)

Maximum depth: 12m (40ft)

Entry to the site off the beach brings you to the fringing reef, at a depth of 5m (16ft). As you follow it around the headland in a westerly direction the depth gradually increases to 12m (40ft). This is a training and introduction site similar to Meridian Reef (Site 1), but shallower and slightly more enjoyable. Barracuda, tuna, jacks and trevally are often present. The reef just breaks the surface in low water. Blue-spotted Ribbontail Rays and Whitetip Reef Sharks are sometimes seen. Reef-fish are present but tend to be scattered over the area rather than dominating particular areas. The site is accessible during inclement weather conditions and suitable for night-diving enthusiasts.

3 KOH PU

★

Location: Just under 1km (¹/₂ n. mile) west of Kata House Reef (Site 2).

Access: Generally by longtail boat: about 15min from Kata Beach. The best section is around the northern shoreline of this tiny islet. There is no buoy to indicate the entry point.

Conditions: Visibility ranges between 8m and 15m (23–50ft). Currents are weak to moderate.

The Hinge-beak shrimp (Rhynchocinetes hiatti) is almost invisible to predators at night.

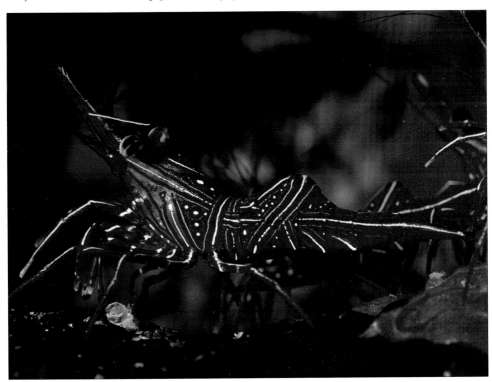

Average depth: 18m (60ft)
Maximum depth: 24m (80ft)
The island is fringed with fallen rocks; these are larger around the northwest area, and are the main feature of the site. The spaces between some of the rocks offer swimthroughs; beneath the rocks are heaps of broken oyster shells, obscure nudibranchs and a few cowrie shells. There are no pelagics or big fish of note, but you are likely to see small schools of fusiliers and snappers, Moorish Idols, squirrelfish and rabbitfish.

4 KOH DOK MAI
★★★

Location: 10km (5 n. mile) west of Hin Musang (Site 6).
Access: About 90min by diveboat from Chalong Bay. There is no mooring buoy.
Conditions: Visibility ranges between 8m (26ft) and above 25m (83ft). Currents can be strong, but are generally moderate.
Average depth: 19m (63ft)
Maximum depth: 31m (103ft)
The east side of the island offers a wall rich in invertebrates and a good representation of tube corals. There are large moray eels, Black-banded Sea Snakes, Honeycomb Groupers and angelfish, and you have a good chance of seeing Leopard Sharks out on the sand. Bivalves cling to sea whips along the deeper sections of the wall. This eastern wall also features two caves. The walls and ceiling of the larger one are rich in soft corals, but it is best to remain outside, exploring the cave's interior safely by torch light.

The western side of the island features a steeply sloping reef rather than the sheer drops that dominate elsewhere. Both Blacktip and Whitetip Reef Sharks have been seen here, and there are healthy seafans and barrel and encrusting sponges. Visiting pelagics are often seen.

5 ANEMONE REEF
★★★★

Location: A completely submerged pinnacle consisting of numerous rocky ledges 30km (16 n. miles) due east of Chalong Bay on Koh Phuket.
Access: This designated Marine Sanctuary is reached in about 2hr from all the recognized departure points. A mooring buoy marks the site's location.
Conditions: Visibility ranges from as low as 4m (13ft) to about 25m (83ft). The full range of currents can be experienced, from mill-pond still through mild to strong to ripping. The stronger currents are fairly predictable.
Average depth: 17m (56ft)
Maximum depth: 26m (86ft)

SHARK POINT MARINE SANCTUARY

Shark Point Marine Sanctuary consists of Shark Point and Anemone Reef which is 1km to the north-west. Designated a Marine Sanctuary in 1992, the sheer profusion of marine life here is justification enough for protected status. The marine park zone extends for a radius of 2.5km around the western limit of Shark Point and all commercial fishing, collecting of marine life, or other harmful activity is prohibited. Official mooring buoys have been installed but if they are in use (which is often the case, given the popularity of these sites), divers must utilize a live-boat dive. On no account should anchors be dropped here.

Anemone Reef is a small rocky plateau with a depth of about 4–7m (13–23ft) beneath the surface at the shallowest parts. As you might guess, the top part of the reef is smothered in sea anemones; there are many resident clownfish, shrimps and Porcelain Crabs. Elsewhere on the reef you find large clusters of soft corals and enormous gorgonian seafans – the latter sheltering dense groupings of Indian Lionfish. The site has a healthy cross-section of marine life, and is one of the few sites featuring Harlequin Ghost Pipefish. At its deepest point a solitary rock is home to a number of juvenile moray eels.

6 HIN MUSANG (SHARK POINT)
★★★★★

Location: A small rocky outcrop 1km (1/2 n. mile) southeast of Anemone Reef (Site 5).
Access: This designated site is reached in about 2hr from all the recognized departure points. There are mooring buoys.
Conditions: Visibility ranges from as low as 4m (13ft) to above 25m (83ft). When currents flow you can drift-dive along the line of pinnacles.
Average depth: 19m (63ft)
Maximum depth: 24m (80ft)
This is justifiably considered one of the premier sites in the area and consequently there are always lots of divers here. A small rock outcrop standing proud of the water marks the spot – this is the top of the northernmost of the three main pinnacles here. All three are dense with colourful marine life, from giant barrel sponges to Honeycomb Groupers, vivid encrusting sponges, moray eels, lobsters, lionfish and even ornate ghost pipefish. Slightly to the west of the northern pinnacle is a large, spectacular arch saturated in the brilliant colours of the soft corals growing on its surfaces. Deeper down, the reef displays black coral, sea whips and gorgonians, with jacks, barracuda, snapper, trevally and mackerel patrolling the fringes. This site was named after the Leopard Sharks often found resting in the sandy sections.

Above: *The Spotfin Lionfish (Pterois antennata) is a master of camouflage.*
Below: *Iridescent soft corals (Dendronepthya sp.) and Featherstar worm (Himerometra robustipinna).*

7 KING CRUISER WRECK
★★★★

Location: 1km (1/2 n. mile) southeast of Anemone Reef (Site 5).

Access: This wreck is reached in about 2hr from all the recognized departure points.

Conditions: If the tide is running, strong currents and low visibility can be expected; at slack tide the site experiences still and much clearer water.

Average depth: 20m (66ft)

Maximum depth: 32m (106ft)

In 1997 the *King Cruiser*, a car ferry operating from Phuket to the Phi Phi Islands, bottomed on Anemone Reef, splitting the marine sanctuary in two. The impact also tore a large hole in the vessel's hull. Today the structure attracts a high diversity of marine life; invertebrates have taken up residence under sheets of peeling paint and juvenile reef fish hover around the now barnacle-encrusted frame. Daylight penetrates the majority of the wreck, though there are some areas that can only be explored with an artificial light source. Beware that a few areas have collapsed ceilings - these should not be entered at all.

8 KOH HI (CORAL ISLAND)
★★★★

Location: The outer of the two islands directly south of Chalong Bay.

Access: About 45min by diveboat from Chalong Bay. Its nearness and its relatively sheltered position mean virtually all year round diving.

Conditions: Visibility is low, with a maximum of about 12m (40ft). Currents are minimal. Beware of boat traffic, especially in the high season.

Average depth: 14m (46ft)

Maximum depth: 20m (66ft)

During the rainy season, Coral Island is the best diving destination from Koh Phuket. The diving and snorkelling is at the eastern end of the northeastern beach. The sloping reef features mainly hard foliaceous corals interspersed with some bubble, staghorn and star corals. The maximum depth here is about 15m (50ft). The usual reef-fish, such as parrotfish and wrasse, are on display, along with urchins and a selection of nudibranchs.

The south of the island is rockier, and this condition continues underwater. This is the best area to dive, not only in terms of safety (no threat from erratic jetskiers!) but also because there is a more diverse presence of marine life, plus healthier corals.

9 KOH RACHA YAI – BUNGALOW BAY
★★★★★

Location: This picturesque island is 20km (15 n. mile) south of Koh Phuket. Bungalow Bay is on its west coast.

Access: About 2hr by diveboat from Chalong Bay. There is no mooring buoy. Snorkellers can access the shallower parts of either reef from the beach.

Conditions: Visibility can exceed 25m (83ft). Currents are generally mild, but can increase in the waters further out in the bay.

Average depth: 17m (56ft)

Maximum depth: 30m (66ft)

Underwater, the western side of the island is slightly superior to the east. This particular site can be split, as

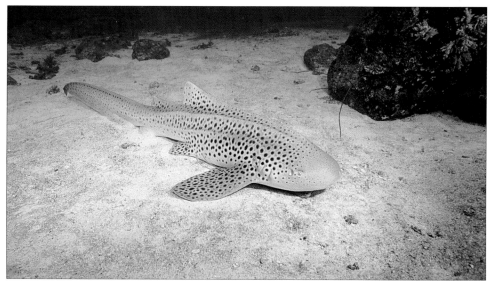

you can choose to follow either of the bay's shorelines. The rocky formations visible above the surface continue underwater, with a good presence of reef-fish. Around the rocks swim surgeonfish and fusiliers, while below you can see inquisitive paired goatfish, nudibranchs, urchins and plenty of Blue-spotted Ribbontail Rays. Coral growth is on average better here than along the east coast.

10 KOH RACHA YAI – EASTERN COAST
★★★★★

Location: The island's eastern side can be considered as two sites: the first begins at the northeast tip and goes south; the second follows the southeastern apex of the island.

Access: About 2hr by diveboat from Chalong Bay. There is no mooring buoy. Access is by `live-boat' dive, after which the boat leaves the fringing reef to drop anchor.

Conditions: Visibility is in the region of 15–20m (50–66ft). Currents vary from weak to moderate.

Average depth: 12m (40ft)

Maximum depth: 22m (73ft)

Koh Racha Yai's eastern side consists of sloping hard coral reefs, mainly foliaceous corals. The shallower sections feature tables and smaller examples of leaf corals; the deeper waters have much the same species, but larger. Many featherstars, lionfish, puffers and a few parrotfish and wrasse are present. The site's southern end has the bonus of octopus and a greater display of reef creatures, including good-sized Titan Triggerfish and moray eels, plus a better selection of colourful fish and invertebrates. Leopard Sharks are sometimes seen.

11 KOH RACHA NOI – NORTHERN TIP
★★★

Location: The uninhabited island of Koh Racha Noi is 33km (18 n. mile) due south of Koh Phuket. The outermost island of the Racha Group. The dive follows around the northern tip of the island.

Access: About 2¹/₂hr by diveboat from Chalong Bay. There is no mooring buoy.

Conditions: Visibility can exceed 25m (83ft). Currents can be incredibly strong, both horizontally and, even more dangerously, downwards. These conditions limit the site to experienced divers.

Average depth: 17m (56ft)

Maximum depth: 30m (100ft)

This is a good multi-level dive site, going around pinnacles and large rocks. There is a fair display of hard and soft corals, and the usual reef-fish are present in reasonable quantities. If you are lucky you should be able to sight reef sharks, but the main attraction is probably

the presence of large Bullethead Parrotfish. However, diving here can be extremely hazardous because of the hostile currents: under no circumstances should this site be attempted by any but the most experienced divers.

12 KOH RACHA NOI – SOUTHERN TIP
★★★

Location: The dive follows around the island's southern tip.

Access: Just over 2¹/₂hr by diveboat from Chalong Bay. There is no mooring buoy. Access is by `live-boat' dive.

Conditions: Visibility can exceed 25m (83ft). Currents can be incredibly strong, both horizontally and, even more dangerously, downwards. These conditions limit the site to experienced divers.

Average depth: 23m (76ft)

Maximum depth: 40m+ (130ft+)

This is a great dive for the experienced diver – in fact, most good operators will bring only divers of advanced level and above. The underwater terrain is similar to that around the island's northern tip (Site 10), but much deeper – the shallowest part of any consequence is at 18m (60ft). Fine soft corals highlight the smooth-sided boulders. Crinoids and featherstars are well represented. There are fairly plentiful, reasonably sized fish, including lionfish, parrotfish, wrasse and triggerfish, as well as large visiting pelagics. Manta Rays and Whale Sharks have been seen here. All in all, this site is similar to those sites around Mu Koh Similan, although not quite as spectacular.

Opposite: *The docile Leopard Shark (Stegostoma fasciatum) will allow divers to approach but please do not touch.*

HOW TO GET THERE

There is a selection of regular transport running between Bangkok and Phuket. It is also possible to directly access the island's International airport from a number of neighbouring countries, or by connecting through Bangkok's Don Muang domestic airport.

By bus: VIP air-conditioned buses depart from Bangkok's southern bus terminal daily at 18.50hrs and arrive at the bus terminal in Phuket Town some fourteen hours later. For further information regarding bus services contact Bangkok southern bus terminal;
tel (02) 435 1199, 435 1200. On arriving at Phuket Town bus station visitors continue their journeys to one of the main beaches unless arrangements have been made for either the dive operator or resort to collect them, by either Tuk Tuk (small open air chartered taxis), local bus or airport limousine.

By Tuk Tuk: There is a T.A.T. charter price schedule in operation but it is unclear whether the swarms of Tuk Tuk drivers awaiting the arrival of tourist-filled buses follow it!

By local bus from Phuket Town bus station: The fares of these buses are standard and not negotiable. There are no designated bus stops or scheduled timetables, but buses should pass every 30 minutes between 06.00hrs and 18.00hrs.

By air: Flights from Bangkok are with Thai International and there are fourteen daily flights which depart the domestic airport every hour, on the hour, between 07.00hrs and 21.00hrs. For further information regarding flights contact Thai Airways International Limited; tel (02) 513 0121/ fax (02) 513 0203. Flights from Koh Samui are with Bangkok Airways; tel (02) 229 3434/fax (02) 229 3454.

For any additional information on Koh Phuket contact the **Tourism Authority of Thailand**; tel (076) 212213, 211036/fax (076) 213582.

WHERE TO STAY

There is a vast range of resorts from five-star hotels to rooms above shops.

PHUKET TOWN

Two hotels worth staying at in Phuket Town itself with swimming pools, comfortable rooms and good Chinese restaurants. **The Metropole Phuket**; tel (076) 215050/fax (076) 215990 and **The Pearl Hotel**; tel (076) 211044/fax (076) 212911.

PATONG BEACH

Novotel Phuket Resort; Kalim Beach Rd, tel (076) 342777/fax (076) 342168 overlooks Patong Beach and has rooms with full amenities. There is a selection of restaurants. Other facilities include a three tier swimming pool. **The Dive Inn**; tel (076) 341927. A friendly atmosphere welcomes the guests here - all rooms have a private bathroom with h/c water, satellite TV, a bar, restaurant and pool table.

KARON BEACH

The Islandia Park Resort; tel (076) 396604/fax (076) 396491 has air-conditioned rooms all with sea views, private bathrooms and h/c water, three restaurants, swimming pool, tennis courts and a fitness centre. **Phuket Golden Sand Inn**; tel (076) 396493-5/fax (076) 396117 has fan-cooled and air-conditioned rooms with private bathrooms with h/c water. There is a good restaurant and laundry service.

KATA BEACH

Marina Cottages; tel (076) 330625/fax (076) 330516 has air-conditioned bungalows with bathrooms, fridge, telephone, and private balcony. The resort has two restaurants, a movie lounge, souvenir shop and a PADI five Star facility diving centre. Big game fishing and horse riding can also be arranged.

NAI HARN BEACH

Phuket Yacht Club; tel (076) 381156-63/fax (076) 381164. All rooms have air-conditioning, private bathroom, hot and cold water, fridge and TV. There is a restaurant and swimming pool.

CORAL ISLAND

Coral Island Resort; tel (076) 214779/fax (076) 216263 has air-conditioned bungalows, all with private bathrooms, h/c water and fridge. Good beach front seafood restaurant.

WHERE TO EAT

There are numerous restaurants spread over the island; below is a small selection of good places to eat. **On the Rock**, **Marina Cottages**; tel (076) 330625 is a seafood and oriental restaurant and is amongst the best on the island. There is a full bar with a good cocktail selection. **Thavorn Palm Beach Hotel**; tel (076) 396090. Old Siam serves Thai cuisine accompanied by authentic Thai music in traditional surroundings. **Baan Rim Pa**; tel (076) 340789. This open terraced Thai restaurant overlooks the bay. The food

here is sensational and should not be missed. **Malee Seafood Village**; tel (076) 341193. Grand open-air sea front restaurant in the centre of Patong. **The Terrace**; tel 01 723 0291 has one of the best views on the island and is a great place to enjoy a cocktail, a glass of wine or a beer and watch the sun go down. **The Dive Cafe**; tel (076) 330323. Great place to meet dive buddies and the Thai food is good too.

DIVE FACILITIES

Scuba diving here is big business, the larger centres cater for divers from all over the world, courses and dive trips are generally supervised by multi-lingual staff, although English remains the predominant language. To ease any transportation worries several of the larger centres provide their own transfer service between their facilities and Phuket International Airport.

Dive Trips

There are two main types of dive trips available around the island. All the diving operators run daily trips, and the larger more established concerns schedule regular live-aboard excursions on their own boats around the Similan and Surin island groups and immediate environs, the Mergui Archipelago and the Andaman islands. Some of the operators occasionally arrange short excursions to the southern destinations around Koh Rok and Hin Daeng. All these trips differ in style and duration with enough variations to suit anyone intending to take a live-aboard excursion. Daily dive trip prices include transfers to and from the resorts, light refreshments and beverages, lunch, two full tanks, weights, weight belt and, if required divemaster services. Equipment rental is extra. Divers who have been out of the water for a period of six months or more will be given the option of either participating in a refresher course or accompanying an instructor during their first dive, there is a minimal charge for this important and necessary service. Snorkellers and non-divers are welcome to join any of the trips for a good discount, which includes all the normal services plus the use of snorkelling equipment.

Live-Aboard excursions

One of the main attractions that bring many divers to Koh Phuket is the selection of regular live-aboard excursions; these allow divers to comfortably access far off and otherwise non accessible dive sites. There are a number of different styles of live-aboard diving excursions available, each with different characteristics and class of boat; but they all share extremely high standards. For schedule details and timetables contact the relevant companies directly. Prices include all diving, meals, snacks, accommodation and any entertainment.

Alcoholic and soft beverages are extra, as is any scuba equipment. Snorkellers and non-divers are again welcome to join any of the trips at a discounted price which includes all the normal services plus the use of all snorkelling equipment. For more information see the Phuket live-aboard feature on page 32.

Dive courses

Local diver training mostly follows the PADI education system, though South East Asia Live-aboards on Patong Beach are also a BSAC Premier School and an IANTD facility. All the internationally recognised certifications are accepted in any of the dive centres and there will be requests for certification cards and log books to be produced. The price structure of the courses remains very similar between the different operators. There are options on where to complete the open water sections of the courses, they can either be completed locally or amalgamated with a live-aboard excursion, allowing the successful students to continue their trip as qualified divers. Average prices are fully inclusive of all instruction, the relevant study materials, equipment, dive trips and certification. The introduction and Open Water Diver Courses include full equipment, all other courses are inclusive of tanks and weight systems only, any additional equipment required for diving courses can be rented from all the centres at a discounted price. All courses necessitate students to provide two passport sized photographs, which can be obtained at the majority of the islands photographic shops.

Dive Operators

Scubaquest (MV *Queen Marine*); 96/23 Moo 3, Kamala Bay, Kathu, Phuket 83000, tel (076) 271113/fax (076) 271113, email: info@scuba-quest.com PADI courses available in a selection of languages. Daily dive trips to all the listed local sites. Live-aboard excursions offered – for services available see Live-aboards feature on page 32. **Dive Asia Pacific** (MV *Sai Mai*, MV *Pelagian*); PO Box 244, Phuket 83000, tel (076) 263732/fax (076) 263733, email: info@dive-asiapacific.com

Top of the range live-aboards – for details see Live-aboards feature on page 32.

Dive Operators on Patong Beach

South East Asia Liveaboards (SY *Crescent*, SY *Wanderlust*, SY *Gaea*); 112/13 Song Roi Pi Road, Patong, Phuket 83150, tel (076) 340406/fax (076) 340586, email: info@sealiveaboards.com PADI, BSAC and IANTD courses available in a variety of languages. Day trips to all the local sites. Good retail outlet including Camero wetsuits. Live-aboard excursions offered – for details see feature on page 32.

Fantasea Divers (MV *Fantasea*); PO Box 22, Patong Beach, Phuket 83150, tel (076) 340088/fax (076) 340309, email: info@fantasea.net The booking office is on Song Roi Pi Road. PADI dive courses available. Two boats serving the local dive sites on day trips. Live-aboard excursions also offered – for services see Live-aboards feature on page 32. **Scuba Cat** (MV *Scubacat*, MV *Scuba Adventure*); PO Box 316, Phuket 83000, tel (076) 293121/fax (076) 293122, email: info@scubacat.com The office and showroom are on the beach road. Great retail outlet offering day trips to all the local sites and live-aboard excursions. For details of live-aboards, see feature on page 32. **Warm Water Divers**; PO Box 81, Patong Beach, Phuket 83150, tel (076) 294150/fax (076) 342453, email: beach@warmwaterdivers.com The showroom is on the beachfront road on Patong Beach. This superb retail outlet also offers day trips to all the local sites. All PADI courses available in a variety of languages. Live-aboard excursions offered on the company's own traditionally restored Junk.

Dive Operators on Kata Beach

Genesis I Liveaboards Co. Ltd (MV *Genesis 1*); PO Box 16, Kata Beach, Phuket 83100, tel/fax (076) 330969, email: dive@genesis1phuket.com Live-aboard excursions only. For services available, see Live-aboards feature on page 32. **Dive Asia** (MV *Choksomboon*); PO Box 79, Phuket 83000, tel (076) 330598/fax (076) 340360, email: info@diveasia.com Offices on both Kata and Karon beaches. PADI 5 star IDC Centre. Reasonable retail outlet, also offering day trips. Live-aboard excursions to Similans on boat capable of carrying 16 guests in 8 twin cabins, with two cold showers. PADI Dive courses available. **Marina Divers** (MV *Marina Dream*); 120/2 Mu 4, Patak Rd, Phuket 83000, tel (076) 330272/fax (076) 330516, email: marinath@phuket.ksc.co.th Located on

the right hand side of the road from Karon to Kata Beach. Day trips to all the local sites. Maximum of 8 divers are catered for on this 19 metre boat in four private double air-conditioned cabins. Live-aboard excursions to Similans and Surin areas. PADI Dive courses available.

Dive Operator on Karon Beach

Kon-Tiki Diving School; 66/3-65/1 Patak Rd, Karon, Phuket 83100, tel (076) 396312/fax (076) 396313, email: kontiki@loxinfo.co.th – PADI 5 star IDC Centre. Day trips to all the local sites, plus live-aboard excursions to the Similan and Surin islands. PADI dive courses available, including in Swedish. The centre also has a small retail outlet.

FILM PROCESSING

The best photographic developing shops are those situated along the Patong Beach Road. Try the Friend Color Lab; tel (01) 723 0127, 956 2519.

HOSPITALS AND RECOMPRESSION CHAMBERS

Phuket International Hospital (Sirirot Second Hospital); tel (076) 249400. **Mission Hospital**; tel (076) 211173, 212386, 212149, **Ruam Paet Hospital**; tel (076) 212950, 214720. **Sirirot First Hospital**; tel (076) 212853. **Wichira Hospital**; tel (076) 211114. The nearest recompression chamber is located on Patong Beach. **Dive Safe Asia**; 113/16 Moo 4, Song Roy Pi Road, Patong Beach, tel (076) 342518/fax (076) 342519. **Tourist Police**; tel (076) 211036, 212213.

LOCAL HIGHLIGHTS

There are countless **excursions** available from Phuket including trips to offshore islands, temple visits, shopping expeditions, beach excursions, snorkelling trips, waterfall tours, bungee jumps, shooting ranges, Go-Kart racing and mini golf courses. Some of the most popular tours include the **Santana Sea and Jungle Canoeing**; tel (076) 340360 - self paddling canoeing tours around National Parks and the local Bays and **Sea Canoe Thailand**; tel (076) 212252 - self paddle canoe excursions, visiting caves and coastal expeditions.

Virtually every tour operator and hotel offers a sightseeing excursion to **Phang Nga Bay**. Boats journey around the bay's spectacular limestone monoliths which provided the backdrop for the James Bond film *The Man with the Golden Gun*.

A full range of **banks** can be found in Phuket Town and are within easy reach anywhere on Patong Beach.

ESTABLISHED OPERATORS AND BOATS

For contact details see Koh Phuket Regional Directory on pp 30-31.

FANTASEA DIVERS

Fantasea Divers offer a trip to the Similans, Surin and the Mergui Archipelago with, whenever possible, unlimited diving. Food on board is a mixture of both Thai and western flavours.

MV *Fantasea*

This 30m (100ft) steel-hulled motor vessel is capable of comfortably holding fifteen guests in double, twin and single air-conditioned cabins. The once-commissioned German vessel was acquired by Fantasea in 1990. It is driven by twin 707 hp engines and has been extensively modified to serve divers comfortably; features now include three heads with hot and cold showers, air-conditioned saloon with video, music centre and a library containing a selection of marine life reference books and even an E6 developing service. Camera batteries can be recharged and camera equipment rented. There is a shaded sundeck on which to relax. The excursion usually offers unlimited diving (dive computers can be hired on the boat) with two feature dives a day; there are comprehensive dive briefings using detailed underwater maps. This vessel visits the Similans, Surin Islands and the Mergui Archipelago.

SOUTH EAST ASIA LIVEABOARDS

This company offers excursions to the Andaman islands, Similan islands, Surin and the Mergui Archipelago. The South East Asia fleet consists of three sailing yachts all skippered by westerners. All boats carry at least one diving staff as well as a cook and one crew. They provide an excellent service, serving delicious Thai and European food. Diving is either led or divers can dive in buddy pairs. The crew are tremendously helpful - on boarding you are told that nothing is to much trouble, and they certainly mean it! As the boats employed by this company are primarily sailing vessels, everything happens in a relaxed manner; there are no real schedules to be followed; meal times, for instance, vary to accommodate the diving.

SY *Wanderlust*

Constructed in 1970, this 16m (51ft) wooden ketch rigged trimaran is capable of carrying eight passengers in double and single berths cooled by individual fans. There is one head with shower as well as a deck shower, and a large sundeck. Camera batteries can be recharged. A TV, video and music centre are all on board. Back-up propulsion comes in the form of an 85 hp engine; tanks are filled by two electric compressors. The yacht visits the Similans and the Mergui Archipelago.

SY *Gaea*

This is the smallest boat of the fleet at 15m (50ft). *Gaea* is a trimaran with a layout similar to Wanderlust and caters for eight guests spread over three fan-cooled cabins. There is one shower and a music centre. Back-up propulsion comes in the form of an 85 hp engine; tanks are filled by a petrol driven compressor. The boat visits the Similans and the Mergui Archipelago.

SY *Crescent*

This 1979 single hulled yacht is 18m (60ft) and constructed in fibreglass. It comfortably caters for ten passengers in four cabins with the option of air-conditioning. There are three heads with hot water showers and a separate deck shower. The yacht is laid out to maximise deck space with convenient diving. There are both sundecks and shaded areas. Back-up power comes courtesy of a 165 hp diesel engine. Tanks are filled by two electric compressors. TV, video and music centre as well as battery charging facilities are all available. There is full navigational equipment, radio and depth sounder. This yacht visits all the listed destinations.

DIVE ASIA PACIFIC

MV *Sai Mai*

This 1987 21m (70ft) wooden motor vessel is capable of carrying a maximum of eight guests in four air-conditioned cabins. There are two heads with hot showers, as well as two more showers on the diving deck. The boat carries oxygen, and full navigational equipment, radio and depth sounder. There is a TV, video, music centre and library in the lounge. Tanks are filled by two electric compressors. Battery charging facilities are available. The food is excellent. This boat gives divers individual treatment; the diving is unlimited with both led dives and buddy-dive options available. Sai Mai visits the Similans and Surin islands and the Mergui Archipelago.

MV *Pelagian*

This is another luxury live-aboard. Up to twelve guests are catered for in six suites, all with private facilities. The boat is due to start operating in the area during 1998, visiting all the sites that her sister ship already covers. One of the overhauls to the boat is the installation of special facilities for photographers.

DIVEMASTER (contact details on page 21)

MV *Divemaster II*

This 19m (63ft) boat comfortably caters for sixteen divers in five air-conditioned cabins. There are three heads with warm water showers, plus a large air-conditioned lounge. Wet and dry camera tables and multi-voltage battery charging facilities are available. The extensive sundeck has a large shaded area with tables for use at meal times. The full range of safety and navigational equipment is on board. *Divemaster II* visits the Similans, Surin Islands, Mergui Archipelago, Koh Tao and Koh Losin.

SCUBA CAT

There are two boats offering different services. The first offers divers who find themselves limited by budget or time scale an alternative means of exploring the Similans.

MV *Scubacat*

This large vessel is based in and shuttles divers around the Similan Islands. Up to twenty-four guests are transferred to and from the boat every other day, offering a short affordable option for accessing the area. The service is good, there is lots of room and it's very comfortable. This vessel visits the Similans and Racha Islands.

MV *Scuba Adventure*

This live-aboard caters for up to ten guests in four air-conditioned cabins. Full entertainment amenities are available on board. Sites visited include the Similans and Surin Islands.

CALYPSO LIVEABOARD

MV *Genesis 1*

Comfortable live-aboard catering for up to twelve divers in eight air-conditioned cabins. The boat is capable of mixing Nitrox, allowing technical diving. Full entertainment amenities are on board. Sites visited include the Similans and Hin Daeng.

SCUBAQUEST

MV *Queen Marine*

Twenty-five metre (80ft) live-aboard capable of carrying up to eighteen divers in twelve fan-cooled berths. This is an economical way to dive the Similans and Surin Islands and the Mergui Archipelago. The boat is spacious and adequately caters for alll on board. Space on the dive platform is always available, even with all the divers on it at the same time.

SY *Phoenix*

This is a 31m (103ft) luxury live-aboard yacht sering the Mergui Archipelago.

The term 'live-aboard' means exactly what the name implies; the boat actually becomes a home or a floating hotel with the divers living onboard. The class and standard of these 'floating hotels' can vary greatly in exactly the same way as land-based accomodation.

The standard of live-aboards in Thailand ranges from a converted fishing boat with a handful of mattresses slung about its decks and a compressor strapped to an old car tyre, through to large spacious yachts with state-of-the-art sailing equipment.

Operators generally sail to the first destination (which in some instances can include further land transfers to and from Koh Phuket) at night. This allows the guests to awaken fresh and ready for the first day's diving after breakfast rather than having to wait for the boat to arrive at the first site. Nightly departures also maximise the daylight hours for diving.

All classes of 'cruise' are regularly scheduled from Koh Phuket but will only sail when there is sufficient demand; it is always best to confirm actual departures in advance. Depending on the intended destination, live-aboard excursions have a duration of between three and fifteen days. The longer the trip, the more important onboard comfort becomes. If it's your first experience of live-aboards it's advisable to select one of the shorter, but extremely enjoyable excursions such as visiting the Similan Islands.

Life onboard the boats is extremely relaxing - the only time guests are required to assemble their diving equipment is on the first day, after that the crew take charge and divers can just don their kit and dive, dive, dive! Another great aspect of live-aboards is that if the intended site is unsuitable due to bad weather, strong currents or even the presence of other boats, it's only a few minutes journey to an equally enjoyable site.

Some operators follow set itineraries, with a minimum of three scheduled dives every day, while others offer unlimited diving. Unlimited diving is only recommended if diving with a computer (which can be rented from the operators).

Night diving is usually possible every night but if you would rather stay on board there are usually other activities to keep you amused such as videos, music centres or just talking with the other passengers. And there is always a log book to be filled out!

Below left: *The range of live-aboards offers a wide selection of diving opportunities.*
Below right: *Live-aboard excursions enable divers to visit otherwise inaccessible sites.*

MU KOH SIMILAN
MARINE NATIONAL PARK

This archipelago of nine small granitic islands sits some 90km (55 n. miles) northwest of Koh Phuket. The islands and their surrounding waters cover an area of about 128 sq km (51 sq miles). They feature lush rainforests inhabited by squirrels and bats. Bird-life is also well represented. There are now two fully staffed park offices (on Koh Miang and Koh Similan), but otherwise the islands are uninhabited.

A noticeable characteristic of the Similans is the huge contrast between the east and west coasts of the islands. The eastern coastlines are in the lee of the prevailing summer weather monsoons, and feature superb sandy beaches and sheltered bays. The western coasts, however, are subject to the full force of the harsh southwesterly monsoons (which blow May–November) and are characterized by rugged shorelines where weatherbeaten granite boulders rise directly from the seabed. As you will see when you dive, this geographical pattern is repeated underwater.

DIVING AROUND THE SIMILANS

The Similans can certainly lay claim to being one of Asia's top dive destinations. The dramatic underwater terrain is highlighted by thriving reefs and abundant soft corals, and the tremendous diversity of marine life includes many of the more exciting, larger pelagics.

During late March and early April, Thailand's hottest period, rising sea temperatures cause plankton blooms, which give the water a greenish tinge and reduce visibility considerably; however, the plankton attracts a wealth of pelagics, with the chance of spotting Whale Sharks, Manta and Eagle Rays and a host of other pelagics.

In general, the east-facing dive sites feature gently sloping reefs and dropoffs with impressive gardens of sea anemones, flourishing hard and soft corals, and teeming fish populations. With negligible currents and mostly moderate depths, these sites are suitable for any level of diver. The sheltered conditions are also perfect for snorkelling.

Diving around the archipelago's western sites is quite the opposite. Here giant boulders tumble down to the seabed to depths of 40m (135ft) or more. Strong currents keep the gaps

---

Opposite: *View to Ao Rawng Tao (Shoe Bay) from Similan Rock, Koh Similan.*
Above: *Brilliant and exotic, the tiny shy Blue ribbon eel (Rhinomuraena quaesita).*

between the boulders free from build-ups of sand, leading to the development of a network of tunnels, archways and caverns that provide exciting swimthroughs. The currents also provide nutrients for masses of gorgonians, crinoids, seafans and lush soft corals.

■1 TRIPLE ARCHES/GOLDEN ARCHES
★★

Location: Some 50m (55yd) off the north coast of Koh Bangu (Island 9).

Access: There is one mooring buoy. The entry point is due north of the island, about 50m (55yd) off the coastline.
Conditions: Beware of strong currents. Visibility ranges from as low as 5m (16ft) up to a much more acceptable 22m (73ft).
Average depth: 11m (36ft)

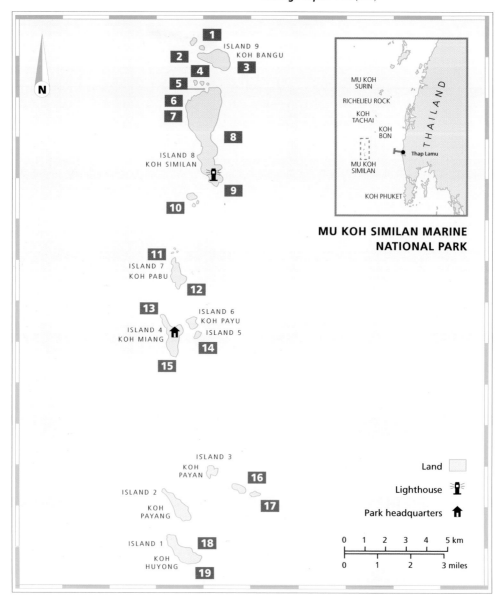

MU KOH SIMILAN MARINE NATIONAL PARK

Maximum depth: 32m (106ft)
The prime location is found by heading north into a depth of 30m (100ft). Here the boulders are bigger and, as the site's name suggests, you find three rock arches. There are vast quantities of Giant Spiny Sea Cucumbers. Branches of colourful soft corals cling to the arches' smooth granite surfaces.

Continuing east, you find schools of adult Oriental Sweetlips and soldierfish in the narrow crevices between the boulders, dodging among the seafans that cling to their almost vertical sides. There are also many Pincushion Starfish. This formation continues but becomes more spread out in the deeper waters, reaching about 27m (90ft).

2 CHRISTMAS POINT
★★★☆

Location: The western apex of Koh Bangu (Island#9),

TRIGGERFISH V SEA URCHINS

If you've ever wondered why the presence of sea urchins can vary enormously in relatively confined areas, the answer is simple - Titan Triggerfish. The spiny sea urchin is the main source of nourishment for these fish, in fact they seem to be their only enemy.

The triggerfish has adopted two methods in order to obtain this food source from its spiny protection. The first method is when the fish blasts a stream of water from its mouth which overturns the sea urchin leaving its unprotected mouth uppermost. The second method is when the urchin is actually plucked from the sea bed in the mouth of the triggerfish and taken towards the surface where it is released to descend, causing the urchin to invert and again leaving the unprotected mouth exposed. The first method is also used for locating small creatures buried beneath the sand as the stream of water clears away surface particles.

Below: *A snorkeller enjoys the splendours beneath the waters.*

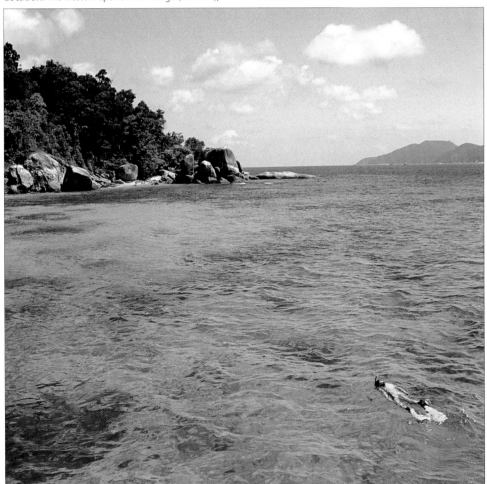

marked by a small collection of outcrops some 50m (55yd) from the island's northern shore.

Access: This site is buoyed.

Conditions: Excellent visibility, often exceeding 25m (83ft). Currents run weak to moderate, occasionally strong.

Average depth: 20m (66ft)

Maximum depth: 34m (113ft)

The western and northern quarters reach 30m (100ft) and the shallower south and east 18m (60ft).

The southwestern section features triangular boulders at 22m (73ft); these continue down to depths greater than 25m (83ft), where you find leaning boulders, offering mazes of swimthroughs. The walls and sides are highlighted by radiant soft corals. Around these are numerous parrotfish of all sizes, small Dog-faced Pufferfish and larger solitary Clown Triggerfish. The overhangs and caves usually sport prides of lionfish travelling below the air pockets as if admiring their own gracefulness.

Northwards there are more soft corals; as you swim around the rocks the penetrating rays of sunlight create interesting contrasts. Sharing the area are mixed amounts of leafy, brain, slipper and lip corals. Groups of Schooling, Pennant and Indian Bannerfish pass close by. Further down, Giant Sea Cucumbers and Blue Seastars decorate the rocky surfaces. Many Indian, Titan and Scythe Triggerfish keep the population of sea urchins minimal. The prolific fish-life includes Raccoon Butterflyfish, large Bicolour Parrotfish, Indian and Spotfin Lionfish and a multitude of wrasse. Further north, Manta Rays, Whale Sharks and barracuda are frequent.

The eastern section is the shallowest, averaging 15m (50ft). The reef is basically formed by terraced foliaceous hard corals. Many tables of staghorns shelter a myriad of tiny reef-fish; the staghorns intersperse a large garden of Gigantic Sea Anemones.

3 BREAKFAST BEND
★★★★★☆☆

Location: Around the southeastern apex of Koh Bangu (Island#9).

Access: There is a couple of permanent mooring buoys about 300m (330yd) due east of the site.

Conditions: Expect calm conditions and great visibility, often above 25m (83ft).

Average depth: 16m (53ft)

Maximum depth: 34m (113ft)

Breakfast Bend is so-called because this is generally done as the first dive of the excursion, immediately after breakfast.

The western section is relatively shallow, averaging 8m (26ft); its sandy bottom is punctuated with scattered rocks. Southeast of here are the beginnings of a reef-

flat, primarily staghorns; these eventually achieve garden-like proportions. They are bigger but much less frequent on the steep reef-slope. The seabed has widespread coral mounds. The corals in this area are relatively healthy, with minimal damage. Lots of sergeant majors dart around in the shallower waters, giving snorkellers a good time.

The reef-slope – also formed by small boulders and coral shelves, with many branches of tree, leafy and brain corals – drops to 18m (60ft); then steeply sloping sand-banks descend to 34m (113ft). As you follow the reef north you pass over some steep sandy slopes, several metres across and bare of coral. There are a good few of these, with stretches of coral between them, before the corals again become completely dominant. Moorish Idols, Raccoon Butterflyfish and Indian Bannerfish – paired rather than solitary – are all present en masse. Colonies of garden eels can be seen on the sandy patches.

Continuing along the reef, bearing slightly northwest, you find a change in the seascape. Large boulders, heavily pitted by numerous bivalves and Christmas-tree Worms, replace the sloping reef; they are highlighted by colourful yellow, white and black featherstars, clinging to the sponge-encrusted surfaces. This is a good place to examine the rocky surfaces carefully, as there are less obvious creatures to see. Often octopuses are present, but you have to look for them, as their coloration provides camouflage.

4 MOORING ROCKS
★★

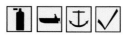

Location: Around the midpoint of Koh Bangu's southwest coast.

Access: The site is unbuoyed.

Conditions: Visibility ranges from 10m to 25m (33–83ft). Currents run weak to moderate. The deeper waters can be chillier, as a cold current often passes through the channel between Koh Bangu (Island#9) and Koh Similan (Island#8).

Average depth: 11m (36ft)

Maximum depth: 27m (90ft)

In daytime this is not one of the better sites on offer: many of the corals have been destroyed by crude dynamite fishing. But it is a good site for night-diving, as it consists of two mountainous coral heads, restricting the number of places where marine life can hide.

Opposite: *Diving buddies explore a swimthrough at Christmas Point, off Koh Bangu.*

5 DONALD DUCK/M16/CAMBELL'S/ SHOE BAY

★ ★ ★ ★

Location: In the small sheltered bay on the northwest coast of Koh Similan (Island#8).

Access: There are several mooring buoys in the bay. The best entry point for divers is directly from the boat. Snorkellers have three options: directly from the boat, from the boat's tender, or by a short surface swim from the sandy beach.

Conditions: Visibility can be as low as 5m (16ft) and as great as 25m (83ft). There is a likelihood of strong currents in the outer bay, generally from the north.

Average depth: 8m (26ft)

Maximum depth: 14m (46ft)

This shallow bay can serve as a good location for early diver training, although there are better locations in the Similans. Divers are sent in all directions around scattered coral mounds and boulders, which provide the sleeping-quarters for a host of marine life, but their formation forces the nocturnal creatures into areas of open sand in search of sustenance. Thus night-divers can observe them with much greater ease and frequency and in larger numbers. Cuttlefish and squid are often

---

BLUE RIBBON EELS (*Rhinomuraena quaesita*)

The Blue Ribbon Eel (p.35) is a member of the moray eel family and can be found amongst the rubble and sand in depths of up to 55m (184 ft), the only evidence of their presence being their heads protruding from their small lairs. As is with all moray's, the body features continuous dorsal and anal fins. Unlike other species of eels it is without pectorals.

These tiny colourful creatures are the only members of the moray family to abruptly change both their colour and sex. This protandrous hermaphrodite begins its life span as a black male with a body length averaging 65cm (25 inches), the juvenile then matures into a radiant blue female with bright yellow fins; the transformation does not necessarily end at this stage, many will continue their development and become completely yellow bodied with lengths averaging between 90 and 120cm (35 and 47 inches).

---

everywhere, as the lights of the diveboats attract them. Crabs, small lobsters and a wealth of other invertebrates, some never seen during daylight, scurry across the sand at night.

Solitary Harlequin sweetlips (Plectorhinchus cinctus) hang motionless in the water.

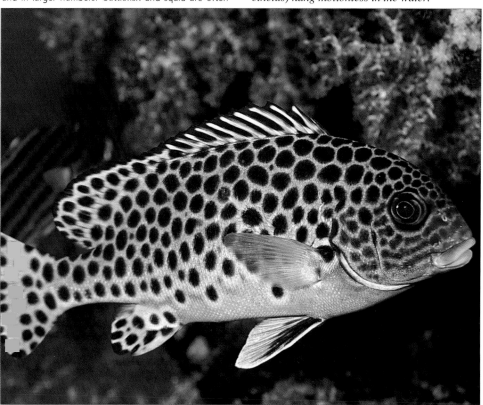

6 TURTLE ROCK

★★

Location: About 50m (55yd) off the rocky northwest coastline of Koh Similan (Island#8), by the larger of the shore's boulders.

Access: The site is unbuoyed.

Conditions: Visibility generally averages about 15m (50ft). Current runs weak to moderate; rare stronger currents transform the site into one suitable only for experienced divers.

Average depth: 20m (66ft)

Maximum depth: 30m (100ft)

Descend directly from the boat to an area of large boulders at about 20m (66ft). The dive will take you around these boulders and through their interconnecting swimthroughs. The boulders are reasonably covered with marine life but show evidence of anchor damage and the depredations of souvenir and curio collectors. However, large numbers of featherstars and clusters of hard and soft corals have escaped damage, so the site is still worth visiting. Powder-blue Surgeonfish and juvenile triggerfish grace the areas close to the boulders; further out are larger triggerfish including Titan and Indian.

Heading northeast is an impressive gorge-like swimthrough, 3m (10ft) across. Gorgonian seafans adorn its walls and provide hiding-places for small groups of lionfish.

7 CHICKEN HAIR REEF/FANTASEA REEF

★★★★★

Location: About 200m (220yd) off the western coast of Koh Similan (Island#8); about twice that distance southwest of Turtle Rock (Site 6).

Access: Two mooring buoys, running east–west, act as securings for diveboats and serve as direct descent points to the site.

Conditions: Visibility is generally high, between 15m (50ft) and well beyond 25m (66ft). There can be quick changes in the currents: weak to moderate currents can suddenly increase in strength, so this tremendous site is suitable for experienced divers only.

Average depth: 18m (60ft)

Maximum depth: 40m+ (130ft+)

Though rivalled by Elephant Head (Site 10), this is one of the favourite dive sites – if not the favourite – in the Similan group. Aside from the lack of any wrecks, there is something here for every diver.

Descending at the eastern (inner) buoy takes you to a rocky plateau at 15m (50ft). This is a great place for underwater photographers. The plateau resembles a

---

TRIGGERFISH (*Balistoides viridescens*)

The large head of the triggerfish covers one third of its rhomboid body; the remaining thick scaled posterior forms a tough leather-like armour which, due to its rigidity, is a non-functional part in the movement of the fish. Propulsion is provided by undulations in the rear dorsal and anal fins, with thrusts of the tail providing extra speed in escape or attack situations. The other function of the tail, along with the pectoral fins, is to direct the fish.

The remaining fin, the first dorsal, also has a very important use. This uniquely trigger-shaped fin is formed by three spines connected together by a thin membrane. The front, or first, spine is the longest and is used by the fish to wedge itself in small hiding places by raising the fin, thus preventing the fish from being dragged out by the tail by any would-be predators.

---

stage on which the abundant fish scuffle for the limelight – they are by no means camera-shy! Among the would-be stars are Powder-blue Surgeonfish, Spinyfoot and Masked Unicornfish and Schooling and Pennant Bannerfish, clashing with the extremely photogenic Moorish Idols and juvenile Titan Triggerfish.

Tapering down towards the southwest is a sheer-walled gully. The entrance is wide enough to venture into, but it soon becomes too narrow; the best way to observe it is to follow slightly above its path. Inside the gully are impressive gorgonian seafans and radiant soft corals; colourful Sea Trout and graceful lionfish are often present in its deeper portions. A giant moray eel is a resident here.

This section is graced by a series of Titan, Undulated and Scythe Triggerfish; also, large numbers of big Bullethead and Bicolour Parrotfish peck away the hard coral skeletons. Yellow-margined Moray Eels, in varying sizes, leave their lairs beneath mounds of lesser star corals to spring on their prey.

Another great area lies slightly northwest of the inner buoy, due north of the outer. A group of three rocks form a pyramid, broken by a narrow gorge running east–west.

The entrance to The Bronx (as one dive operator calls it) is like an enormous fish bowl. There are passing schools of jacks and Humpback, Single-spot, White and Blue-striped Snappers, and always colourful reef-fish like Red Coral Trout, Indian Lionfish and Oriental Sweetlips. These are backdropped by seafans, sponges, splendid yellow crinoids, featherstars and soft coral.

Follow The Bronx west, pass over the single geometrical rock, and immediately turn right; the water here is 26m (85ft) deep. Continue north until you reach a scattered area of short underwater pinnacles. The bottom is composed of fragmented coral substrate. Peer hard into it: this is home to the tiny but magnificent Blue-ribbon Eel (*Rhinomuraena quaesita*). This site demands more than one visit.

8 BEACON BEACH REEF/MORNING EDGE
★★★☆☆☆☆

Location: This and Beacon Point (Site 9) are on the longest continual coral structure in the island group. The reef spans the length of the southeastern coastline of Koh Similan (Island#8), about 200m (220yd) offshore.

Access: A number of mooring buoys dotted along the reef-crest provide convenient entry points.

Conditions: Visibility is generally very high, with an average in excess of 20m (66ft). Currents, when present, are weak to moderate, and flow north–south.

Average depth: 12-18m (39-59ft)

Maximum depth: 34m (113ft)

The reef-flat, in just over 5m (16ft) of water, features many small boulders of lesser star and brain corals, interspersed with familiar clusters of staghorns, all rich in colourful reef-fish like damsels, wrasse, parrotfish and surgeonfish, as well as large numbers of inquisitive Indian and Titan Triggerfish. The coral formations remain fairly constant over the southern section of the reef, increasing in size with depth. At around 20m (66ft) they are large enough to provide shelter for a number of Red Coral Trout.

As you head north along the reef, you come to areas of foliaceous corals, like lettuce and carnation, where there are many colourful reef-fish: Bird and Lunar Wrasse, Powder-blue Surgeonfish, squirrelfish, soldierfish and the Indian Bannerfish are all plentiful. The bottom is punctuated with large, impressive coral mounds and rocks covered with soft corals in diverse hues, encrusting sponges and various tubeworms and featherstars. Gorgonian and black seafans cling to the sides, which are further highlighted by small schools of lionfish.

9 BEACON POINT
★★★★☆

Location: The southern extension of Beacon Beach Reef (Site 8), this fringes Koh Similan's (Island#8) southern apex.

Access: No mooring buoys offer a convenient and direct descent to the site. The best method is by a 'live-boat' dive.

Conditions: Visibility is generally good, averaging 20m (66ft). Currents are weak to moderate.

Average depth: 16m (53ft)

Maximum depth: 55m (180ft)

The site is very like Site 8 but with more fish and much healthier and larger corals, especially in the deeper waters. Also, you have a better chance at this site of seeing Manta and large Eagle Rays, plus large pelagics, in the deeper southern waters, away from the headland.

The reef-flat features many small boulders of lesser star and brain corals, interspersed with familiar clusters of staghorn corals, all rich in colourful reef-fish like chromis, wrasse, parrotfish and surgeonfish, as well as large numbers of inquisitive Indian and Titan Triggerfish. The coral cover remains constant around the apex, with individuals increasing in size with depth – especially gorgonian seafans at about 30m (100ft). In the shallower waters, lettuce and carnation corals abound, their complementary reef-fish including Bird and Lunar Wrasse, Powder-blue Surgeonfish, squirrelfish, soldierfish and Indian Bannerfish.

10 ELEPHANT HEAD (HIN PUSA)
★★★★★

Location: The giant rocky outcrop off Koh Similan's (Island#8) southern tip. As you approach the site from the west the outcrop resembles a partially submerged elephant – hence the name.

Access: There is one permanent mooring buoy off the western face; descending to about 18m (60ft), directly onto the site.

Conditions: Visibility is good, ranging from 15m (50ft) to in excess of 25m (83ft). Currents can be strong, flowing north–south. There can be strong surge.

Average depth: 24m (80ft)

Maximum depth: 70m (235ft)

The underwater terrain is breathtaking. The dive takes you around huge boulders, some with frames measuring over 30m (100ft), sitting individually or stacked high to form daring swimthroughs comprising arches, caverns, gullies and tunnels at all depths. There is plenty of marine life and hard and soft corals abound, the former residing in the site's shallower sections, the latter clinging to the undersides of the boulders.

You descend at the mooring buoy and head east to the first of the colossal granite boulders; many parrotfish adorn this part of the site. The eastern faces of the boulders have far more soft corals than the exposed western faces.

Southwards, the boulders take a different formation, single boulders some 3m (10ft) wide lying with sandy pathways between them. Around these boulders are Emperor and Imperial Angelfish, Titan Triggerfish and sheltering schools of Yellowtail Fusiliers and juvenile Yellow Snappers.

The southernmost point of the site is a tiny group of submerged pinnacles in very deep water. These are a great place to observe small reef sharks.

Opposite: *Soft corals appear in a multitude of iridescent colours.*

11 DEEP SIX
★★

Location: Following the northern shore of Koh Pabu (Island#7).

Access: There is no mooring buoy.

Conditions: Visibility ranges between 16m and 25m (53–83ft). Currents can be strong.

Average depth: 18m (60ft)

Maximum depth: 40m (130ft)

This is another deep dive, following a ridge that features large seafans (typical of the area) in its deeper sections. Turtles and Leopard Sharks can be found on the sand, and you can see plenty of featherstars as well as small mounds of patch corals. The diversity of the fish-life is average, with angelfish and bannerfish making their presence felt. On the side of the ridge you can see a profusion of interesting bivalves.

12 EAST OF EDEN
★★★

Location: Following the reef that fringes the southeastern section of Koh Pabu (Island#7).

Access: There is no mooring buoy. Access is by 'live-boat' dive.

Conditions: Currents can be very strong, but are usually moderate. Visibility ranges from about 6m (20ft) to over 25m (83ft).

Average depth: 22m (73ft)

Maximum depth: 34m (113ft)

This is a steep sloping hard coral reef consisting of mostly hard-coral laminates. However, unusually for an east-facing reef, there are soft corals in the shallower waters at about 12m (40ft). This is one of the few sites where it is possible to observe the rarely seen Bow-mouth Guitarfish. Also on view are schools of snappers and fusiliers, and turtles and Leopard Sharks are occasionally seen. There is a stunning bommie (coral head) in the middle of the reef, starting in around 9m and going down to 30m; it features one of the finest concentrations of corals in the Similans.

13 STONEHENGE
★★★

Location: Directly off the northern point of Koh Miang (Island#4).

Access: There is no mooring buoy.

Conditions: Currents are moderate to strong. Visibility is typical of the area, at about 15–25m (50–83ft).

Average depth: 28m (93ft)

Maximum depth: 40m (130ft)

This is a deep dive, its best features being below 25m (83ft). The site consists of large towering rocks. The alleyways between these host large seafans and barrel sponges. This is a particularly good site for lobsters, and lionfish and Bearded Scorpionfish are likewise plentiful. Unicorn Surgeonfish and large angelfish are other common denizens, while pelagics like tuna, barracuda and trevally are frequent visitors. Leopard Sharks are often found on the sand in the deeper parts of this site. There is also a resident shovel-nosed shark here.

14 BARRACUDA POINT
★★★

Location: Around the two rocky islets about 500m (550yd) due east of Koh Miang (Island#4).

Access: There is no mooring buoy. Drift or follow the rocks. Boats generally send their tenders out to retrieve divers.

Conditions: Currents are moderate to strong; the site can be drift-dived when currents run north–south or south–north. Visibility ranges between 15m (50ft) and 25m (83ft).

Average depth: 14m (46ft)

Maximum depth: 34m (113ft)

The deepest section of this area is the southern part where there are lots of large boulders on the seafloor; in the deeper waters these are adorned with seafans and sea whips. The shallower section of this area features hard corals, and there are normally plenty of batfish in evidence.

The site's northern part is shallower, with a maximum depth of about 22m (73ft). The seascape is similar to that on the south, but the rocks surrounding you are more prominently highlighted by colourful seastars, anemones and crinoids in radiant reds and yellows. The batfish you encountered at the southern section of this site may follow you to this area.

15 BIRD ROCK
★★★

Location: A collection of large submerged granite boulders immediately south of Koh Miang (Island#4).

Access: There is no mooring buoy. Access is by 'live-boat' dive.

Conditions: Strong currents can prevail, sweeping divers away from the site. Visibility can be up to about 25m (83ft).

Average depth: 18m (60ft)

Maximum depth: 40m (130ft)

The site consists of large granite boulders tumbling to a depth of 40m (130ft). This bouldered continuation of the island features many barrel sponges and patches of encrusting sponges. The presence of reef-fish is adequate, with all the regulars of the region represented. There are a number of average swimthroughs at about 16m (53ft).

16 SHARK FIN REEF (HIN PHAE)
★★★★

Location: Around the small collection of rocks, which breaks the water at low tide, 3km (1.6 n. miles) southeast of Koh Payan (Island#3).

Access: This site remains unbouyed.

Conditions: Visibility runs from as low as 5m (16ft) to over 25m (83ft). As with many of the area's more open sites, there is a likelihood of strong currents.

Average depth: 16m (53ft)

Maximum depth: 40m (130ft)

The best locations to enter the water are off either end of the line of small rocky outcrops. The dive circumnavigates these outcrops. The northeastern side features a sloping reef, the southwestern side a more dramatically sheer dropoff: rocks resembling fallen hexagonal pillars, the highlight of this side of the site. At the southeastern end of these formations, in about 16m (53ft), is a large swimthrough; this provides an almost purpose-built opening, whichever way you are going, to the site's opposite side.

The marine life at this site is much more intense and

Emperor shrimp (Periclimenes imperator) and host Prickly sea cucumber (Thelanota ananas).

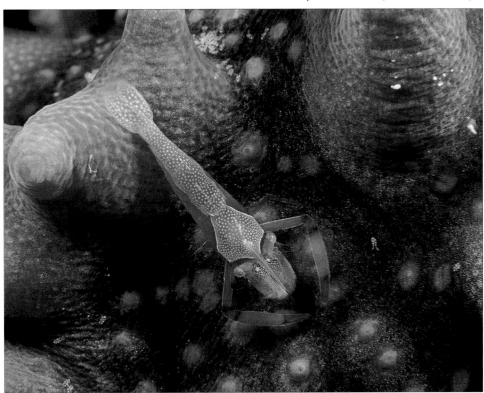

diverse along and below the sloping northeastern reef. Regular inhabitants include schools of batfish, surgeonfish, Moorish Idols and bannerfish. Large Napoleon Wrasse have also been seen. This section of the site is a very good place to spot passing sharks and large rays.

BOULDER CITY
★★★

Location: Immediately south of Shark Fin Reef (Site 16).
Access: The permanent mooring buoy is located over the northeast section of the site in about 27m (90ft) of water.
Conditions: In favourable conditions you can expect good visibility – occasionally over 30m (100ft). The site can experience strong currents from the north.
Average depth: 19m (63ft)
Maximum depth: 32m (106ft)
The site consists of a collection of enormous submerged granite boulders running southeast–northwest and more typical of a west-facing, rather than an east-facing, coastal rock formation in this area. As you approach them they fancifully resemble rocky mountains separated by wide valleys.

Descending directly from the boat, head southwest to pass over some large scattered rocks before you reach the rocky plateaux. This area has many gorgonian seafans and sea whips, plus small table corals, with Chocolate-dip Chromis, and a diversity of fire corals. If you maintain this heading you will then come to the smooth plateau.

The plateaux are smooth, their sheer sides punctuated occasionally by clusters of soft coral and radiant crinoids; small crevices house a diversity of marine life, with lionfish, Blue-spotted Groupers, Red Coral Trout and Bearded Scorpionfish all adopting them as havens in the stronger currents. Schools of Pinnate Batfish meander aimlessly in the shallows, beyond which Great Barracuda constantly patrol.

18 CORAL GARDENS/HOBBITLAND
★★★✩✩✩

Location: Following the eastern side of Koh Huyong (Island#1).
Access: There is no mooring buoy.
Conditions: Visibility ranges between 15m and 25m (50–83ft). Currents can be strong, a great drift-dive.
Average depth: 5m (16ft)
Maximum depth: 24m (80ft)
This relatively attractive shallow site is good for novice divers. It has the typical formation of an east-facing site

in this area. There are good examples of branching and table corals on the reef-flat, which lies in very shallow water. The surrounding deeper waters have the usual seafans and whips, and these feature in the shallower waters as well. There are many fire corals on the reef-slope, along with anemones hosting various clownfish, mainly Clarks Saddleback. There is a good representation of colourful reef-fish, including damselfish, butterflyfish and basslets.

19 SURGEON ROCKS
★★★

Location: Around the southern apex of Koh Huyong (Island#1).
Access: There is no mooring buoy.
Conditions: Visibility here averages about 20m (66ft), but the strong northerly currents that can be present not only limit visibility but render the site totally unsafe for novice divers.
Average depth: 18m (60ft)
Maximum depth: 35m (115ft)
This site comprises mainly large scattered boulders interspersed by patches of sand of equivalent size. The hard corals here are by no means prolific, but there are good examples of soft corals and barrel sponges. All in all, though, this serves merely as a convenient spot for the last dive of an excursion before diveboats head back to Koh Phuket, the pause reducing the length of the final stage of the homeward journey. This site, as its name suggests, hosts impressive numbers of different surgeonfish, with Powder-blue and Elongate being the more prominent of the species represented.

In the site's eastern section the large boulders are at an average 28m (93ft). Look beyond these into the deeper waters, as this could be your final chance – at least on this excursion – to spot large underwater creatures like Manta Rays and Whale Sharks, which frequent this area; so too do large schools of Great Barracuda. Around the rocks are schools of juvenile Blue-striped Snappers and a range of groupers.

WHITETIP REEF SHARK
(*TRIAENODON OBESUS*)

Length: Up to 210 cm
Normal Depth: 5-300m
Appearance: Brown/grey with white tipped dorsal fin and slender body.
These sharks are generally timid but can become excitable when the waters are baited. Often found in pairs or small groups. They are viviparous (produce living young) and a thirteen month gestation period can result in up to five juveniles. This shark is nocturnal and feeds on sleeping parrotfish, goatfishes, snappers and triggers. They always return to the same cave at dawn.

How to Get There

For information regarding travelling to Mu Koh Similan Marine National Park please refer to the Koh Phuket section (p 30) as this is the main take- off point. From there access is by live-aboard boat. An alternative is to board the Sea Tran Express which departs Patong and arrives 2¹/₂ hours later.

For any additional information on Mu Koh Similan contact the **Tourism Authority of Thailand**; tel (076) 212213, 211036/fax (076) 213582.

Where to Stay

Accommodation on Koh Miang (island #4) is in the form of purpose-built dormitory style bungalows, each capable of housing twenty people. Permission to stay in these bungalows must be obtained in advance from either the Royal Forestry Department or the Marine National Parks Division of the Royal Forestry Department. It is also possible, with permission, to camp on the island's main beach. Koh Miang also has a small outdoor restaurant and beach bar run by the staff of the **Royal Forestry Department**. Tents can be pitched for a small fee. For further information contact the **Royal Forestry Department**, Thap Lamu office; tel (076) 411914 or the Royal Forestry Department; tel (02) 579 1151/60 or the **Marine National Parks Division of the Royal Forestry Department**, Bangkok; tel (02) 579 7048/fax 579 7047.

Dive Facilities

There are no dive operators situated on any of the islands. The majority of the operators based on Koh Phuket will either schedule, or act as booking agents, for live-aboard excursions. Day trips are offered by some of the smaller operators on Phuket - but there is world class diving to be found here and day trips cannot really do the sites justice. For details of exact services provided see pp 31, 32. Trips are also organised by **Divelink Thailand** in Bangkok (see details on page 21).

Dive operator at Phang Nga
Sea Dragon Dive Centre, Phang Nga; tel (01) 723 1418/fax (01) 723 1418. This operator is located to the north of Thap Lamu and concentrates on budget live-aboard excursions and diver training. The company schedules 3-day 2-night excursions which depart from Khao Luk twice weekly. Two boats are capable of carrying eight guests each. Also included in the price are all regular services, soft drinks and, unusually, any required diving equipment. The range of PADI dive courses are also available. Non divers are welcome to join the trip for a price which includes snorkelling equipment.

Film Processing

Photographic services are not available on any of the islands. The nearest are on Koh Phuket and their details are listed in the Phuket regional directory on page 31.

Hospitals and Recompression Chamber

There are no medical facilities on any of the islands. The nearest ones are those listed in the Phuket regional directory on p 31. The nearest recompression chamber is also the same one listed in the Phuket regional directory (p 31).

Local Highlights

As is the case with Mu Koh Surin the main reason to come here is for the diving. However, there are many beaches dotted along the eastern sides of the larger islands, giving families and friends or non-diving visitors plenty of opportunities to relax in the sun whilst taking the occasional plunge in the clear seas. Beaches can be reached by Longtail boats. **Koh Miang** (island #4) has a pleasant nature trek that follows a narrow path cutting right through the island from east to west. This trail provides plenty of opportunities to observe the many fine examples of flora and fauna on this picturesque island. **Koh Similan** (island #8) has is a wonderful sandy beach at Campbell's Bay; at the northern end of this beach is **Similan Rock**, an enormous granite boulder perched high on top of smooth rocky shelves. It is possible to climb up to this monolith via a walkway of planks and ladders. From the top there are stunning views overlooking both this and the northernmost island of Koh Bangu (island #9). The climb is well worth the effort, but be warned that is often slippery; always ensure good foot and hand holds, and climb slowly.

A yacht meanders between Islands 8 and 9 in the Similans.

MU KOH SURIN MARINE NATIONAL PARK

MU KOH SURIN AND ENVIRONS

Mu Koh Surin Marine National Park is located 80km (48 n. miles) due west of Ranong Province on the west coast of Thailand.

The five granite islands sit in 135 sq km (80 sq miles) of water. The largest, Koh Surin Nua, has an area of 19 sq km (11 sq miles) and a highest point 240m (800ft) above sea level. To its immediate southwest lies Koh Surin Tai; between the two is a strait only 200m (220yd) wide which can be crossed on foot during low waters. Koh Surin Tai is slightly smaller, 12 sq km (9 sq miles), but has a highest point of 350m (1169ft) above sea level.

Both of these islands are covered with verdant primary evergreen forest. The supporting canopies average 32m (104ft) in height. Amid the forest are a few fruit trees and a collection of deciduous trees rich in epiphytes. Some 10–20% of Koh Surin Nua has a coverage of secondary growth, the primary forest having suffered from not only harsh monsoon conditions but also, during the 1960s, logging. The only residents on Koh Surin Nua are the National Park officials. Koh Surin Tai has a small community of Chao Ley Sea Gypsies on some of its eastern beaches.

DIVING AROUND MU KOH SURIN

The Mu Koh Surin sites are visited by live-aboard excursions from Koh Phuket. Many of the sites follow fringing reefs which slope gently to the sea-bed; others take you around small islets and along the walls of sheer submerged pinnacles.

Two local sites are as diverse as they are interesting. Koh Tachai (Site 11) features a series of multi-level reefs, each one different in both its formation and its resident marine life. Further south, the rocky outcrop of Koh Bon (Site 12) features regular visits from mantas and whale sharks.

The coral and marine life of Muh Koh Surin are now, thankfully, under protection, but there is still evidence of damage caused by a range of different fishing techniques. Dynamite fishing has certainly left its mark.

Opposite: *The tranquil beauty of a glorious Koh Surin sunset.*
Above: *Healthy reefs are once more thriving in this area.*

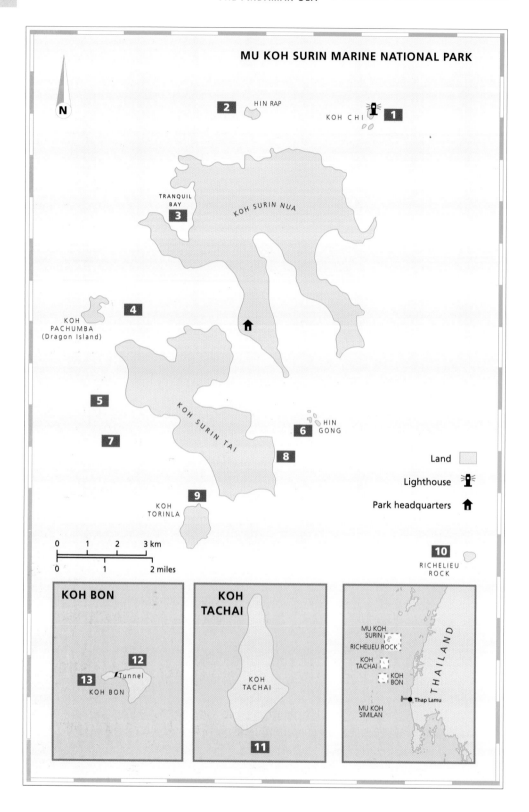

MU KOH SURIN MARINE NATIONAL PARK

N

2 HIN RAP

KOH CHI **1**

TRANQUIL
BAY
3

KOH SURIN NUA

4

KOH
PACHUMBA
(Dragon Island)

5

KOH SURIN TAI

HIN
6 GONG

7

8

9

KOH
TORINLA

Land

Lighthouse

Park headquarters

10

RICHELIEU
ROCK

0   1   2   3 km

0   1   2 miles

KOH BON

12

13 Tunnel

KOH BON

**KOH
TACHAI**

KOH
TACHAI

11

MU KOH
SURIN
RICHELIEU ROCK

KOH
TACHAI

KOH
BON

THAILAND

Thap Lamu

MU KOH
SIMILAN

1 KOH CHI (NUN ISLAND)

★★☆☆

Location: The site follows the eastern coast of the rocky islet some 2km (1 n. mile) northeast of Koh Surin Nua.
Access: The site is unbuoyed. The point of entry, is governed by conditions, being at either the north or the south end of the coast.
Conditions: Strong currents can flow south–north or vice versa; either way, in such conditions the site is suitable for drift-diving. Visibility averages 15m (50ft).
Average depth: 18m (60ft)
Maximum depth: 23m (76ft)
The main reason for visiting this collection of rocky outcrops is that it is one of the classic locations to observe large visiting pelagics, such as Great Barracuda, Dog-faced tuna, Threadfin Trevally, Big-eye Jack, mackerel and tuna; it is also one of the area's better locations for observing turtles, especially late in the day as they come closer to shore to feed or, in season, to lay their eggs. The main turtle species observed here are Hawksbill, Olive Ridley and Green, plus the very occasional Leatherback.

The dive follows a fringing reef of foliaceous and

CHAO LEY - SEA GYPSIES

'Sea gypsies' live in a small community on the northern half of Koh Surin Tai's eastern beach. Known as Chao Ley (from the Thai chao talay, meaning people of the sea), these nomadic fisherfolk originated in Indonesia and now live on a handful of the many islands in the Andaman Sea. During the period of the March full moon they celebrate their ancestors with a ceremony involving the launch of flamboyantly-decorated, miniature boats from the beach. These boats represent the fortunes of the clans and if they return to the same beach the Chao Ley will move to settle a new location.

Many Chao Ley here supplement their income by collecting shells which are sold on to tourists as souvenirs, and this accounts for the rarity of large shells within the Park. They have also been responsible for denuding reefs of large seafans (which are collected using hookah apparatus) and have been implicated in the illegal practise of dynamite fishing.

The Park authorities can do little to prevent these activities, since the Chao Ley are a law unto themselves. They help turtle conservation by collecting eggs which are hatched out in the 'Head Start' project on Koh Surin Nua, but the motive is purely commercial since they are paid for the eggs.

Oriental sweetlips (Plectorhinchus orientalis) in victory formation.

laminate hard corals among fallen rocks. The shallower sections are dominated by a number of tables of stag and elkhorn corals.

2 HIN RAP
★★☆☆☆

Location: The large rocky outcrop about 2km (1 n. mile) due north of Koh Surin Nua.

Access: The site is unbuoyed. The best entry point is 50m (55yd) from the outcrop at either the southwest or southeast point.

Conditions: Visibility is generally good – 15m (50ft) – but can be as low as 2m (6½ft) in stronger currents.

Average depth: 15m (50ft)

Maximum depth: 24m (80ft)

On the north the bottom drops to 24m (80ft), then gradually slopes back along the eastern coast to be at 15m (50ft) around the islet's southern apex. The north part itself features large scattered boulders over sand, some so close together they have formed small caverns and archways you can cautiously pass through. The eastern coast features a shallow sloping reef of mainly foliaceous corals, the deeper portions being host to large numbers of gorgonian seafans and coral whips. This reef, like many other of the island group's eastern-facing reefs, is good for spotting Green, Hawksbill and other Turtles.

Beyond the northern face the waters deepen quite dramatically; Great Barracuda, some over 2m (6½ft) long, school here. Whale Sharks and Manta Rays are often seen in the shallower waters.

Snorkellers can enjoy the shallow waters along the outcrop's western face. The terrain below this face remains more or less constant at 5m (16ft), and features

---

It is not easy to keep up with a Whale shark (Rhinocodon typus).

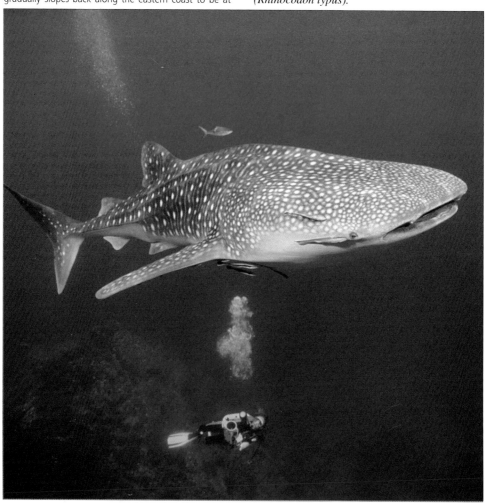

a plentiful diversity of small colourful reef-fish. This shallower shelf stretches along almost the entire length of the coastline.

3 TRANQUIL BAY
★★

Location: Tranquil Bay is on the western coast of Koh Surin Nua. The site is along its rocky southwestern coastline.
Access: Boats generally anchor for the night at one of the bay's permanent mooring buoys.
Conditions: This sheltered bay has low currents and high visibility – ideal for night-diving.
Average depth: 9m (30ft)
Maximum depth: 16m (53ft)
Taking you around the outer perimeters of large submerged boulders, this is solely a night-dive site, and a great location to observe all manners of nocturnal marine life. Turtles, rays, crabs, shrimps and juvenile reef sharks abound. Later at night you can see parrotfish encased in the cocoons they create in order to cloak their scent from would-be predators while they sleep. Black-spined Sea Urchins move slowly across the rocks, and the closed polyps of sea whips and small gorgonian seafans slowly open to filter nutrients from the waters.

4 DRAGON ISLAND (KOH PACHUMBA)
★★

Location: A small uninhabited island 3km (2 n. miles) northwest of the sound that divides the two Surin islands. The site is around a submerged pinnacle – reaching 4m (13ft) below the surface – directly off the island's north coast.
Access: The site is unbuoyed. The preferred method of entry is a 'live boat' dive.
Conditions: Visibility is generally 15–24m (50–83ft). A strong south–north current can flow.
Average depth: 18m (60ft)
Maximum depth: 22m (73ft)
An average wall-dive around a submerged pinnacle. In the shallower waters around the upper section of the pinnacle are a number of batfish. Away from the main rocky structure are some large, rounded, fallen boulders, where Blacktip Reef and Nurse Sharks cruise.

There are few soft corals, and most examples are relatively small; the rocks are actually more highlighted with orange and blue encrusting sponges. Marine life is dominated by medium-sized snappers, fusiliers, jacks, mackerel, tuna and barracuda.

The diversity of reef inhabitants is relatively poor, probably because of past overfishing and the collection of shells and shellfish which has been a real problem in these parts.

5 BREAKER REEF
★

Location: About 1km (1/2 n. miles) off the northern section of the west coast of Koh Surin Tai, where a completely submerged pinnacle lies an average 4m (13ft) below the surface.
Access: The site is unbuoyed.
Conditions: Visibility ranges from 10m (33ft) to 20m (66ft). This site can have extremely strong swirling currents, which not only rapidly change direction but also regularly fluctuate in strength.
Average depth: 18m (60ft)
Maximum depth: 22m (73ft)
The corals here are in very poor condition: those in the shallower waters near the pinnacle have been severely damaged by harsh monsoon conditions, while those in deeper waters, away from the pinnacle, have in past years fallen foul of dynamite fishing.

The site should not be ruled out completely, though, as soft corals in the deeper waters of the southeastern area are slowly beginning to flourish, but it will be a long time before it fully recovers and marine life returns.

6 HIN GONG
★★

Location: A small collection of granite outcrops in the southeastern approach to the sound separating Koh Surin Nua and Tai.
Access: The entry point is around 50m (170ft) off the southwest face of the dominating rocky outcrop. As with the majority of local sites, the preferred method of entry is a 'live-boat' dive.
Conditions: Visibility ranges from around 4m (13ft) to over 20m (66ft). Strong currents are frequent.
Average depth: 10m (33ft)
Maximum depth: 21m (70ft)
An average site for the area, with minimal marine life.

The dive follows the southwestern perimeter of an area of large submerged boulders. There are a number of swimthroughs, but they are by no means as impressive as those found at various sites in the Mu Koh Similan area. The rocks' upper surfaces are fringed with many featherstars and sea anemones. Scatterings of soft corals have regrown above gorgonian seafans in the deeper waters. The sea-bed has patches of hard corals, but little else to offer. However, the site has a good representation of shells, mainly cowries, oysters and Giant Clams in the shallows.

7 MARSHALL REEF

★

Location: About 3km (¹/₂ n. miles) off the western coast of Koh Surin Tai and 2km (1 n. mile) southwest of Breaker Reef (Site 5). A submerged pinnacle lies approximately 4m (13ft) below the surface.

Access: The site is unbuoyed. The preferred method of entry is a 'live-boat' dive.

Conditions: Visibility ranges from 10m (33ft) to 20m (66ft). This site can have extremely strong swirling currents, which not only rapidly change direction but also regularly fluctuate in strength.

Average depth: 18m (60ft)

Maximum depth: 22m (73ft)

This site is just like its northeastern neighbour, Breaker Reef (Site 5), but with extensive dynamite damage in the deeper waters. The healthiest corals are around the pinnacle's eastern wall.

8 TURTLE LEDGE

★★★★★★

Location: A fringing reef running along Koh Surin Tai's southeastern coastline, stretching north from the southern headland to a single secluded beach.

Access: The reef remains unbuoyed. Divers and snorkellers enter about 50m (55yd) offshore.

Conditions: Visibility may be as low as 10m (33ft) but is much more often beyond 30m (100ft). Strong currents can transform it into an enjoyable drift-dive, simply following the fringing reef along the shoreline.

Average depth: 8m (26ft)

Maximum depth: 20m (66ft)

The reef-flat sits in only 3m (10ft) of water, allowing excellent snorkelling. The higher portions of the reef-slope have numerous gardens of sea anemones, below which are large Magnificent Sea Anemones, most inhabited by Clark's Anemonefish. Clusters of stag and elkhorn corals shelter Giant Clams and encrusting sponges from the predation of Bullethead Parrotfish.

The site offers a wide diversity of marine life, but it is not concentrated in any one particular area. The recommended approach is to cover a reasonable portion of the reef; generally unadvised elsewhere (except when drifting in stronger currents), this approach here does not impair your enjoyment, as the majority of the reef inhabitants can be witnessed at a distance – they do not require close inspection!

The site got its name from the frequent sightings of turtles, in particular Hawksbill.

This is a really good place for night-diving. One interesting feature is away from the reef, over the sand

---

WHALE SHARK (*Rhincodontidae*)

The impressive Whale Shark (p.52), although intimidating in appearance, is a harmless filter feeder which obtains nutrition by filtering minute planktonic creatures from the water as they pass through its open, prominent mouth.

The planktonic creatures are then retained from literally gallons of water as they pass through the swimming fish before they are expelled through its gills in vast amounts. Feeding times are easy to recognise as the expiration of water causes the gills of the shark to shudder in large undulating movements.

Whale Sharks are often spotted in somewhat limited visibility when the waters become a cloudy green due to the increased presence of planktonic creatures.

---

in deeper water: a number of heavily pitted rocks provide warrens for sleeping parrotfish. As you approach these rocks they look like covered baskets of fish with only the tails in view!

9 KOH TORINLA

★★★★★

Location: About 1km (¹/₂ n. miles) off the southwest tip of Koh Surin Tai.

Access: The unbuoyed entry point is 50m (167ft) off the north coast of Koh Torinla.

Conditions: Current, when present, is generally moderate, flowing west–east. Visibility ranges between 15m (50ft) and 25m (83ft).

Average depth: 12m (40ft)

Maximum depth: 27m (90ft)

After a descent of 20m (66ft) you head southeasterly and follow a sloping reef, which has a crest in 10m (33ft) of water (the more favourable area for snorkellers). In the eastern area is a small garden of Magnificent Sea Anemones hosting Pink Skunk and Clark's Anemonefish. Blue Spot Groupers and Red Coral Trout shelter beneath many fine flower corals; many members of the Chromis family dart among large tables of staghorns. Away from the reef are coral patches.

As you head westwards back over the reef you find a shallow section carpeted with staghorns in excellent condition. Small hard-coral coronets top many rocks between soft-coral gardens. Beyond the gardens, bearing south, are numerous smooth porous corals – including Lesser and Greater Star Corals – with Giant Wrasse, large Bicolour Parrotfish, Blue-spotted Groupers, Imperial Angelfish and Bird Wrasse venturing between the rocks.

There are many shelves of rocks at varying depths, all with different features. The shallower ones host Hermit Crabs, Crown Urchins and Cleaner Shrimp, and are rich with colourful green featherstars. Over the ledges in the deeper waters there are many moray eels and larger groupers to be encountered.

10 RICHELIEU ROCK
★★★★★

Location: Off Khuraburi, on Thailand's west coast, and 14km (7¹/₂n. miles) east of Mu Koh Surin.

Access: The rock can be reached in about 3hr from Khuraburi pier and in just over 1hr from Koh Surin Nua.

There is no permanent mooring. The pinnacles are visible only at low tide, so it is dangerous for boats to approach too close.

Conditions: As the rock is in open seas there can be very strong currents. Visibility ranges from 5m (16ft) to beyond 30m (100ft).

Average depth: 19m (63ft)

Maximum depth: 45m (147ft)

This is among the world's top listed locations for sighting

Artificial light can reveal colours otherwise lost at depth.

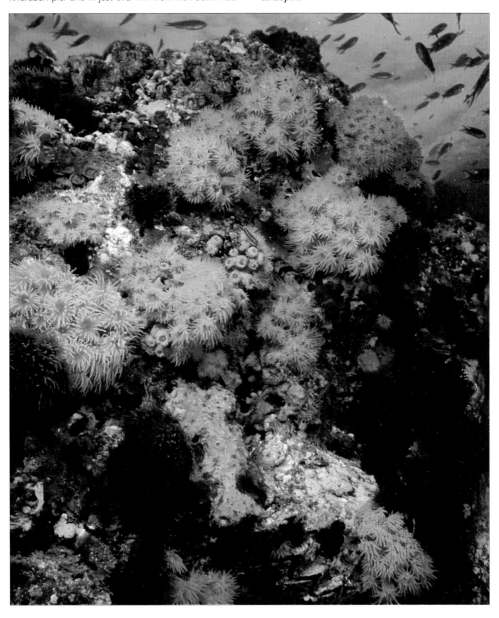

Whale Sharks. One of Thailand's best sites, this is a wall-dive around the main outcrop, which is surrounded by smaller submerged pinnacles whose peaks range from 3m (10ft) to 10m (33ft) below the surface. The pinnacles have numerous shelves and ledges at all depths.

The three southern pinnacles are in 22m (73ft); at this depth you find orange gorgonian seafans, immediately beneath radiant hermetypic corals. Around the corals is a wide diversity of marine life: residents include Schooling Bannerfish, Single-spot and Giant Snappers, Indian and Spotfin Lionfish, Moorish Idols, Titan Triggerfish, and Shovelnose Rays. Also present are Bearded Scorpionfish, stonefish, moray eels, Long-spined Sea Urchins, seahorses, shrimps, crabs and colourful nudibranchs.

As this is the only food source in the immediate area, it is excellent for large pelagics. Rainbow runners, Great Barracuda, trevallies, tuna and jacks are frequently seen. On one of the eastern shelves an enormous Carpet Anemone is home to a family of tiny Porcelain Crabs.

11 KOH TACHAI
★★★★☆☆☆

Location:: 40km (22 n. miles) south of Koh Surin Tai.
Access: Koh Tachai is about 2hr from Koh Surin Tai. The entry point lies 200m (220yd) due south of the island's southernmost point. There are no outcrops to mark its location: mooring buoys have been placed here.
Conditions: The current here runs weak to moderate. Visibility ranges from 9m (30ft) to above 30m (100ft).
Average depth: 22m (73ft)
Maximum depth: 30m (100ft)
This site is divided into three reefs, each dominating a different depth with different structures and reef inhabitants. If you want a single-depth dive, the optimum position is slightly above the inner pinnacle in the site's average depth of 22m (73ft).

Off the island's southern point, two submerged pinnacles stand proud of many large boulders and rocks, providing great swimthroughs. This area is part of the first and deepest of the three reefs, ranging from 25m (83ft) to 30m (100ft). It continues to fringe the island, mainly in the form of bold rocks featuring swimthroughs of varying sizes.

The second, or middle, reef is found in 19m (63ft). It is constructed mainly of hard corals and large rocks, around which schools of spadefish – such as the Pinnate Batfish – are tended by Common Cleanerfish. Clinging to the rocks are gorgonian seafans, featherstars, colourful crinoids and carpets of sea anemones. Large Bullethead Parrotfish and even larger Napoleon Wrasse share the waters with Titan and Orange-striped Triggerfish, Moorish Idols, Schooling Bannerfish and small schools of juvenile snappers.

The third and shallowest reef sits in 12m (40ft). Here you find Indian Lionfish, Giant Clams and schools of juvenile Yellowtail Barracuda.

12 KOH BON PINNACLE
★★

Location: About 22km (12 n. miles) south of Koh Tachai and 46km (25 n. miles) northeast of the Similan islands.
Access: Off the northern coastline of Koh Bon; the site can only be located by using a GPS.
Conditions: Visibility ranges from fair to excellent. Currents can be anything from non-existent to strong.
Average depth: 24m (80ft)
Maximum depth: 34m (113ft)
This submerged pinnacle lies beneath 18m (56ft) and cannot be seen from the surface. The main attraction is the healthy numbers of Whale Sharks, other sharks and Manta Rays which for some reason are attracted to the waters surrounding this otherwise plain feature.

13 KOH BON
★★★

Location: Off the southwestern end of Koh Bon.
Access: The entry point is at the southwest tip of the lime-stone cliffs; otherwise, a 'live-boat' dive is recommended.
Conditions: Visibility is good, often reaching 30m (100ft) in sheltered areas. Currents can run quite rapidly.
Average depth: 21m (70ft)
Maximum depth: 40m (130ft)
The reef bottoms at 32m (106ft) then sharply drops to 40m (130ft) to reach gently sloping sand. Huge sponges can be found in depths of 30-40m (100-130ft).

Beneath the entry point the rocks are carpeted with golden star corals and the island's perimeter takes the form of a wall covered with sea anemones and encrusting sponges. There are octopus, resting cuttlefish, and Coral Trout. On closer inspection a variety of Cleaner Shrimps are apparent tending to their hosts at cleaning stations. To the southwest you can follow a splendid reef covered in corals teeming with marine life.

ANCHORAGE PROBLEMS

The conditions of corals in Thai waters has, especially over the last few decades, sadly deteriorated. One cause of the deterioration is the constant dropping and raising of anchors, not only directly onto corals but in close proximity which causes just as much damage. Anchors dig into the silt when they are dropped so, of course, when they are raised, large amounts of silt get raised with them. As the falling silt drifts, it buries otherwise healthy corals; the bigger the anchor the more serious the damage.

However, nowadays the situation is definitely improving due to the numerous permanent mooring buoys which have been installed by both dive operators and the Royal Forestry Department. If the permanent buoys are fully utilized coral damage will be greatly reduced.

HOW TO GET THERE

For any additional information regarding travelling to Mu Koh Surin Marine National Park please refer to the Koh Phuket section on page 30 as this is the main take-off point.

By bus: VIP air-conditioned buses leave Bangkok's southern bus terminal daily at 18.50hrs and arrive at the National Park Office pier some twelve hours later. The pier is located 6km (3.5 miles) north of Khuraburi Town. For further information regarding bus services contact Bangkok southern bus terminal; tel (02) 435 1199, 435 1200, Phuket Central Tour; tel (02) 435 5019, 434 3233.

By boat: It is possible to reach Koh Surin Nua directly from the National Park Office pier. Passengers congregate at the pier at 08.00hrs for the journey which takes approximately 3 hours. Tickets can be purchased from the National Park Office at the pier. For more information contact Royal Forestry Department, Kuraburi office; tel (076) 491378. Royal Forestry Department, Koh Surin Nua; tel 01 723 1424.

For any additional information on Mu Koh Surin contact **Tourism Authority of Thailand**, Phuket office; tel (076) 212213, 211036/fax (076) 213582.

WHERE TO STAY

There is accommodation on Koh Surin Nua in the southern bay of Ao Mae Yai in the form of purpose built dormitory style bungalows (sleeping between six and eight people). The sleeping arrangements are basic and consist of mattresses lined up on the wooden floors. It is possible to stay in these bungalows but permission must be granted from either the Royal Forestry

Department or the National Parks Division of the Royal Forestry Department in advance. It is also allowed (when permission has been granted) to camp on the western beach. You can use your own tent or rent a two-man tent from the Royal Forestry Department.

Island guests are served by a restaurant and small bar run by the staff of the Royal Forestry Department. Contact the **Royal Forestry Department**, Bangkok; tel (02) 579 1151/60 or the National Parks Division of the Royal Forestry Department at the same address in Bangkok.

DIVE FACILITIES

There are no dive operators situated on either of the islands. The majority of the operators based on Koh Phuket either schedule or will act as booking agents for live-aboard excursions. For details of exact services provided please see the Phuket section.

Dive Trips

The best way to dive the area is to join the relaxed atmosphere on board one of Phuket's live-aboard excursions, as listed in the Phuket section p. 31. Trips can also be arranged through **Divelink Thailand** in Bangkok, see page 21.

FILM PROCESSING

Photographic Services are not available on these islands. The nearest are on Koh Phuket, see page 31.

HOSPITALS AND RECOMPRESSION CHAMBER

There are no medical facilities on either of the islands. The nearest ones are those listed in the Koh Phuket section on p. 31. The

WILDLIFE

The forest canopy on the two Surin islands reaches some 30m in height and supports a variety of wildlife including pig tailed macaques, grey-bellied squirrels, mouse deer, Malaysian flying lemurs and flying foxes.

nearest **recompression chamber** is Dive Safe Asia on Koh Phuket.

LOCAL HIGHLIGHTS

The major highlights of this island group are underwater and are detailed in the site descriptions. Non-divers can enjoy the reefs by renting **snorkelling gear** and a **Longtail boat** from the National Park Office.

There are also a number of land-based distractions to enjoy, centred mainly on or around the larger of the Surin Islands, the northern island of **Koh Surin Nua**. There is a **nature trail** which takes visitors across the island from the Park Official's Office in the south to the rangers sub-station in the north.

At the Park Official's office there is an interesting exhibition of the **marine life** to be found in the park's surrounding waters.

Across the sound, on the adjacent beach of Koh Surin Tai is an interesting **sea gypsies fishing village**. It is possible to visit the island and wander amongst these people but please respect their privacy.

Male Pharoah cuttlefish (Sepia pharaonis) give their attention to a single female.

THE MERGUI ARCHIPELAGO

In 1997 the Mergui Archipelago in the south of Myanmar (Burma) was opened up to foreigners for the first time in over fifty years. The port of Mergui used to be the main gateway to the Gulf of Siam and beyond – back in the 17th Century all passing boats came into the port to offload cargo or replenish supplies. Since then the Mergui Archipelago has been left largely alone and today it is an area of some mystery. Numerous islands remain unexplored, and the region presents the possibility of hundreds of exciting new dive sites. Trips here certainly have an exploratory feel, with visitors being amongst the first foreign faces ever seen by local nomadic Moken people (Burmese sea gypsies).

The topography of the area comprises mainly undulating hills, no higher than 600m (2000ft), allowing for exploration of the islands. There are literally hundreds of islands, islets and outcrops, many of the larger ones boasting glorious beaches fringed by rich mangroves and with streams flowing down from the elevated land. Wildlife is profuse, with Brahminy Kites and White-bellied Sea Eagles circling in contention for fish. Over the primary rainforest small green parakeets are common and Wreathed, Pied and Great Hornbills frequently patrol the skies.

Diving the Mergui Archipelago

All diving here is done from live-aboard boats operating out of Thailand. Charters on luxury yachts offer the chance to combine diving and island exploratory cruises for durations of between three and seven days.

Coral representation is sporadic, and the underwater terrain is quite rugged. However, the area's great attraction is diving with big fish, namely sharks, rays and a wealth of pelagics. The excitement at a number of the open ocean sites is indescribable. The Burma Banks and Black Rock attract a huge variety of sharks as well as frequent schools of Manta Rays. There is a healthy array of smaller reef life at many sites, and several are good for snorkelling. North Eastern Little Torres, for instance, has a relatively shallow plateau with plenty to see, while fringing reefs off the beaches on larger islands are also suitable.

Opposite: *A quiet, relaxed atmosphere prevails at the port of Mergui.*
Above: *Ole' Scarface, a familiar Silvertip shark (Carcharhinus albimarginatus) at Silvertip Bank.*

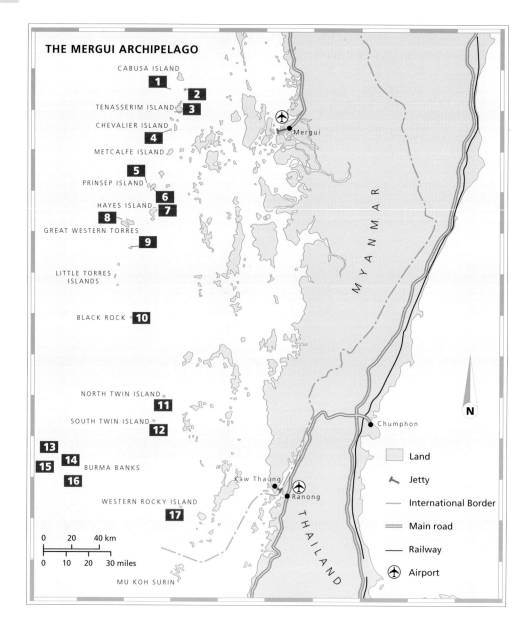

THE MERGUI ARCHIPELAGO

CABUSA ISLAND **1**
2
TENASSERIM ISLAND **3**
CHEVALIER ISLAND
4
METCALFE ISLAND
5
PRINSEP ISLAND
6
HAYES ISLAND **7**
8
GREAT WESTERN TORRES
9

LITTLE TORRES
ISLANDS

BLACK ROCK **10**

Mergui

MYANMAR

NORTH TWIN ISLAND
11
SOUTH TWIN ISLAND
12
13
14
15 BURMA BANKS
16
WESTERN ROCKY ISLAND
17

Chumphon

N

Kaw Thaung
Ranong

THAILAND

MU KOH SURIN

0   20   40 km
0   10   20   30 miles

Land

Jetty

International Border

Main road

Railway

Airport

1 NORTH AND SOUTH PINNACLES

★★★

Location: A series of pinnacles 8km (4n. miles) to the south of Cabusa Island.
Access: Live-aboard only. Entry is off the west of the southernmost pinnacle.
Conditions: Currents and visibility vary according to tidal behaviour at this open ocean site. The length of the reef formation makes it a terrific drift dive.

Average depth: 18m (60ft)
Maximum depth: 38m (126ft)
This dive follows around a jumble of rocks, with Whitetip Sharks, Indian Triggerfish and fusiliers often present. On the western ridge at a depth of between 14 and 17m (46–56ft) is a cleaning station, regularly attended by Eagle Rays, Dusky Batfish and Oriental Sweetlips. The eastern slope has large oysters embedded in its rocky structure, and below these numerous small fish dart between patches of sea whips. Large fish such as Giant and Humpback Snappers are commonplace. Scorpionfish lurk everywhere – in crevices, on ledges and under rocky overhangs.

2 FREAK ISLAND
★★☆

Location: A small 30m (100ft) high outcrop crowned by a tree, between Cabusa and Tenasserim Islands.
Access: Live-aboard only. Entry point depends on weather.
Conditions: Visibility ranges from 5m (16ft) to beyond 30m (100ft).The full range of currents can flow.
Average depth: 12m (40ft)
Maximum depth: 26m (86ft)
Following the structure clockwise from a western entry, numerous triggerfish and a couple of Giant Groupers can be seen frolicking in the deeper waters. Schools of tangs and Spiny Foot, fusiliers and juvenile snappers are also present. There is a lavish gorgonian seafan garden at 24m (80ft) off the northern point, where giant Barrel Sponges and copious mature Giant Snappers, Sea Bass, Moorish Idols and Pennant Bannerfish can be found. Heading east, fish life remains diverse, though Sergeant Majors become more dominant. Lionfish hover and swoop over an impressive garden of Magnificent Sea Anemones blanketing the rocks.

3 SMUGGLERS FOLLY
★★

Location: The north edge of the large western bay of Tenasserim Island.
Access: Live-aboard only. Descend midway along the inlet.
Conditions: Visibility generally exceeds 5m (16ft), to above 30m (100ft). Waters are generally calm.
Average depth: 16m (53ft)
Maximum depth: 30m (100ft)
This bay was a hiding place in the 17th century for pirates intercepting ships on their approach to Mergui harbour, and the allure of lost booty makes it an intriguing dive. Local marine life includes Blue-ring Angelfish, Moorish Idols, Yellow-lined Snappers, and Bicolour and Bullet-head Parrotfish, while Blue-spotted Ribbontail Rays can be seen gliding over the coral substrate bottom.

4 CHEVALIER ROCK
★★★★

Location: Immediately south of Chevalier Island. Two rocky pinnacles break the surface, with a shallow reef running southeast–northwest between them.
Access: Live-aboard only. The easiest entry point is to the south.
Conditions: In calm conditions drift diving is possible, but strong surge can make things difficult. Visibility is good.
Average depth: 20m (66ft)
Maximum depth: 34m (113ft)

Heading northwest from the entry point takes you over an extensive field of gorgonian seafans in varying shades of orange, all regimentally standing in rows perpendicular to the wall so as to filter nutrients from the flowing waters. This configuration continues through a gorge which leads up to 24m (80ft). Fish life here consists mainly of small Checkerboard and Lunar Wrasse, with seafans swaying to and fro in the swell as the current passes up and over the wall. At this depth the south of the rocky structure seems fairly barren, but ascending to a depth of 11m (36ft) brings you to 'Maurice Ledge', a rocky plateau, with shelves at varying depths all interconnected by a matrix of slopes, steps and caverns. This area is much more radiant than the others, and features a high presence and diversity of marine life, plus large patches of orange and yellow encrusting sponges.

5 TOWER ROCK
★★★

Location: At the western end of the north coastline of Prinsep Island.
Access: Live-aboard only. Entry is directly off the rock face in the narrow strait separating Pebble Rock; head east.
Conditions: An acceptable visibility range, with generally calm waters.
Average depth: 18m (60ft)
Maximum depth: 32m (106ft)
Above water this formidable rocky karst conjures up all sorts of images of what to expect in the depths below. This is primarily a wall dive, although there are scattered rocks worth exploring away from the wall itself, frequented by more than a few large Black and Whitetip Sharks. The wall itself features small green branch corals, with lots of holes and crags forming protective lairs for crayfish and other small invertebrates. Solitary juvenile Blue ring and Emporer angelfish can be seen fluttering around. There can be a lot of wave action here and the roar of the water crashing into the caverns and caves above the surface echoes around the site.

6 SERGEANT ISLAND
★★

Location: The sister island of Prinsep Island.
Access: Live-aboard only. Entry is off the northeast coast.
Conditions: Average visibility of 10m (33ft). Generally calm.
Average depth: 17m (56ft)
Maximum depth: 25m (83ft)
At the northern point is a slope of small rubble stretching some 80m (240ft) across, possibly caused by an enormous landslide many years ago. It descends to 25m (83ft), ploughing a furrow through the entire reef. There is an assortment of schooling marine life here including cuttlefish, fusiliers and large Devil Rays, occasionally as

many as forty. The largest coral feature is a mound of lesser star corals, with a giant moray eel beneath, and some green Tubastraea. Butterflyfish are present, though these are only medium-sized. A small crevice at 10m (33ft) hosts a tremendous diversity of marine life, including two large porcelain crabs, and an extended family of Clark's Anemonefish milling around a carpet anemone.

7 BULL SHARK OUTCROP
★★★

Location: A tiny outcrop immediately east of Hayes Island.
Access: Live-aboard only. The preferred entry point is off the east face in 22m (73ft) of water.
Conditions: Visibility is fair to good. Strong currents often run, but there are sheltered areas.
Average depth: 16m (53ft)
Maximum depth: 22m (75ft)
Strong currents bring this site to life. Devil Rays can sometimes be seen circling overhead, while Whitetip Sharks are often present in nearby deeper waters and closer in. On the reef numerous lionfish mingle amongst green branches of corals highlighted by a few soft coral bushes in deep reds and mauves. Following clockwise around the outcrop into more sheltered waters on our first dive here, a Bull Shark also suddenly made an appearance. Away from the reef's edge here, there is a shallow area of table corals and sea anemones, where you can see Black-banded Sea Snakes, Bearded Scorpionfish and a small octopus.

8 GREAT WESTERN TORRES
★★☆☆

Location: Off the rugged northwest coast of the western of the two islands.
Access: Live-aboard only. Enter off the northwest shoreline and follow it northwards.
Conditions: Clear and calm seas mostly, though strong currents run around the full moon.
Average depth: 22m (66ft)
Maximum depth: 60m (198ft)
This dive first meanders around a number of enormous submerged boulders, with the depth dropping beyond 50m (167ft). The centrepiece is a submerged pinnacle rising from around 40m (133ft) to 20m (66ft) with sheer, barren walls, which provide a great observation station. Yellow-margined triggerfish can be seen scouring the seabed below, occasionally retreating from sight as a patrolling Whitetip or Blacktip Shark looms into view. Big rays are also sometimes visible in deeper waters. This first section can be done as an exciting drift dive, around, over and occasionally through all manner of boulders.

The second, eastern section of the site is shallower and somewhat more protected from currents by the

layout of the underwater terrain. There is a good representation of hard corals, dotted with sea anemones.

This is a terrific dive site offering a high presence of pelagics in flowing waters and a variety of smaller colourful creatures in the more sheltered waters.

9 NORTHEASTERN LITTLE TORRES
★★☆☆☆

Location: The nearest of the Little Torres islands to Great Western Torres.
Access: Live-aboard only. The entry point is south of the row of small rocky outcrops off the southwest coast.
Conditions: Very good in all respects.
Average depth: 18m (60ft)
Maximum depth: 50m+ (167ft+)
This is a highly enjoyable dive, with a rich diversity of marine life and good opportunities for seeing sharks and rays. Grey Reef, Black and Whitetip Sharks all frequently cruise by, while rays include large Black-spot ribbon-tailed Stingray and Black Marbled. Heading north from the entry point, an introductory area of soft corals and sea fans prepares divers for the glorious coral gardens ahead. At 22m (73ft) there are numerous coral boulders and mounds and coral laminates; brain corals, lesser and greater star corals, tables of stag and elkhorn, small gorgonians and sea whips are all represented. Titan Triggerfish race around off the reef, Blue and Orange Starfish laze on the rocks and Black-banded Sea Snakes wriggle past. The shallower southeast section of this coral garden has Sergeant Majors, and crayfish concealed in narrow crevices. This is amongst the archipelago's better snorkelling sites.

10 BLACK ROCK
★★★★★

Location: A 50m (165ft) wide outcrop equidistant between North Eastern Little Torres and North Twin Island.
Access: Live-aboard only. Entry is off the southern face.
Conditions: Visibility ranges from as little as 5m (16ft) to excellent. Strong currents can run.
Average depth: 22m (73ft)
Maximum depth: 40m+ (133ft+)
This is a tremendously exciting dive site, with a never ending stream of sharks of different sizes and species. It is primarily a wall dive, underlined with small boulders. This is the place to observe larger sharks such as Scalloped Hammerhead, Bull and Grey Reef. The sharks patrol waters away from the rocky mass, passing through and between patch reefs and boulders that have settled to form wide U-shaped gullies on the seabed. Large barracudas provide a wake-up call for any divers thinking of investigating the rocks. Reef fish are prolific all around this open ocean site, but this is not a place for anyone who feels uncomfortable with sharks.

11 NORTH TWIN
★★★☆

Location: 86km (55n. miles) to the south of Black Rock.
Access: Live-aboard only. The entry point is immediately off the north shore.
Conditions: Fair to good.
Average depth: 15m (50ft)
Maximum depth: 22m (73ft)
Below the entry point is a wide plateau at 20m (66ft), covered by numerous hard and soft corals, crinoids and small reef fish. Eggshell and Tiger Cowrie Shells sit on display, while small groups of goatfish fidget about between the rocks and over the coral substrate bottom. Juvenile Harlequin Sweetlips are in evidence, and around one particularly compact cluster of seafans, schools of Checkerboard Wrasse and small fish fry congregate. There are larger table corals and porite mounds dotted with multi-coloured plume worms, and below the mounds crayfish concealed in darker overhangs. Heading from north to south is a gully at 15m (50ft), inside which live a selection of surgeonfish including Masked and Powderblue. Parrotfish, Spiny Foot and Dog-faced Pufferfish have also taken up residency. The waters away from the island appear to be part of one of the many routes for Burmese Barracudas and small Whitetip Reef Sharks. The barracuda in particular often come in close to check out divers and on occasion escort them round the site.

12 SOUTH TWIN ISLAND
★★

Location: 20km (12n. miles) south of North Twin Island.
Access: Live-aboard only. Entry is off the northern end of the bay on the east coast.
Conditions: Visibility ranges from 10m (33ft) to 20m (66ft). Currents are generally calm.
Average depth: 16m (53ft)
Maximum depth: 25m (83ft)
Numerous large scattered boulders abound, covered with elk and staghorn corals as well as many small colourful reef fish including Queen Triggerfish and juvenile Moorish Idols. The rocks not only provide shelter in strong currents but also play home to several Painted Crayfish who have made their lair under one of the ledges. Away from these configurations, large schools of mackerel can be seen passing by, along with jacks, tuna and trevally.

Opposite: *A Coral grouper (Cephalopholis mimiata) waits at a cleaning station.*

13 ROE BANK
★★★

Location: The most northwesterly of four divable banks.
Access: There is no mooring buoy to indicate the bank's position. Operators carefully locate an area away from any corals and drop anchor.
Conditions: Visibility varies from 10m to 30m (33–100ft), with an average of 15m (50ft). Current ranges from zero to very strong.
Average depth: 15m (50ft)
Maximum depth: 60m (200ft)
This is the furthest bank from Koh Phuket. The top of this submerged plateau starts about 15m (50ft) below the surface, sloping down gradually to 30m (100ft) at the edges before dropping dramatically to the ocean floor, more than 300m (1000ft) below. The top surface has sandy areas between large table corals and coral mounds and pillars, with soft corals on the underside of overhangs. There are reef-fish aplenty, mingling with – or trying to avoid – passing pelagic predators, and reef and oceanic sharks.

14 BIG BANK
★★★

Location: Just over 7km (4 n. miles) southeast of Roe Bank (Site 13).
Access: Via a live-aboard diving cruise.
Conditions: Visibility varies from 10m to 30m (33–100ft). Current ranges from zero to very strong. This is the largest of the banks, and in stronger currents you can drift-dive.
Average depth: 18m (60ft)
Maximum depth: 30m (100ft)
The bank covers an area of almost 2 sq km (0.8 sq miles). Its plateau is the deepest of the four banks', averaging 18m (60ft), with sides sloping down to 30m (100ft), then a wall down to 300m (1000ft). The elevated section of this site is scattered with coral mounds, some rising to 12m (40ft) and being 5m (16ft) across. Some are divided by impressive gullies and canyons wide enough for divers to pass through; seafans adorn their walls, and lesser star corals provide an undulating floor. Numerous sharks roam this site. Tawny Nurse Sharks are the most common.

15 RAINBOW REEF
★★★

Location: About 5km (3 n. miles) southwest of Big Bank.
Access: Live-boat dive with divers being retrieved by small tenders, especially in strong currents.
Conditions: Visibility varies from 10m to 30m (33–100ft), with an average of 15m (50ft). Current ranges from zero to very strong.

Average depth: 15m (50ft)
Maximum depth: 60m (200ft)
This site has possibly the highest proportion of hard-coral cover of all the banks, with some magnificent table corals spreading to 5m (16m) or more in diameter. There are also huge coral mounds and boulders on top of the platform, as well as patches of elkhorn and staghorn coral and gorgonian seafans. The fish life here is typical of the area.

16 SILVERTIP BANK
★★★

Location: The easternmost of the four divable banks.
Access: Occasionally mooring buoys mark this site, but if the buoys are missing, operators carefully locate an area away from any corals and drop anchor; a competent diving member of the crew then descends and secures it further.
Conditions: The current here can be zero, but it can be very strong. Visibility can vary from 10m to 30m (33-100ft).
Average depth: 14m (46ft)
Maximum depth: 60m (200ft)
Silvertip Bank is the most frequently visited of the banks. Covering about 1 sq km (0.4 sq miles), the bank is a flat platform with patches of dense hard corals and coral heads, as well as rock grottoes and tunnels where soft corals predominate.

The main attraction at this site, however, is its sharks – and there are plenty of them. Reef sharks here include Silvertips, Whitetips, Grey and Nurse Sharks, while oceanic visitors include Tiger Sharks and Hammerheads. Enormous Whale Sharks are sometimes seen.

17 WESTERN ROCKY
★★★★★★

Location: A collection of small rocky outcrops 82km (50n. miles) southwest of Kaw Thaung, Victoria Point.
Access: Live-aboard only. There are several entry points.
Conditions: Conditions can vary rapidly.
Average depth: 20 m (20 ft)
Maximum depth: 30m (100ft)
This site is generally dived either to or from the Burma Banks. The underwater terrain here consists of pinnacles, both outcropping and submerged. The largest outcrop has a cave that cuts right through it and branches into a narrow and low exit; this tunnel is filled with crayfish and other invertebrates, but is best avoided since its exit is blocked by two large though harmless resident Nurse Sharks. Around the other pinnacles Porcelain Crabs and sea anemones abound, with a variety of small sharks visible in the deeper waters.

HOW TO GET THERE

The live-aboard trips that access the Mergui Archipelago all take as their real starting point the port of Kaw Thaung on Myanmar's Victoria Point. Kaw Thaung is situated just across from the Thai town of Ranong, easily accessible by domestic flight or overland from within Thailand.

From Bangkok to Ranong there are two flights a day, four times a week; the flight time is 1hr 20 min. For further information about flights from Bangkok, contact Bangkok Airways, tel (02) 2293434.

Ranong can also be reached by road from Phuket Island, which is in fact where many of the relevant live-aboard operators are based. Phuket itself is served by both international flights and up to fourteen domestic flights from Bangkok a day. It is sensible is to make a prior arrangement to be then collected at the airport by your dive operator.

On arrival in Ranong and after a brief immigration procedure, boats make the 30 min crossing to Kaw Thaung, where another immigration procedure is required. For immigration clearance you need two copies of your passport and four passport-sized photographs. The live-aboard boats and their passengers are then cleared to leave, though some trips choose to take the opportunity to enjoy a typical Burmese dinner before departure or bedding down for the night.

WHERE TO STAY

As all of the trips are live-aboard excursions, accommodation is on-board. The only exception is if guests choose to join or leave their excursion at the port of Mergui. Flights leave for Mergui from Kaw Thaung in the early hours, making a single night's accommodation in Kaw Thaung necessary; this can be pre-arranged by the operator.

DIVE FACILITIES

There are no dive facilities in the region; the only way of diving here is by live-aboard. No less than seven boats serve the area, from a total of four operators, three based on Phuket and the other in Bangkok. All provide a first-class service, with variations only in cost, time scale and preference of boat. For full details see the Live-aboard feature on page 32.

South East Asia Liveaboards (SY *Gaea*, SY *Crescent*); 112/13 Song Roi Pi Road, Patong, Phuket, 83150, Thailand, tel (076) 340406/fax (076) 340586, email: info@sealiveaboards.com

Dive Asia Pacific (MV *Sai Mai*, MV *Pelagian*), PO Box 244, Phuket, 83000, Thailand, tel (076) 263732/fax (06) 263733, email: info@dive-asiapacific.com

Fantasea Divers (MV *Fantasea*), P.O. Box 20, Patong Beach, Phuket 83150, Thailand, tel (076) 340088, 295511/fax (076) 340309, email: info@fantasea.net

Divemaster (MV *Divemaster II*), 110/63 Lardprao Soi 18, Lardprao, Bangkok 10900, Thailand, tel (02) 9384216-7/fax (02) 9384218, email: divemstr@ksc9.th.com

FILM PROCESSING

Photographic Services are not available here. The nearest are on Koh Phuket, see page 31.

HOSPITALS AND RECOMPRESSION CHAMBER

There are no medical facilities on any of the islands. The nearest are those listed in the Koh Phuket section on p. 31. The nearest **recompression chamber** is on Koh Phuket.

LOCAL HIGHLIGHTS

The Mergui Archipelago offers a chance to see a rich diversity of flora and birdlife. The historic port of Mergui is worth exploring.

The SY Crescent *at anchor off Prinsep Island.*

THE ANDAMAN ISLANDS

The Andamans are in Indian territorial waters but due to the fact that they are far closer to Thailand (with Phuket some 450km (280 miles) to the south east) than to India itself (with the mainland well over 1000km (620 miles) to the northwest), diving here has, so far, been pioneered by long-range live-aboards from Koh Phuket.

The forward programmes of Koh Phuket dive operators are continually being thrown into doubt by the obfuscations of Indian bureaucracy, and it would be a brave soul indeed who was willing to predict a date when regular cruises will take place.

Covering an area of just over 8,000 sq km, there are at least 500 islands, islets and rocky outcrops in the archipelago, with just 26 of these currently inhabited. The larger islands are fairly mountainous and blanketed with dense rainforest. A high proportion of these forests are protected, with a confusing network of Tribal Reserves, six National Parks and Coastal Belts, and no less than 94 wildlife sanctuaries.

DIVING AROUND THE ANDAMAN ISLANDS

Many of the islands are surrounded by fringing reefs, often several hundred metres wide and separated from the shore by a lagoon of similar width. There are also more steeply sloping reef walls, and coral pinnacles or knolls. Divers can follow around undulating hills of raven black volcanic lava, which makes for some unusual diving. There are also plenty of shallow reefs suitable for snorkelling.

Large pelagics are plentiful in these waters, as are a variety of sharks: large schools of hammerheads often patrol the waters away from the reefs and Grey, Whitetip, Nurse and Leopard sharks are found closer inshore. Silvertip and Oceanic Whitetips also sometimes appear out of the deep blue beyond. Species not usually seen in Thai waters (such as Bumphead Parrotfish and Napoleon Wrasse) are frequently seen here.

Another feature of the Andamans are the impressive cleaning stations where Giant barracuda hover silently waiting for their teeth to be picked. Enormous Manta Rays are also often seen, sometimes by the dozen.

Opposite: *A live-aboard at Fish Ledges.*
Above: *Two Chromodorididae nudibranchs share a meal of bryozoan branches.*

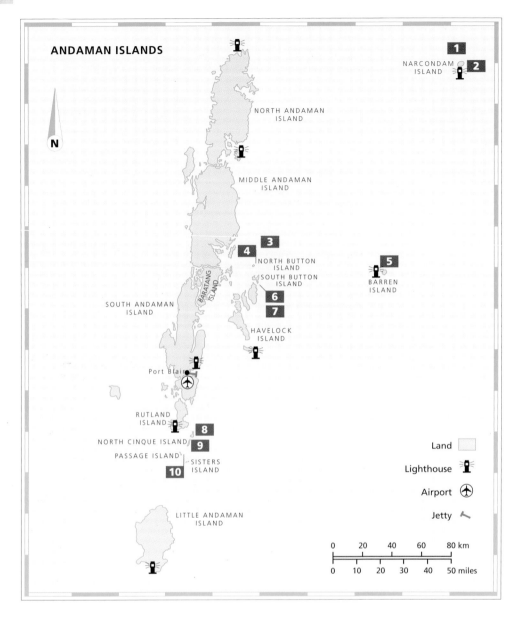

ANDAMAN ISLANDS

1

NARCONDAM
ISLAND
2

NORTH ANDAMAN
ISLAND

N

MIDDLE ANDAMAN
ISLAND

3

4

NORTH BUTTON
ISLAND

SOUTH BUTTON
ISLAND

5

BARREN
ISLAND

BARATANG
ISLAND

SOUTH ANDAMAN
ISLAND

6

7

HAVELOCK
ISLAND

Port Blair

RUTLAND
ISLAND

NORTH CINQUE ISLAND

PASSAGE ISLAND

8

9

SISTERS
ISLAND

10

LITTLE ANDAMAN
ISLAND

Land

Lighthouse

Airport

Jetty

0	20	40	60	80 km

0	10	20	30	40	50 miles

1 NARCONDAM ISLAND –
LIGHTHOUSE POINT

★★★★

Location: 135km (73 n. miles) east of N. Andaman Island.
Access: Entry is by 'live-boat' dive or from a dinghy.
Conditions: Visibility is good, averaging 25m (83ft).
Currents can be strong; only for more experienced divers.
Average depth: 25m (83ft)
Maximum depth: 32m (106ft)

This is a superb, exciting dive site with plenty of big fish action. A coral ridge runs north from the point some 150m (165yd), interspersed with canyons; the bay itself has a mass of white sponges and healthy hard corals, whilst the reef is covered in large seafans with several kinds of barrel sponges. Reef dwellers are plentiful, with numerous surgeonfish, fusiliers, snapper, coral trout, angelfish, parrotfish, and oriental, giant and spotted sweetlips.

There's plenty to see here, with Manta rays, Eagle rays, Rainbow runners, Bluefin trevally, Bumphead parrotfish, giant Napoleon wrasse, Silvertips, Whitetips and even Whale Sharks.

2 NARCONDAM ISLAND – NEIL'S PRIDE
★★★★★

Location: About 135km (73 n. miles) east of North Andaman Island. The dive follows a ridge that drops west–east, beginning off the island's northeast point.
Access: Access is by 'live-boat' dive.
Conditions: Visibility usually exceeds 20m (66ft). This site has irregular currents, and is suitable only for experienced divers.
Average depth: 28m (93ft)
Maximum depth: 40m (130ft)
The bottom of this site is very pleasant, consisting of coral-covered rocks and pinnacles with lots of beautiful hard and soft corals. The reef slopes very steeply seawards. There is an excellent diversity and representation of marine life, including Giant Sweetlips – about 1.5m (5ft) long – Manta Rays, fusiliers, Leatherback Turtles and Silvertip Reef Sharks. Among the visiting pelagics are schools of Bluefin Trevally and tuna.

3 CAMPBELL SHOAL
★★★

Location: About 20km (10 n. miles) east of the southeastern coast of Middle Andaman Island.
Access: Access is by 'live-boat' dive.
Conditions: Visibility varies between 5m and 16m (16–53ft). Currents are weak to moderate.
Average depth: 17m (56ft)
Maximum depth: 22m (73ft)
The bottom of this site is covered in mainly hard corals, with sporadic sandy patches, and hosts a multitude of reef animals.

The reef-flat has many mounds of hard corals, again with a big population of marine life. Hard corals also predominate on the reef-slope. It has been said that the hard corals here are the best so far discovered in the waters around the Andaman Islands. The marine life includes Whitetip Reef Sharks, large cod and groupers, Coral Trout, Blue- and Golden-banded Fusiliers.

4 NORTH BUTTON ISLAND
★★★

Location: About 10km (5½ n. miles) east of Middle Andaman Island, south of Campbell Shoal (Site 14) and immediately north of Diligent Strait.
Access: Access is by 'live-boat' dive.
Conditions: Visibility is fair, between 10m and 15m (33–50ft). Currents are weak to moderate.

Average depth: 17m (56ft)
Maximum depth: 20m (66ft)
This is a very easy dive, in conditions that are relatively favourable. The bottom mainly comprises coral-covered rocks with patches of sand. Here you can find Humpback Snappers, Giant Groupers and schools of Spinyfoot and Unicornfish among mostly hard corals, with a few seafans. The corals are in good condition. There is a very good diversity and representation of reef-fish, including many different species of angelfish, butterflyfish, damselfish, snappers and cod. A great spot for observing the smaller reef-fish, as they hide and dart among the coral branches. On the reef-flat are boulder corals, staghorns, coral laminates and finger corals.

5 BARREN ISLAND – WALLS 'N' ASHES
★★★

Location: About 82km (45 n. miles) east of North Button Island (Site 15). The best site is off the rocky northwest point, there is an underwater ridge at 30m (100ft).
Access: Access is by 'live-boat' dive.
Conditions: Visibility is good, often exceeding 30m (100ft). Currents can be strong, so this site is for experienced divers only.
Average depth: 27m (90ft)
Maximum depth: 44m (147ft)
The island is an active volcano, and the coral here is still recovering from a 1995 eruption. The site offers a series of wall dives, with the main bottom in a depth exceeding 90m (300ft). This is an interesting dive, but there is little coral on the walls. Between the walls are enormous areas of sloping black volcanic ash with many semi-buried dead and broken trees. Black seafans, colourful crinoids and bushes of white stinging hydroids are in evidence, and hosts of orange encrusting sponges cover the rocks. Silvertip Reef Sharks come up in numbers from the depths to investigate. Large schools of pelagics – including sharks, Dog-tooth Tuna, Giant Barracuda, Rainbow runners and trevally – are a characteristic of this site, which also has plenty of Black-banded Sea Snakes.

6 SOUTH BUTTON ISLAND
★★★★☆

Location: Between Baratang and Outram islands; the dive follows a wall on the island's south side.
Access: Access is by 'live-boat' dive.
Conditions: Visibility averages above 10m (33ft). Currents are weak to moderate.
Average depth: 12m (40ft)
Maximum depth: 25m (83ft)

This is a good site, with nice hard corals in the shallower waters and coral mounds at greater depths – snorkellers can see these when conditions are calm. This southern wall drops to 15m (50ft), from where a sandy slope continues down. Schooling Hammerhead Sharks can often be seen in the distance.

The eastern and northern sides of the island can also be dived. These are shallower – about 12m (40ft) – and feature coral gardens with, below, mainly sand and rubble. You see only the occasional seafan, but there is lots of fish-life – Grey Reef Sharks, Bluefin and Yellowfin Trevally, Giant Napoleon Wrasse, angelfish, surgeonfish and a wealth of small colourful reef fishes.

7 MINERVA LEDGE
★★★☆☆

Location: About 15km (8 n. miles) southeast of Henry Lawrence Island.
Access: Access is by 'live-boat' dive.
Conditions: Visibility generally exceeds 20m (66ft). In weak currents this open-ocean dive is easy, but in stronger ones it should be limited to more experienced divers.
Average depth: 13m (43ft)
Maximum depth: 17m (56ft)
This gently sloping offshore reef affords a nice shallow dive. The bottom here is mostly rocky, with some healthy corals. The reef-flat is at a depth of 9m (30ft), and in calm conditions can be enjoyed by snorkellers. Many reef-fish are in evidence, as are visiting pelagics – look out for Large Potato Cod, Whitetip Reef Sharks, big schools of Blue-fin Trevally and various spadefish.

8 INVISIBLE BANK – FLAT ROCK
★★★★★

Location: At the southern end of Invisible Bank, about 90km (49 n. miles) southeast of Rutland Island.
Access: Access is by 'live-boat' dive.
Conditions: Visibility averages 30m (100ft). There can be strong currents.
Average depth: 12m (40ft)
Maximum depth: 16m (53ft)
Invisible Bank itself has few live corals except in a handful of sheltered areas, and marine life is poor apart from occasional rays and sharks. Flat Rock, however, is a different story altogether. Again, there are few corals but the topography is fairly dramatic, with scattered rocks over a sandy bottom, and the concentration of fish is incredible. The pelagics are especially noteworthy. It is difficult to know where to start, but you can expect to see schools of Black Unicornfish, surgeonfish, mackerel, tuna

and trevally. Grey and Whitetip Reef Sharks are likely to be in evidence, as are Nurse Sharks, Dog-tooth Tuna, Great Barracuda and Giant and Bluefin Trevally. As if that were not enough, look out for the moray eels, Napoleon Wrasse and large stingrays! A fabulous dive spot, with plenty of big fish.

9 NORTH CINQUE ISLAND – SOUTHEAST REEF
★★★

Location: About 9km (5 n. miles) southeast of South Andaman Island. The dive follows around the southeastern apex and along the eastern side of the island to its eastern point.
Access: Access is by 'live-boat' dive.
Conditions: Visibility is very good, often about 30m (100ft). Currents are minimal.
Average depth: 15m (50ft)
Maximum depth: 22m (73ft)
The southeastern part of the reef consists of tremendous hard and soft corals; these are very dense on the rocks down to about 16m (53ft), below which there is far more sand than rocks. The corals are very healthy and completely free of damage; they are among the healthiest in the region. There are many fish in evidence. Most are small fusiliers and snappers, but you can expect to see also Napoleon Wrasse, large groupers and Hawksbill Turtles.

10 PASSAGE ISLAND – FISH ROCK
★★★★★

Location: The small outcrop to the north of Passage Island.
Access: Access is by 'live-boat' dive.
Conditions: Visibility varies between 10m and 40m (33–130ft). There can be strong surface currents.
Average depth: 21m (70ft)
Maximum depth: 35m (116ft)
This aptly named site offers an extremely colourful dive, with millions of fish. The topography consists of rocky slopes, boulders and drop-offs, featuring large fan corals and plenty of basket sponges. Below 25m (82ft) the rocks are covered in small bushy soft corals in numerous hues. Grey and Whitetip Reef Sharks are almost always in the vicinity, as are Nurse Sharks.

Among the rest of the marine life are Eagle Rays, Potato Cod, large Coral Groupers, fusiliers, sweetlips, turtles, batfish, Bumphead Parrotfish, Squirrelfish, curious and friendly Oriental Sweetlips, surgeonfish, Yellow Tangs, Indian and Titan Triggerfish, tuna, Rainbow runners and many species of trevally.

How to Get There

There are two ways of accessing these islands.
By boat: Live-aboard excursions travel directly from and return to Koh Phuket in Thailand. This passage requires a lengthy sea journey - from 24 to 48 hours each way.
By air: The second option is fly to India's mainland and take a connecting flight to the Andaman Islands. India Air depart from Calcutta and Madras airports; the flight time is 2 hrs. Planes depart Calcutta every Monday, Tuesday, Thursday and Saturday and Madras every Sunday, Wednesday, Thursday and Friday.

Visas are required by anyone intending to visit India. Andaman Island visas are issued automatically on arrival at Port Blair. Applications for Indian visas are surrendered to the Immigration Authorities at any of the Indian Embassies.

Where to Stay

There are a couple of establishments which have adequate amenities and are reasonably priced. **The Bay Island Hotel**, Marine Hill, Port Blair; tel 20881. Comfortable air-conditioned rooms and bungalows, traditionally constructed using local timbers. **Andaman Beach Resort**, Corbyn's Cove, Port Blair 744 101; tel 20599, 21381.

Located on the coast at the south end of town, air-conditioned cottages set amongst landscaped gardens overlooking the sea.

Where to Eat

The two resorts listed above have very good restaurants. The majority of the island cuisine originates in South India, with local delicacies including venison, lobsters and shrimps.

Dive Facilities

Live-aboards are the only feasible and available way of travelling in this area. The companies vary their routes to the islands; firstly they sail and return directly from Koh Phuket, with either the outward or inward passages being broken up with diving around Mu Koh Similan, Surin and the Burma Banks or alternatively, divers transfer to the Andaman islands by air and join boats at Port Blair on South Andaman Island. For detailed schedules and the various options on offer contact the operators directly. The two operators are: **Scubaquest** and **South East Asia Liveaboards**. See page 32 for contact details.

Film Processing

It is advisable to purchase enough film for the trip in advance; developing is best done in Thailand.

Hospitals & Recompression Chamber

G.B. Pant Hospital, Port Blair, South Andaman Island. There is no recompression chamber on or around the islands, so dive safely.

Local Highlights

Port Blair, the capital of the Andamans and Nicobar Islands has a multi-racial populous; they even celebrate each other's festivals. Daily excursions can be arranged through the islands' resort or hotels or at any one of the travel service shops in Port Blair.

Chiriya Tapu, locally known as **Bird Island**, is located off the southernmost tip of South Andaman Island. There is good snorkelling in the shallower waters. Visitors can enjoy fishing amongst thick mangroves. It is also a great location for bird watchers.

Corbyn's Cove, a palm fringed white sandy beach, is one of the most popular weekend spots on the islands; located around 7km (4 miles) south east of Port Blair, it is great for swimming, snorkelling and even surfing.

Ross Island was the British administrative headquarters of the territory for fifty years. It is now occupied by spotted deer and peacocks.

A diver observes a school of Dusky Batfish (Platax teira).

KOH PHI PHI
(Had Nopparat Marine National Park)

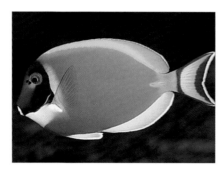

The two Phi Phi Islands have long been a popular destination for budget travellers, drawn by their fabulous beaches, crystal-clear waters and dramatic limestone landscapes. Snorkelling around the islands' reefs is another major attraction, and scuba diving has taken off here in a big way. The islands are 50km (30 miles) southeast of Phuket and 40km (25 miles) south of Krabi.

KOH PHI PHI DON AND KOH PHI PHI LEY

The larger of the two islands is Koh Phi Phi Don, a stunning outcrop whose two halves are linked by a narrow isthmus. The elevated landmass on the eastern section of the island is covered in dense forest, criss-crossed by tracks, while the western half is virtually inaccessible due to the steep, hilly terrain. Most of the development on Koh Phi Phi Don has been concentrated on the sand-flats around the isthmus.

Koh Phi Phi Ley is uninhabited. The rugged limestone cliffs of the island are home to populations of edible nest swiftlets, whose nests are collected from inside large caves by local sea gypsies.

DIVING AROUND KOH PHI PHI

There has been a huge growth in the diving business here over the past few years and there are now at least a dozen dive operators in the growing township of Ao Ton Sai. The area offers a good variety of different types of diving with abundant hard and soft corals and healthy fish populations. Local operators use either Longtails or larger, specially converted boats. The larger boats here also offer day trips to the more far-flung sites of Hin Musang, Anemone Ree, Koh Dok Mai and the King Cruiser Wreck.

Snorkelling around the islands is excellent, with plenty of shallow coral gardens on the fringing reefs which are alive with colourful fish. Sadly considerable anchor damage was inflicted on some of the popular snorkelling areas in the past.

Opposite: *Daytrippers sail past the sheer limestone cliffs of Koh Phi Phi Ley.*
Above: *The Powder blue surgeonfish is a trademark of the Andaman Sea.*

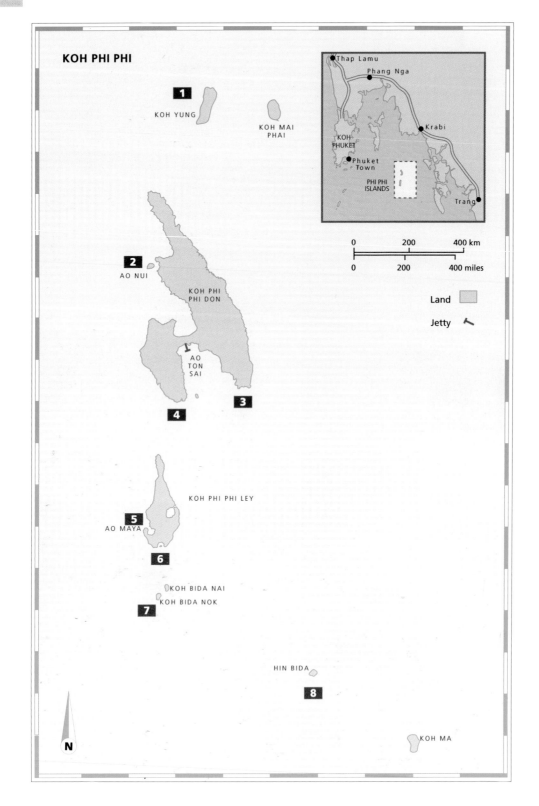

KOH PHI PHI

1   KOH YUNG

KOH MAI PHAI

Thap Lamu
Phang Nga
Krabi
KOH PHUKET
Phuket Town
PHI PHI ISLANDS
Trang

| 0 | 200 | 400 km |
| 0 | 200 | 400 miles |

Land
Jetty

2   AO NUI

KOH PHI PHI DON

AO TON SAI

3

4

KOH PHI PHI LEY

5   AO MAYA

6

KOH BIDA NAI
KOH BIDA NOK

7

HIN BIDA

8

KOH MA

N

1 KOH YUNG (MOSQUITO ISLAND)
★★☆

Location: 5km (3 n. miles) due north of Koh Phi Phi Don. The dive follows around the island's northwestern apex. There is also an underwater pinnacle off the northeast shore.

Access: Less than 1hr from Ton Sai bay on Koh Phi Phi Don.

Conditions: Visibility averages 15m (50ft). Strong surface currents are frequent– sometimes rendering this site suitable for experienced divers only.

Average depth: 16m (53ft)

Maximum depth: 20m (66ft)

This site features abundant white soft corals covering the rocks everywhere. In addition, there are sea whips on the gentler slopes on the southwestern side. It is also well worth investigating the sandy bottom, since you will almost certainly discover large rays there, and have a good chance of spotting Leopard Sharks. A couple of big groupers are in residence, and the reef inhabitants include lionfish, wrasse, Rock Basslets, Moorish Idols, small moray eels, shrimps, hermit crabs and lobsters. Among the pelagics frequently seen passing by are barracuda, jacks and trevallies.

The splendid Jewel box sea urchin (Mespilia globulus).

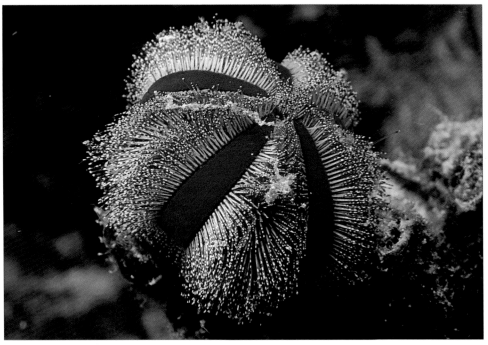

CLEANER WATER CAMPAIGN

The islands of Phi Phi, pronounced 'pee pee', are now attracting around 3,000 tourists every day in high season, along with a growing Thai community which means that sewage pollution is increasing and six thousand cubic metres of waste water per day are being discharged into the surrounding seas. In an attempt to avert the environmental risk this poses to the islands and their coral reefs, the authorities in Krabi have initiated a programme to improve water quality and garbage disposal on the islands. A total of over US$1.3 million is being invested in this project, with around US$800,000 allocated for a water treatment system, incinerator and disposal site. This sorely needed programme will hopefully ensure a sustainable future for tourism on the Phi Phi Islands as well as protecting the reefs.

2 AO NUI (NUI BAY)
★★★★★★

Location: On the northwest coast of Koh Phi Phi Don. The dive circumnavigates the large rocky outcrop just outside the bay.

Access: About 30min by (larger) diveboat and 1hr by Longtail from Ton Sai Bay. The site can be entered off either the eastern or the western face of the rock. Diveboats wait for the divers and snorkellers in the sheltered bay to the east of the outcrop.

Conditions: Currents generally run weak to moderate,

but there is always a leeward side to this site. Visibility is in the range 5–30m (16–100ft). This makes a great night-diving selection.

Average depth: 15m (50ft)
Maximum depth: 21m (70ft)

This really is an enjoyable dive. The waters around the eastern face are shallow and ideal for snorkelling: there are lots of corals and colourful reef-fish among small boulders and rocks, encrusted with patches of sponges and interspersed with a multitude of Christmas-tree Worms. The western section, by contrast, features a wall that descends to a depth of 20m (66ft). At the bottom of the southern end of the rock you encounter tumbled rocks that climb dramatically towards the shallower eastern rocks. At the northwestern apex you find large boulders, balanced on top of each other; more experienced divers can explore a number of relatively tight swimthroughs.

The wall features a wealth of marine life: many moray eels, squadrons of lionfish and Blue-ringed Imperial and Emperor Angelfish. The site is also a reliable place to see Ghost Pipefish.

3 HIN PHAE
★★☆☆☆

Location: The rocky outcrop off Koh Phi Phi Don's southeastern headland.
Access: About 15min by diveboat or 30min by Longtail from Ton Sai Bay. Diveboats can moor to either of the mooring buoys.
Conditions: Visibility, at about 7–15m (23–50ft), is acceptable. This is a good sheltered site with minimal current.

Average depth: 8m (26ft)
Maximum depth: 16m (53ft)

This shallow location is often a stopping-off point during the return journey from the southern sites; it offers good snorkelling and diving. The main feature is a shallow fringing reef. The flat, crest and upper slope attract snorkellers while divers can enjoy the whole spectrum of the site.

Coral laminates dominate the reef, and there are some patch reefs. On the slope you see brain corals and staghorns above soft corals. There are many holes and tunnels for moray eels to pass through in their quest for food. Look out for invertebrates, too: small crabs and the occasional lobster mingle with busy cleaner shrimps. Damselfish, angelfish, small rock groupers, snappers, surgeonfish and basslets are other residents.

---

4 HIN DOT
★★★

Location: The submerged pinnacle off Koh Phi Phi Don's southwestern headlands.
Access: About 15min by diveboat or 30min by Longtail from Ton Sai Bay. A buoy marks the top of the pinnacle, and Longtails can moor to it; however, due to the shallow water above the pinnacle, larger diveboats will drop anchor away from the site.
Conditions: Visibility is very current-dependent, averaging about 8m (26ft) and peaking at just above 20m (66ft). Strong currents are generally present; this dive should be done by experienced divers only as currents can rise abruptly.

Average depth: 12m (40ft)
Maximum depth: 28m (93ft)

This, conditions permitting, is a great multi-level dive. The pinnacle is dominated by three interesting shelves – at 3m (10ft), 12m (40ft) and 15m (50ft). This provides ample and varied underwater scenery at all levels as you spiral upwards. There are good soft corals at all depths. The hard corals are represented by tubes and laminates. The deeper sections of the walls have numerous oysters and clams clinging to, and embedded in, the craggy surface.

Many reef-fish are in evidence, including Lunar Wrasse, parrotfish, Honeycomb Groupers and Spotfin and Indian Lionfish. There are Bearded Scorpionfish, too, lurking among the coralline-encrusted rocks as they await their prey of tiny fish.

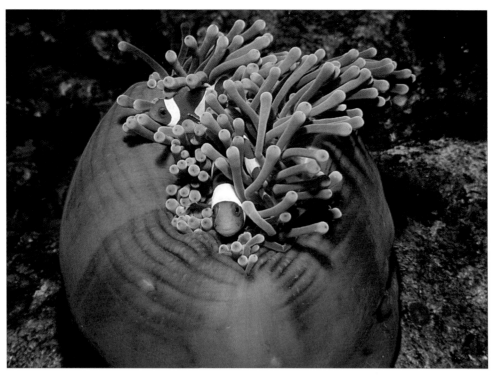

Above: *Anemonefish tend to a Magnificent sea anemone (Heteractis magnifica).*
Below: *Crown-of-thorns starfish (Acanthaster planci) can cause irreparable damage to corals.*

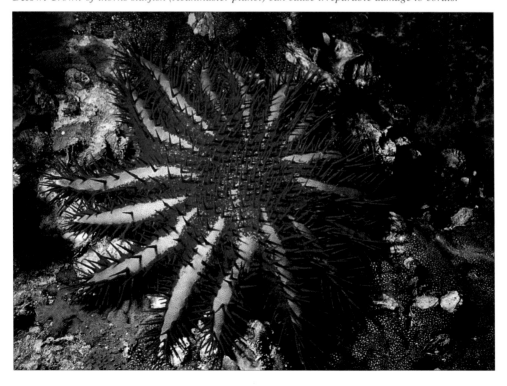

5 AO MAYA (MAYA BAY)

★★★☆☆☆☆

Location: The large, sheer-cliffed lagoon at the southwestern end of Phi Phi Ley.

Access: About 30min by (larger) diveboat or at least 45min by longtail from Ton Sai Bay. Divers enter the water at the mooring buoy in the bay's northern entrance, and follow the coastline north.

Conditions: Visibility ranges from 8m and 30m (26–100ft). Current plays a big part in this dive: it can transform it from a gentle relaxed underwater tour to an exciting drift-dive. There would be good snorkelling anywhere in the bay were it not for the boat traffic.

Average depth: 16m (53ft)

Maximum depth: 24m (80ft)

The dive follows the coast along a steep shelved reef, with occasional sections of wall; hard corals, sea whips and various species of sea anemones cover the elevated shelves. The wall sections are fairly barren, but fortunately are in the minority. There are also small offshore pinnacles and submerged rocks to explore.

Colourful wrasse of all sizes and schools of Moorish Idols and bannerfish constantly pass by. You can see lots of mating cuttlefish below the central cliff section. Above, on the lower ledges, are scattered Crown-of-Thorns Starfish and Jewel-box Sea Urchins.

6 AO LOSAMAH (LOSAMAH BAY)

★★★☆☆☆

Location: Around the towering offshore limestone structure in the bay that cuts into the southern coastline of Phi Phi Ley.

Access: About 40min by diveboat or 90min by Longtail from Ton Sai Bay. The preferred entry point is directly off the outcrop's northern face. Scattered mooring buoys provide overnight securings for yachts. This site is recommended for night-diving.

Conditions: Visibility averages 15m (50ft). Currents, if any, are minimal along the northern face but can be moderate along the rock's more open southern wall.

Average depth: 14m (46ft)

Maximum depth: 20m (66ft)

The sandy bottom, at 8m (26ft), is punctuated by rocky ledges among which are numerous Bearded Scorpionfish.

Fringing the rocks are numerous sea whips, some bent over by the aggregations of wing oysters clinging to them. The southern section of the site is deeper, at 20m (66ft), and follows a wall where many bivalves and clusters of soft corals are in evidence. Pairs of large Blue-ringed Angelfish explore the nooks and crannies.

7 KOH BIDA NOK

★★★★☆

Location: The outer of the two large outcrops directly south of Phi Phi Ley.

Access: About 50min by diveboat or 1hr 40min by longtail from Ton Sai Bay. No mooring buoy.

Conditions: Visibility is in the 20m (66ft) range. Currents are weak to moderate.

Average depth: 19m (63ft)

Maximum depth: 30m (66ft)

The prime spot is the southwest section, where large rocks form a mountainous terrain, featuring walls that drop to elevated ledges. There are many gorgonian seafans, sea whips and colourful soft corals. Lots of Bearded Scorpionfish disguise themselves amid the rocks, and various species of lionfish hover between. Varying sizes and species of colourful parrotfish and wrasse, along with large schools of Moorish Idols, seem to be at all depths. The higher ledges have numerous sea anemones well populated by clownfish. As if this were not enough, this site offers, over the sand, Leopard Sharks and various blennies and gobies. Another bonus is that Manta Rays and Whale Sharks are often here .

8 HIN BIDA (PHI PHI SHARK POINT)

★★★☆☆☆

Location: A small rocky outcrop some 8km (4 n. miles) southeast of Phi Phi Ley. It stands proud of the water by a mere 1m (40in).

Access: Just over 1hr from Phi Phi Don, just over 1½hr from Koh Lanta and about 2hr from Koh Phuket. There is no mooring buoy.

Conditions: Visibility is good, averaging about 20m (66ft). Current generally weak to moderate.

Average depth: 12m (40ft)

Maximum depth: 18m (60ft)

This easy dive follows an area of submerged rocks immediately northeast of the outcrop. These gently slope down northwards to sand at 18m (60ft). The area due north of the outcrop is covered with scattered rocks and is shallower, at about 5m (16ft); in calm conditions snorkellers can enjoy schools of colourful reef-fish, including Blue-lined Snapper and Harlequin Sweetlips, not to mention more static attractions like multicoloured Plumeworms, featherstars and crinoids.

This location's secondary name refers to the overwhelming presence of Leopard Sharks. There are also lots of cuttlefish, squid and Titan Triggerfish. Large Undulated and Golden Moray Eels, Spiny Lobsters and octopuses attempt to obscure themselves within the many craggy holes and crevices.

Above: *The feeding polyps of this Tubastraea faulkneri coral are frequently mistaken for soft coral.*
Below: *Plankton feeders thrive in brisk currents.*

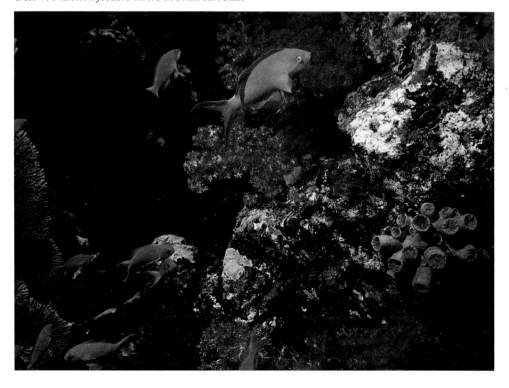

Longtail boats play an important role in diving around Thailand and are always much in evidence either transferring divers from the shores to await dive boats or being used as dive boats themselves.

Originally these boats served as fishing and trading vessels; now they also provide day trips for tourists and divers. The majority of boats work in popular diving resorts such as around the shores of Koh Phuket or in the waters around the Phi Phi Islands and along the beaches of Ao Nang and Railae in Krabi Province. Here they play a major role in everyday life and remain the sole method of delivering supplies and trafficking guests to distant beaches on the offshore islands. However the area boasting the largest number of Longtails remains the collective beaches around Koh Phuket with over five hundred boats operating in the surrounding waters.

Few technical innovations or advancements have been made to the boats over the centuries. Two changes of significance occurred during the last fifty years. Originally, all the wooden parts were pinned together by dowels, forced into place and secured with glue; these were replaced by steel nails in the 1960s making construction quicker and therefore more convenient.

The second change is really more of a technical advancement. The boats were primarily designed to operate as sailing vessels, however nowadays they are usually propelled by engines.

The engines, usually diesel, are at the stern, mounted on a rotating bracket which swivels from left to right. It is also centrally mounted between two steel plates allowing it to freely pivot vertically about its axis. This simple two-stage universal joint allows the boat to be steered port and starboard and also allows the engine to be raised and lowered in order for the propeller, which is on the end of a three metre shaft, to avoid rocks and corals in the shallower waters and entanglement in nets or ropes.

In the past, Longtails were constructed using only locally obtained timber but, due to a logging ban of the required hardwoods throughout Thailand, there has been a drastic decline in the number of boats being made. The shortage of the necessary hardwoods has forced the import of more expensive timbers from Malaysia making construction of the

boats a more costly exercise. Previously the boats were extremely cost effective with a minimum life-expectancy of around thirty years which meant they outlasted their engines three times over! Today the boats are still built using age-old techniques; the preferred tool for the majority of the work remains the ancient axe chisel.

Construction begins with the keel, followed by the bow, stern and finally the outer plankings. Completed vessels are caulked and then finished with either brightly coloured paint or clear varnish. Cautious owners reinforce their boats by applying a mixture of bound broken shells and coral substrate to the hulls in order to add a stronger protection against knocks and scratches.

Completed Longtails vary proportionately in both length and width. Hulls can range from anything between five to fifteen metres. The only other variation is that some have protection from the sun and rain by long canopies covering the central two thirds of the boat and some are equipped with sun parasols. An average sized boat will comfortably cater for four divers, two diving staff, full diving equipment including two

tanks each, and of course the captain.

As far as diving is concerned there are really only three different entry techniques which are suitable from these boats. The backward roll is very popular but some divers prefer the controlled seated entry or to 'kit-up' in the water – the giant stride is definitely unsuitable. Whichever technique is used, ensure that tanks and other belongings are secured first and not allowed to roll about in the boat causing it to rock as the divers enter the water.

Exiting the water is restricted to one simple method; first the diver removes his weight belt and scuba gear, then holds on to the side of the boat and kicks out of the water and into the boat. (Very few Longtails have ladders as there is no suitable place to store them.) Fins are removed once the diver is safely back inside the boat.

Opposite: *The long 'tails' of the boats give off a spectacular water spray.*
Below: *Longtail boats are not only used for transport, they also serve as diving vessels.*

HOW TO GET THERE

There are no direct routes to these islands. The easiest way is via Koh Phuket, although they can also be accessed from Krabi Town or its beaches via Express boat.

By bus: VIP air-conditioned buses leave Bangkok's southern bus terminal daily at 18.50hrs and arrive at the bus terminal in Phuket Town some fourteen hours later. For further information regarding bus services contact Bangkok southern bus terminal; tel (02) 435 1199, 435 1200 or Phuket Central Tour; tel (02) 435 5019, 434 3233. In Phuket, contact Phuket bus terminal; tel (076) 211480, Phuket Central Tour; tel (076) 213 615, 214335 or Phuket Travel Service; tel (076) 222107-9. On arrival at the bus terminal it is possible to buy boat tickets from any of the surrounding travel shops.

By air: via Phuket. Flights are with Thai International. There are fourteen daily flights which depart the domestic airport every hour, on the hour between 07.00hrs and 21.00hrs. They are conveniently arranged to coincide with incoming International flights, allowing immediate connections. The flight time is seventy-five minutes.

On arrival at Phuket International Airport it will be necessary to transfer to either Phuket Town or one of the major southern beaches to purchase boat tickets to Koh Phi Phi Don.

Boats are run daily and they depart between 07.00hrs and 10.00hrs depending on which tour operator is used. Travel times vary between companies but on average, journeys last ninety minutes. Boats depart from the deep sea port and Chalong Bay.

For further information contact Thai Airways International Ltd, 89 Vibhavadi Rangsit Road, Bangkok 10900; tel (02) 513 0121/fax (02) 513 0203.

By car and taxis: this takes over twelve hours to reach Phuket alone and is not advisable.

By boat from Krabi: The boat leaves daily from Ao Nang beach at 09.00hrs and from Railae beach fifteen minutes later. Boats also leave the pier in Krabi Town twice daily at 09.00hrs and 02.30hrs. The one-way journey last approximately ninety minutes. For further information contact Phi Phi Marine Travel Co, 201/3-4 Uttarakij Road, Krabi Town; tel (075) 611496.

For any additional information on Koh Phi Phi contact the **Tourism Authority of Thailand**, Phuket Office; tel (076) 212213, 211036/fax (076) 213582.

WHERE TO STAY

There is plenty of accommodation on Phi Phi to choose from, ranging from small fan-cooled huts and bungalows to a large air-conditioned hotel. Prices greatly increase during the high season but this does not seem to deter the numerous holiday makers and accommodation is always full during this period. The majority of bungalow resorts fringe the beaches of Loh Dalum Bay, whereas the hotel overlooks Ton Sai Bay. There are other resorts scattered around this central area of the island

LOH DALUM BAY BEACH

Charlie Beach Resort; tel (075) 620615. This is a popular resort with 87 bungalows and its own restaurant.
PP Princess Resort; tel (075) 612188. A total of 96 lovely air-conditioned bungalows with plenty of natural light. Good restaurant and a handful of small on-site shopping facilities.

TON SAI BAY

Phi Phi Hotel; tel (075) 611233. This is presently the only hotel on the island, located in the centre of the tiny town. There are 64 air-conditioned rooms, a coffee shop, karaoke lounge and restaurant.

LAEM HIN BEACH

Bay View Resort; tel (01) 229 1134. Around 30 fan-cooled rooms overlook Koh Phi Phi Ley. There is also a good outdoor restaurant.

PHI PHI PALM BEACH

Laem Thong Beach; tel (01) 229 0052. Luxury air-conditioned bungalows with good sports facilities including a diving centre.

WHERE TO EAT

There are many restaurants offering a selection of Thai, Italian, Danish, French, Swiss and Japanese food. There is also a wonderful bakery with excellent cakes and mouth-watering savouries.

DIVE FACILITIES

There are around a dozen diving operations on the island, mostly located in the small, and only, town in Ton Sai Bay on Koh Phi Phi Don. The range of shops is not as broad as it is on Koh Tao; most of the operations are of a similar size and carry similar amounts of equipment. The Phi Phi dive sites are also visited as daily excursions by operators in Krabi and on Koh Phuket.

Dive trips

Dive trips are conducted on board converted vessels and Longtail boats. Trips run on a twice daily basis, departing from the pier in Ton Sala Bay at around 08.00hrs and 14.00hrs; most come complete with light refreshments, fruit, lunch and divemaster services. Not all operators include equipment in the trip price. The larger dive boats carry fresh water tanks for rinsing photographic equipment, but the Longtail boats do not. Day trips to the more distant destinations of Shark Point, Anemone Reef, Koh Dok Mai and Hin Bida are on board the larger diveboats. Snorkellers and non-divers are welcome to join any of the scheduled diving trips; masks and fins are available for hire. If you want to organise your own snorkelling trip you can hire a Longtail from Ao Ton Sai or Hat Yao for a reasonable charge.

Dive Courses

All local instruction follows either PADI or NAUI training programmes. Prices quoted are fully inclusive of all equipment and certification. Single day non certification Discover Scuba experience programmes are available, as are PADI Open Water Diver courses which run over three to four days and NAUI Open Water Diver courses which run over four to five days. PADI Advanced Open Water Diver courses and NAUI Advanced Open Water Diver courses run over two to three days. There are also speciality diver courses with a wide range to choose from.

Dive Operators

Aquanauts, Ton Sai Bay, Phi Phi Don, Krabi 81000; tel (01) 229 4707. Established in 1994, PADI instruction is available in English, French, German, Italian, Japanese and Swedish. Daily dive trips on board speedboat and Longtails. **Barakuda Diving Centre**, Ton Sai Bay, Phi Phi Don, Krabi 81000; tel (075) 620698. German-run centre, established in 1992. PADI education available in English, French and German. Dive trips are on board own dive boat. **Dragon Divers**, Ton Sai Bay, Phi Phi Don; tel (075) 381304. PADI education is available in English, French, German and Swedish. Dive trips on Longtail boat. **Moskito Diving**, PO Box 359, Phuket Town 83000; tel (01) 229 1361/fax (01) 229 2802. PADI IDC Centre. This is the largest operation on the island. They even have a small swimming pool for training. PADI education is available in English, French, German, Swedish and Thai. Daily dive trips on board own diveboat. There is a good retail outlet and an associated pub and barbecue garden.

Phi Phi Scuba Diving Centre, Ton Sai Bay, Phi Phi Don, Krabi 81000. Friendly diving centre, established in 1991. PADI education is available in English, French, German and Swedish. Daily dive trips onboard centre's own 16m dive boat. Good retail selection. **Sea Frog (Thai) Co Ltd**, Ton Sai Bay, Phi Phi Don; tel (02) 259 7553/fax (02) 7553. Established in 1989 in Bangkok, this Thai-run dive company offers PADI instruction in English, Japanese and Thai. NAUI instruction is available in Thai. Dive trips on board own small dive boat and Longtail boat. Retail selection.

Film Processing

Print film can be developed and copied at any of the photographic services in Ton Sai Bay. As yet there are no facilities for the development of slides. The nearest developing services are on Koh Phuket (see page 31).

Hospitals and Recompression Chamber

There are no hospitals on the island, but there is a small health centre at the western end of Ton Sai Bay. The nearest hospitals are those listed in the Phuket and Krabi regional directories (see page 31).

The nearest recompression chamber is on Koh Phuket and could be reached by Express Boat in around 2hrs. Contact **Dive Safe Asia**, Patong Beach, Phuket; tel (076) 342518/fax (076) 342519.

Local Highlights

Koh Phi Phi Don is renowned for its beaches, the best of which is the superb Hat Yao (Long Beach), which can be reached in around ten minutes by Longtail or by a half-hour walk over the hillside from Ao Ton Sai. There is also accommodation here.

Ao Loh Dalum, the northern crescent on the isthmus, is also an attractive beach, with a superb panorama at its eastern end which is reached via a sign posted track behind the Chao Ley settlement. It takes around half-an-hour to walk up the hill, and there's a cafe at the summit.

Sailing and windsurfing are both available from Ao Ton Sai, and you can also go **rock-climbing or big-game fishing**. Contact: Windy City Service; tel 01 229 0483/01 229 1074.

Most of the daily excursions concentrate on island tours and snorkelling, with trips to see the limestone caves on Koh Phi Phi Ley and snorkelling in Ao Maya Bay being one of the most popular. These trips also visit the Viking Cave near Ao Maya, which feature 400-year old drawings of Chinese junks on the walls. **Glass-bottom boat tours** are also available, as are six-hour, round the island excursions.

There are a range of tourist-oriented shops in Ao Ton Sai, as well as others selling basic provisions. One problem on the island is a lack of fresh drinking water but this situation may be improved in the future.

Car hire
There are no roads on Phi Phi Don, just a series of tracks. From Ao Ton Sai, Longtail boats run regularly to the other beaches.

The isthmus of Phi Phi Don is where all the island's facilities are located.

KRABI
(Had Nopparat Marine National Park)

This area undoubtedly features some of Thailand's most stunning landscape and forms part of the Had Nopparat Marine National Park. Sheer rocky cliffs are crowned with elevated jungles, and coconut palms clad the hillsides above glorious beaches. The rusty red and gray limestone cliff-faces are scarred with numerous caves and crevices, some of which can be climbed by the more adventurous to reach a mountain-top lagoon.

Away from the mainland, in Ao Nang Bay, large outcrops tower from the water to form curious monoliths; you can see how the abrading seas have shaped the limestone into a series of jutting overhangs, with limestone 'icicles' that offer natural mooring holds.

As yet tourism remains in its infancy. Krabi province is some 940km (590 miles) south of Bangkok. The extremely picturesque Phang Nga Bay is 100km (62 miles) north; it, and its surrounding limestone outcrops were the featured location for the film *The Man with the Golden Gun*, and Koh Phing Kan is affectionately known as 'James Bond Island'.

The area's general activities, including diving, are centred on the two beaches of Ao Nang and Railae, located 16km (10 miles) to the north of Krabi town.

DIVING AROUND KRABI

Directly off Ao Nang Bay there are two islands, Koh Podah Nai and Nok, and a handful of limestone outcrops – most of the area's diving is concentrated around these. All the local diving, which is relatively shallow, can be reached in an average of 45min by Longtail boat or in around 20min by the larger dive boats.

Like tourism, diving in this area is very much in its infancy. The local reefs have suffered minimal damage except in the north of the bay. Schools of dolphins used to swim into the area to feed, but sightings of these graceful creatures are now quite rare.

Divers can enjoy an abundance of radiant soft corals and a tremendous diversity of marine life. There are gently sloping reefs, caves and exciting swimthroughs. The shallow reefs also offer opportunities for some tremendous snorkelling which is quite possibly among the best in the country.

Opposite: *The limestone outcrop of Koh Phing Kan is affectionately known as 'James Bond Island'.*
Above: *A male Orange striped triggerfish (Balistapus undulatus).*

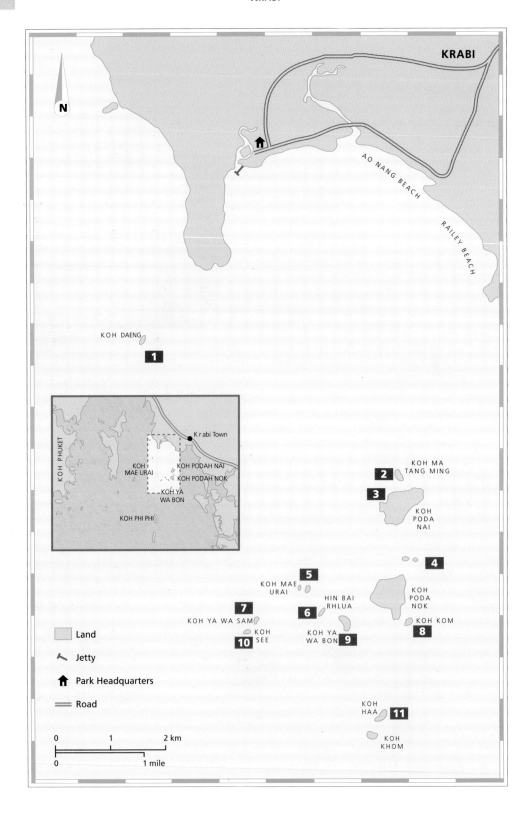

KRABI

N

AO NANG BEACH

RAILEY BEACH

KOH DAENG
1

KOH PHUKET

Krabi Town

KOH
MAE URAI

KOH PODAH NAI

KOH PODAH NOK

KOH YA
WA BON

KOH PHI PHI

KOH MA
TANG MING
2

3

KOH
PODA
NAI

4

5

KOH MAE
URAI

KOH
PODA
NOK

HIN BAI
RHLUA
6

7

KOH YA WA SAM

KOH KOM

KOH
SEE
10

KOH YA
WA BON
9

8

Land

Jetty

Park Headquarters

Road

KOH
HAA
11

0   1   2 km

KOH
KHOM

0   1 mile

1   KOH DAENG (RED ISLAND)
★★☆☆

Location: 3km (1.6 n. miles) southwest of Ao Nang Beach.

Access: About 15min from Ao Nang Beach and 25min from Railae. Large submerged boulders and rocks to the south of the island offer the best diving. A mooring buoy about 50m (55yd) south of the island marks the descent position.

Conditions: As Koh Daeng is sheltered from the open seas by the mainland, minimal currents flow; alas, the proximity also means visibility is restricted to about 5m (16ft).

Average depth: 6m (20ft)

Maximum depth: 12m (40ft)

There is much to see. Hawksbill, Green and other turtles come here, as do sea snakes, Blue-spotted Ribbontail Stingrays and juvenile reef sharks. The sides of the rocks and boulders are rich in soft corals, and the boulder-tops host a variety of hard-coral laminates. Northwards, away from the boulders towards the island, lies a vast meadow of radiant orange soft corals.

In the sandy bottom small burrows are the homes of shy Sabre-toothed Blennies and a variety of gobies with their symbiotic hosts, blind Alpheid Shrimp.

2   KOH MA TANG MING
★★☆☆☆

Location: The outcrop 100m (110yd) off the northern shoreline of Koh Po Da Nai.

Access: About 35min from either Ao Nang or Railae Beach. Divers enter the water from the boat. The site is unbuoyed; the best place to anchor is off the western side.

Conditions: Visibility averages 8m (26ft). Because Koh Ma Tang Ming is small there is sheltered diving away from any strong current.

Average depth: 6m (20ft)

Maximum depth: 14m (46ft)

This is not one of the area's better sites, but certainly merits mention as it has reasonable diversities of both marine life and hard corals. Close inspection of the submerged rocks is recommended, as numerous members of the Scorpaenidae family – such as Bearded Scorpionfish and stonefish – are concealed on the rocky ledges.

Small Yellow Boxfish, Rock Basslets, Moorish Idols and bannerfish add colour, as do trees of soft corals, although these are few and far between. Hard corals are represented by staghorn, brain and some small boulders of coral porites. The best area for snorkellers is around the eastern side where, close to the rock, there are many sea whips, large plate corals and associated reef inhabitants.

3   KOH PODAH NAI
★☆☆☆☆☆

Location: The largest of the offshore islands and islets, just over 6km (3.2 n. miles) south of Ao Nang Beach.

Access: About 35min from either Ao Nang or Railae Beach. Several mooring buoys, all suitable moorings, are scattered along the reef. **Warning: Due to a large presence of boat traffic, extreme care must be taken when snorkelling at this site.**

Conditions: The waters are generally very calm. Visibility ranges from 5m to 12m (16–40ft).

Average depth: 5m (16ft)

Maximum depth: 12m (40ft)

The northern beach of Koh Podah Nai slopes gently down to an extensive reef-flat, which continues outwards for a further 50m (55yd) before it reaches an almost sheer slope which drops to 12m (40ft). The main attraction is the reef-flat. At high tide the corals are covered with only 2m (6ft) of water or less; at lower tides many coral heads break the surface. These conditions render this particular area suitable only for snorkelling. Better corals and marine life are found a little way out. The reef consists mainly of small clusters of staghorn, cauliflower and a number of leaf and plate corals. Enquire at the local dive shop as to the whereabouts of seahorses.

The diving here follows the reef-slope anticlockwise.

4   KOH PODAH NOK (CHICKEN ISLAND)
★★★★★

Location: 500m (0.25 n. miles) due south of Koh Podah Nai (Site 3).

Access: About 35min from either Ao Nang or Railae Beach. To reach the site, simply enter from the island's eastern beach and head north.

Conditions: Visibility is always good. The seas occasionally become rough by late afternoon.

Average depth: 1m (40in)

Maximum depth: 4m (13ft)

This site is immensely popular. Coral fringes the eastern beach, forming an almost patch-like reef. The marine life is more prolific round the eastern shore of the small islet at the beach's northern end. As the water is shallow and generally calm, the underwater views are spectacular. The seascape is mostly punctuated with rocky boulder and coral laminates, but the main attraction is the large diversity of marine life. Lots of small colourful reef-fish –

like damselfish, parrotfish and wrasse – share the waters with reasonable-sized Giant Clams and a wealth of smaller invertebrates.

5 KOH MAE URAI (KOH TARU)
★★★

Location: 1km (0.5 n. miles) due west of Koh Podah Nok (Site 4).

Access: About 40min from either Ao Nang or Railae Beach. There are two mooring buoys; the one on the western cliff serves as the entry point.

Conditions: Visibility ranges between 6m and 18m (20–60ft). Currents can be strong, but are predictably low during slack tides.

Average depth: 9m (30ft)

Maximum depth: 16m (53ft)

Above the water this rocky outcrop resembles a giant cobra's head, 30m (100ft) high, rearing from the depths. It features two underwater tunnels, each penetrating right through the rock from east to west. With the rock on your right, approach the nearer tunnel – swimming through it takes you over mounds of shingle where there are clusters of soft corals and small gorgonian seafans. Bannerfish, Moorish Idols and Blue-ringed Angelfish ignore you as you pass through. The exit itself has two large boulders on either side; they and the flat ground between them act as a natural frame for glorious soft corals in whites, pinks, blues, oranges and yellows. Their brilliance is enhanced by the sunlight in the water.

Beyond the coral gardens, the sea-bed tapers gradually down past shelves of rocks crowned with green, black and yellow featherstars, orange encrusting sponges and Magnificent Sea Anemones; the latter host various guests, including the endemic Two-banded Maroon and Skunk Anemonefish.

6 HIN BIA RHLUA (BOAT-SHAPED ROCK)
★★★★★

Location: 500m (0.25 n. miles) southeast of Koh Mae Urai (Site 5).

Access: About 45min from either Ao Nang or Railae Beach. There are two mooring buoys.

Conditions: Visibility ranges between 4m and 15m (13–50ft). Currents can be strong.

Average depth: 9m (30ft)

Maximum depth: 16m (53ft)

One of the local favourites. The southern side of the outcrop is the deepest section of the dive, which gradually gets shallower as it follows round clockwise to the north. In some sections the depth is under 4m (13ft),

so snorkellers have an ideal opportunity to observe the reef-flat and -crests, which are dominated by staghorn corals and a host of colourful reef-fish, including basslets, chromis, parrot and small wrasse.

The northern side is mainly dominated by terraces of foliaceous corals. Below these are many small boulders of lesser and greater stars, with the familiar punctuation of sea whips. Keeping on westward you lose the reef, which continues to fringe the outcrop. Straight ahead are two large, parallel mounds; you can swim between them to find many members of the scorpionfish family, including camouflaged Bearded Scorpionfish and flamboyant lionfish.

Back at the reef, set a bearing of due north. There is a lovely gorge to swim down. Its left side is a sheer wall covered in multicoloured soft corals; its right is a continuation of the reef-slope. The marine life is very intense here. Along the gorge's floor parrotfish peck away the hard skeletal layer of the corals.

7 KOH YA WA SAM
★★★

Location: About 2km (1¼ miles) west of Koh Podah Nok (Site 4).

Access: About 45min from either Ao Nang or Railae Beach. Two islets, 500m (¼ n. miles) apart, run north–south. The preferred diving is in the shallower waters around the southern outcrop. Off the east coast of each outcrop is a single mooring buoy.

Conditions: Current can occasionally be strong, transforming this usually relaxing site into quite a challenge. Visibility ranges between 5m and 15m (16–50ft).

Average depth: 9m (30ft)

Maximum depth: 17m (56ft)

The recommended entry point is at the mooring buoy off the southern outcrop. Follow the mooring line and head west towards the sloping reef, then follow it southwards. The reef-slope climbs over many fallen rocks which provide the main structure and heavily punctuate the minimal corals. An elevated area of corals between the two outcrops is more densely populated, but does not justify the longer journey; there are much better areas of corals around the islets nearer the shore.

Juvenile Blacktip Reef and Grey Nurse Sharks often rest among the rocks, with Leopard Sharks out on the sand – the main attraction of the site.

8 KOH KOM
★★★

Location: The sheer rocky outcrop 100m (110yd) off the

southeastern apex of Koh Podah Nok (Site 4).

Access: The surrounding waters are reached in about 35min from either Ao Nang or Railae Beach. The dive circumnavigates the outcrop. Two mooring buoys mark the site, one off the western face and the other off the east; the favoured entry point is the former.

Conditions: Visibility is often restricted to 5–10m (16–33ft). Currents can occasionally be strong.

Average depth: 12m (40ft)

Maximum depth: 20m (66ft)

The depth below the western mooring buoy averages about 14m (46ft). The seascape around this side of the outcrop features numerous terraced shelves which drop down to a number of large fallen rocks. Moorish Idols and Schooling Bannerfish patrol among many sea whips and bushy black corals. The gaps between the rocks act as shelters for a selection of medium-sized vertebrates including large Dog-faced Pufferfish and groupers. Beyond this area is a small cave; following through its gully clockwise you double back to exit at an elevated rocky plateau densely carpeted with Magnificent Sea Anemones which themselves are occupied by collections of Saddleback and Tomato Anemonefish.

The southern apex of this site has a beautiful elevated staghorn garden. Hosts of colourful reef-fish dart to protect themselves from predators under the sharp and stinging branches.

9 KOH YA WA BON
★★

Location: 1km (1/2 n. miles) west of Koh Podah Nok.

Access: About 40min from either Ao Nang or Railae Beach. There is no mooring buoy. The entry point is halfway along the eastern side.

A school of Head-band butterflyfish (Chaetodon collare).

Conditions: Visibility ranges between 6m and 18m (20–60ft). Currents can be strong but are predictably low during slack tides.

Average depth: 12m (40ft)

Maximum depth: 20m (66ft)

The descent hits the bottom at 15m (50ft); from here you can go either north or south around the parabolic outcrop. To the north an impressive archway cuts through the face of the rock for about 10m (33ft); the entrance is at 6m (20ft) and the exit at 12m (40ft). This is a good swimthrough, but wide enough for only one diver at a time. The site's northern area gradually slopes down over coral laminates interspersed with sea anemones (with a variety of tenants) and rocks. Away from the reef are three large submerged boulders, whose southern faces are carpeted in anemones; their many crevices act as homes and lairs to a variety of invertebrates, including Banded and Boxing Shrimp. These are also good places to spot small Snowflake Moray Eels meandering among the rocky ledges.

Heading south after entry makes the site more of a wall dive. Wrasse, parrotfish and lionfish abound.

10 KOH SEE
★★★

Location: Three outcrops in a step formation, rising from south to north, about 10min due south of Koh Podah Nok (Site 4).

Access: About 45min from either Ao Nang or Railae Beach. The sole mooring buoy is off the southwestern extremity.

Conditions: Visibility ranges between 5m and 22m (16–73ft). Large waves and strong winds generally bring in much stronger currents, rendering the site suitable for only more experienced divers. It is best to dive at slack tide.

Average depth: 6m (20ft)

Maximum depth: 16m (53ft)

There is a tremendous diversity of corals and marine life here. Descending from the boat to a depth of 9m (30ft) off the eastern face you find a wall. To the west this gradually declines into close formations of large rocks.

Back along the reef-slope itself, at a steady depth of 11m (36ft), a ribbonlike effect is created by various brain corals which have anchored themselves into the limestone.

The coral assortment changes towards the site's western end. The familiar hard species are replaced by bubble corals and zoanthids, occasionally fooling visitors with their anemone-like appearance. These continue to the western apex, which is highlighted by a spectacular shelved slope of leaf corals. In good visibility this presents an indescribable sight.

PRINCESS CAVE

During the reign of Alexander the Great, a trading ship carrying two Indian princesses sank off the Phra Nang coast. Local legend has it that ever since then one of the deceased, Princess Srikula-tavee, has returned to visit at each full moon a certain cave on Phra Nang beach.

Villagers believe their prosperity is directly linked to the spirit of the princess. With every full moon local inhabitants gather together at the cave in question to honor her spirit. Numerous candles and incense are burnt, and offerings of fruit, flowers and water placed around a shrine which was erected by local fishermen just inside the cave's entrance. Also inside the cave are curious phallic carvings, placed there by local fishermen's wives to ensure their husband's safe passage at sea.

---

11 KOH HAA
★★

Location: A rocky outcrop about 500m (¼ n. miles) south of Koh See (Site 10).

Access: Just over 45min from either Ao Nang or Railae Beach. There is no mooring buoy.

Conditions: These can vary quite considerably. Visibility drops to between 4m and 15m (13–50ft). Unkinder currents are rather frequent.

Average depth: 12m (40ft)

Maximum depth: 20m (66ft)

If the boat is correctly positioned there will be two large rocks beneath it at a depth of 9m (30ft). These are covered in soft corals, with oysters clinging to the rocky surface and to sea whip corals. The craggy surfaces of these small pinnacles host various moray eels.

As you go south, there are many sea anemones, mainly Magnificent and Gigantic; there is an equally impressive number of tenant anemonefish. If you look closely at the anemones you usually find other, smaller hosts such as the Anemone Crab and the translucent Anemone Shrimp.

One reef resident is worth looking out for – a solitary Siam Mantis Shrimp (or, aptly, Bone Crusher Shrimp) dug into the sand around the site's northern section.

Opposite: *A coral formation typical of the type found in the waters of Krabi province.*

HOW TO GET THERE

There are unfortunately no direct routes to this beautiful part of the country but this should not deter those intending to visit as all journeys have straight-forward connections. There are plans for a local airport to open in 1999.

By bus: VIP air-conditioned buses leave Bangkok's southern bus terminal daily at 18.00 and 18.30hrs. The local bus terminal is just outside Krabi Town and takes twelve hours to reach. A fully reclining seat on the more spacious 24 seat bus costs more than a fully reclining seat on the adequate 32 seat bus. Note that both ticket prices increase for the return journey, so it is advisable to book both journeys in Bangkok prior to departure. For further information regarding any bus services ring Bangkok southern bus terminal; tel (02) 435 1199, 435 1200, Lignite Tours; tel (02) 435 5017. For any information or bookings regarding further travel from Krabi there are two reliable companies: Songserm Travel Centre, Krabi Town; tel (075) 612665-6/fax (075) 612318 and P.P. Family Co. Krabi Town; tel (075) 611717, 612463. In Krabi Town visitors connect to one of the beaches by either road or sea. Connect with a local bus (Songthaew) to Ao Nang Beach. This journey is done in two stages, both are in Songthaews which are no more than converted pickup trucks with two benches and a roof on the back. The fares are standard and not negotiable. There are no designated stops and the buses can be flagged down anywhere - passengers tap against the iron framework with a coin when they want to get off. Fares are paid at the destination. The short journey from the bus station to Krabi Town takes ten minutes. In Krabi Town passengers exchange buses to reach Ao Nang beach which takes another forty five minutes. The last bus leaves the town at 17.30hrs so if visitors arrive later than this they can find accommodation in the town and continue their journey in the morning.

By boat: By Longtail boat to Railae or Ao Nang beach. Boats leave the estuary in town when the boatman decides there are enough passengers to warrant the journey - timetables do not exist. Boats take forty minutes to reach Railae beach - the price is negotiable - and take another fifteen minutes to the next beach of Ao Nang. Boats also provide a regular service between the two beaches. The last boat departs from either beach at around 17.30hrs.

By air: Until Krabi gets its own local airport, the nearest flights are to Phuket with Thai International. There are fourteen daily flights which depart the domestic airport every hour, on the hour, between 07.00hrs and 21.00hrs they are conveniently arranged to coincide with incoming International flights, allowing immediate connections. The flight time is seventy five minutes. On arrival at Phuket International Airport it will be necessary to transfer to a taxi or local air-conditioned bus for a further 3 hour journey to Krabi. The regular air-conditioned VIP Bus service leaves from the end of the airport road. A taxi is necessary to get to the bus stop from the airport. For further information contact Thai Airways International Limited; tel (02) 513 0121/fax (02) 513 0203.

By car and taxis: This takes over twelve hours and is not advisable.

For any additional information on the Krabi area contact the **Tourism Authority of Thailand**; tel (076) 212213, 211036/fax (076) 213582.

WHERE TO STAY

Ao Nang Beach

The accommodation along Ao Nang beach ranges from small huts with communal bathrooms up to comfortable hotels. The best time to find somewhere to stay is in the mornings immediately after guests have checked out. If staying at one of the very basic bungalow resorts it is recommended to leave diving gear at an alternative secure place, such as a dive shop. **Phra Nang Inn**; tel (075) 612173/fax (075) 612174. Located towards the southern end of the beach, this resort is full of local character. The Inn decor is in traditional Thai style as is the open air restaurant and bar. The rooms surround either an attractive garden or the small swimming pool - all have air-conditioning, TV and fridge. **Gift's Bungalows**; tel (01) 723 1128. Located at the jungles edge are 26 bamboo and brick bungalows laid out in a landscaped tropical garden. The rooms are cooled by roof fans. There is a restaurant serving first-class European and Thai food.

Railae Beach

The east and west beaches both have a good range of accommodation. The smaller resorts do not have a constant electricity supply and their generators are switched off at around midnight. This is however changing as more resorts are upgrading to include air-conditioned bungalows. This has the disadvantage of making all the bungalows more expensive. **Sand Sea Bungalows**; tel (075) 611944. Twenty bungalows nestle under coconut trees. **Sun Rise Bungalows**, Amphur Muang, Krabi, has an on-site diving centre and twenty bungalows set out parallel to Sand Sea bungalows. **Dusit Rayavadee**, 67 Moo 5, Sai Thai-Susan Hoi road, Amphur Muang, Krabi 81000, tel (075) 620740-3/fax (075) 620630. 98 luxurious, spacious air-conditioned bunglows. There are several on-site shops, bars, first-class restaurants and a large swimming pool.

WHERE TO EAT

Ao Nang Beach

There is a beach front walkway at the northern end of Ao Nang with about 10 restaurants - all of which are definitely worth a visit. The larger hotels have their own restaurants but by the time service and tax have been added to the bill they are not cheap. **Sala Thai Restaurant** is the last restaurant at the far end of the walkway and is the most popular and welcoming restaurant on the beach. The food is excellent, varied and very reasonably priced. **Ya Ya Plaza** attracts many divers, who come here to enjoy the sunsets while sipping delicious cocktails. **The Last Cafe** is secluded amongst trees at the opposite end of the beach - an excellent place for meals or beach snacks. Closes after sunset.

Railae Beach

This beach differs from its northern neighbour of Ao Nang in as all the restaurants are associated with resorts. Two important things to remember when visiting this beach is that the pace is slow and restaurants often close at 21.00hrs. **Sand and Sea** is right on the western beach. The menu here is like a book, with delicious cheap selections. Be warned of the dishes with Holy Basil leaves as they are red hot.

DIVE FACILITIES

The dive operators on Ao Nang and Railae beaches are all very friendly and provide a wonderful personal service. Local trips use Longtail boats while larger boats are chartered to the more distant sites and for overnight excursions.

Dive Trips

Dive trips run on a daily basis. All trips depart from Ao Nang and Railae beaches and include light refreshments, fruit, drinking water, lunch, Divemaster services.

On the majority of the local diving trips, the surface interval can be spent on the island of Koh Podah Nai, either sunbathing or eating at the restaurant. Snorkellers can enjoy the reefs around this and Chicken Island. Day trips to the further destinations of Shark Point, Anemone Reef, King Cruiser Wreck and the Phi Phi Islands are available. Snorkellers and non divers are welcome to join any of the scheduled diving trips - masks and fins are available.

Dive courses

Courses for the complete beginner are very popular here with a good selection of shallow sites. All local instruction follows one of three diver training programmes in either PADI, NAUI or SSI; prices are similar. Prices quoted are fully inclusive of all equipment and certification. Students are required to provide two passport sized photographs. Check with individual dive operators about which courses they offer.

Dive Operators

Phra Nang Divers; 47/7 Moo 2, Ao Nang Beach, Krabi 81000, tel (075) 637064/fax (075) 620630, email: pndivers@loxinfo.co.th Brand new offices on both Railae West and Ao Nang beaches. They also run a live-aboard with trips to the southern sites of Koh Ha Yai, the Koh Rok group and Hin Daeng and Muang. Excursions to Koh Tarutao Marine National Park have recently been added. There is a retail centre as well as a number of rooms for let. **Ao Nang Divers**; c/o Krabi Seaview Resort, 143 Moo 2, Ao Nang Beach, Krabi 81000, tel (075) 637242-5/fax (075) 637246, email: aonang@loxinfo.co.th   PADI 5-star Centre. MV *Chok Suda* serves both day trips and, on demand, live-aboard excursions to the far southern sites. There is a good retail outlet and associated resort. **Aqua Vision,** 32/1 Moo 2, Ao Nang Beach, Krabi 81000, tel/fax (075) 637415. First-class, very friendly dive shop, professionally run by German, Swiss and Japanese management. Day trips and live-aboard excursions to all the listed southern destinations on own dive boat. A full range of PADI courses is offered in a variety of languages. Good retail selection. **Poseidon International Diving School,** 23/1 Moo 2, Ao Nang Beach, Krabi 81000, Thailand, tel (075) 637147/fax (075) 637350. PADI Dive Centre. PADI courses are available in English, German and Swedish. Good retail outlet and equipment repair service. **Seafan's Divers**, 207-208 Moo 2, Ao Nang Beach, Krabi 81000, tel (075) 637214/fax (038) 880439. Located above

Phra Nang Inn on Ao Nang beach. PADI Instruction is available in English and NAUI in Thai. There is a small retail selection. **Calypso Diving**, 202 Moo 2, Ao Nang Beach, Krabi 81000, tel (075) 637 056. PADI 5-star Dive Centre. PADI courses in German. Dive trips on board Longtails and the company's own small boat. **Coral Diving**, Krabi Resort, Moo 2, Ao Nang Beach, Krabi 81000, tel/fax (075) 637465. Located in Krabi Resort. The complete range of PADI courses are taught in German. Dive trips to all the main sites on board the centre's own dive boat. **Freeland Divers**, Moo 2, Ao Nang Beach, Krabi 81000, Thailand, tel (075) 637172. This is a small Italian-run venture offering day trips on board their own small dive boat and Longtails. SSI diver training is on offer. **Baby Shark Divers**, P.O. Box 32, Main Post Office, Krabi Town, Krabi 81000, fax (075) 612914. Located on Railae beach, halfway along the path connecting the east and west beaches next to Sunrise Bungalows. Range of NAUI courses conducted in English by a first-class Canadian instructor. Dive trips are scheduled for all the local sites on board Longtails. Snorkelling gear is available for hire.

FILM PROCESSING

The nearest developing services are in Krabi Town but slides cannot be processed there.

HOSPITAL AND RECOMPRESSION CHAMBER

Krabi Provincial Hospital; tel (075) 611227, 611228 is the only hospital in Krabi Town. It is extremely basic and not particularly clean so if you do require treatment it is advisable if at all possible to get to one of the hospitals in Phuket (see p. 31). The nearest recompression chamber is situated on Koh Phuket. It takes between 3 and 4hrs to reach the chamber by road. Contact **Dive Safe Asia**; tel (076) 342518/fax (076) 342519.

LOCAL HIGHLIGHTS

The majority of Krabi's visitors seem content to stay put on the beaches but day excursions and shopping trips are available. The superb beaches on the mainland and the small off-shore islands of **Koh Podah Nai** and **Koh Podah Nok** are the main reason people visit Krabi. Both of the islands have beautiful beaches and terrific views of the mountainous mainland landscape. It is possible to stay on the island of Koh Podah Nai, in one of the thirteen bungalows spread along the mountains edge in the centre of the island, it is advised to check their availability at Krabi Resort on Ao Nang beach before arrival as they quickly become full. Longtail boats to either of

the islands can be arranged privately or they can be visited as part of a five islands tour which includes these and three other locations, snorkelling gear, fruit and lunch. Trips can be booked at the majority of resorts. On the mainland there are many other impressive beaches, all of them blissfully free from watersports and regimented rows of sun umbrellas.

At the western end is **Had Noppharat Thara**, a 5km (3 mile) long beach fringed with casuarina trees providing shade for picnics. There are a number of offshore limestone islets which can be explored on foot during the lower tides. You can also take a trip by Longtail boat through the mangrove forests around the estuary at the northern end of the beach. Boats can be hired from the wooden jetty by the National Park's Head Office and Information Centre for two hours. **Ao Nang Beach** is the most popular beach in the area. There are a number of bungalow resorts and independent restaurants which span the narrow asphalt beach road. Daily excursions leave from the beach and can all be arranged and booked through the resorts.

Railae Beach, the western beach was once voted the second most beautiful in the world. It can only be reached by boat and there is ample accommodation, restaurants and shops selling basic provisions.

Phra Nang Beach is part of the National Park and there is a collection of caves at the southern end of the beach, the largest of which is Princess Cave.

Krabi Town is small and can be walked around in twenty minutes but it offers a reasonable range of shops and there is also a good market selling vegetables, meats and locally caught fresh fish. All the main banks are conveniently located along Uttarakit road, all of which offer a currency exchange service.

Car and motorbike rental

Motor bikes and jeeps can be rented directly from most resorts. An International driving permit may be required as will a passport for deposit.

SEVENTY FIVE MILLION YEAR SHELL CEMETERY

One of the most famous landmarks in the area is Su San Hoi Shell Cemetery. Located 17 km (10 miles) from Krabi town beyond the headland east of Railae beach, this fossil shell beach is one of only three in the world (the others being in the USA and Japan).

KOH LANTA MARINE NATIONAL PARK

There are dozens of islands off the Krabi coast, many of them only just beginning to open up to adventurous backpackers searching for the quintessential bamboo hut on the perfect beach. Fifteen of these islands make up the Koh Lanta Marine National Park, which covers about 135 sq km (52 sq miles) across four main island groups – Koh Lanta Yai and Koh Lanta Noi, Koh Ngai, Koh Rok Nok and Koh Rok Nai, and the Koh Ha group of islands.

The island with the most facilities – including about a dozen bungalow 'resorts' and four dive operators – is Koh Lanta Yai, which is some 25km (15 miles) long, with a hilly central section and a string of superb sandy beaches. The main settlement is Amphoe Koh Lanta, on the east coast, a small township with limited amenities – a few grocery stores and a couple of noodle shops and little else. At the northern end of the island, Saladan is ostensibly a fishing port, but has a post office, a foreign currency exchange, grocery shops and restaurants.

DIVING AROUND KOH LANTA

The diving around Koh Lanta and the adjacent islands is exceptionally good, and this is definitely regarded as one of the best areas in the country. There is a good variety of diving, with reef-walls, fringing reefs, caves and a wreck to explore around the offshore islands, islets and rocks.

Marine life is abundant, with a healthy cross-section of reef species as well as pelagics. Visibility is a respectable 20m (66ft) on the dive sites furthest from the mainland, sometimes reaching 30m (100ft).

Only four local operators and two visiting live-aboards from Koh Phuket currently utilize these sites, so they are uncrowded and show few signs of damage: some deterioration is evident on areas nearer the mainland, due to bottom trawling and dynamite fishing, but enforcement of National Park regulations is now helping curb these practices.

Two sites, Hin Mouang (Site 8) and Hin Daeng (Site 9), are among the top handful of Thailand's dive sites, largely thanks to the presence of Manta Rays, Whale Sharks, oceanic

Opposite: *The incredible sky at night, Koh Lanta.*
Above: *Hermit crabs (Diogenidae) are familiar dwellers at most dive sites.*

sharks and other pelagic visitors; Hin Mouang is distinguished also by having one of the most spectacular reef-walls in the country, dropping down some 70m (230ft).

As an added bonus, the Koh Lanta Marine National Park is one of the few places in the world which still has substantial numbers of Dugongs in the coastal waters.

ISLAND OF LONG BEACHES

The inhabitants of Koh Lanta Yai are mainly Muslim; mixed-race descendants of Malaysian settlers and the chao ley (sea gypsies) who live along the eastern coastline. Aside from fishing and shrimp farming, the other main economic activities on the island focus on rice, rubber and coconuts. The name given to the island by the chao ley is Paulao Satak, which means 'the island of the long beaches'. Most of these beaches fringe the western coastline, lapped by clear, unpolluted waters which are perfect for swimming and snorkelling.

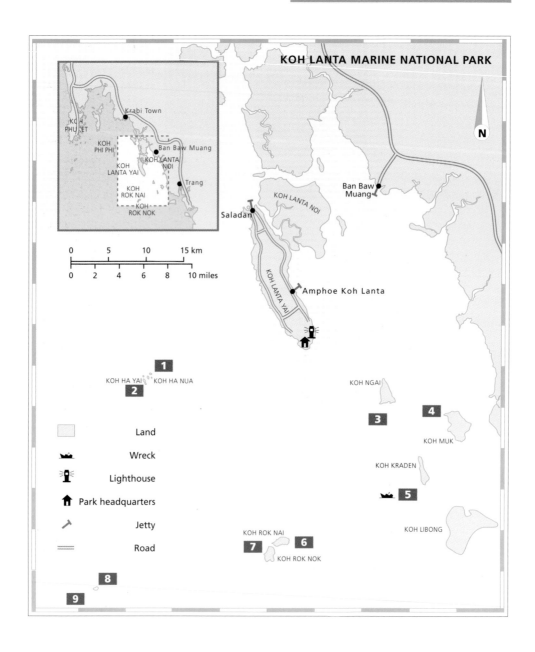

KOH LANTA MARINE NATIONAL PARK

1 KOH HA NUA – NORTHERN OUTCROP
★★

Location: This is the northernmost of the Koh Ha group.
Access: Just over 1hr by diveboat from Saladan Pier, over 4hr by live-aboard from Chalong Bay on Koh Phuket. There is no permanent mooring buoy.
Conditions: Because of its positioning and size, there is always a favourable section of this site, with calm conditions and visibility ranging up to 25m (83ft).
Average depth: 20m (66ft)
Maximum depth: 34m (113ft)
One point of individuality is that the site is characterized by a scattering of geometrically shaped rocks. Sea whips and seafans are much in evidence, as are featherstars and nudibranchs. The reef-life offers nothing particularly special, but this is as good a place as any to see Indian and Spotfin Lionfish, Bearded Scorpionfish and Imperial Angelfish. There is a small cave off the South West wall.

2 KOH HA YAI
★★★

Location: The southernmost of the Koh Ha islands.
Access: The entry point is off the south west face. This small island is unbuoyed.
Conditions: Visibility ranges from 5m to 20m (16–66ft). Current, if any, is generally only weak to moderate.
Average depth: 18m (60ft)
Maximum depth: 25m (83ft)
There is excellent adventure here. The south western face has a brilliant cave with two entrances. The western (left) of these is a hole in the rock at a depth of 5m (16ft). This immediately enters the larger of two connected 'cathedrals', which rise an impressive 30m (100ft) above sea-level. The other entrance/exit, at the eastern end, is deeper, at 16m (53ft). It is not dark in the cathedrals: light enters from the waters below, creating rather strange illusions.

3 KOH NGAI
★★★★

Location: This island lies about 11km (6 n. miles) off the southern tip of Koh Lanta Yai. The site is centred on the group of rocky outcrops 100m (110yd) off Koh Ngai's southwest tip.
Access: Just over 1hr from Saladan. There is no permanent mooring buoy. Entry can be anywhere around the jagged outcrops.
Conditions: Due to the proximity of the mainland,

visibility is not great, averaging about 8m (26ft). Currents are often strong.
Average depth: 6m (20ft)
Maximum depth: 16m (53ft)
The best bit of this site is in the south, where you perform a shallow dive around rocks and a gently sloping fringing reef. Nurse Sharks lurk under the rocks, and occasionally you can see Leopard sharks. There are plenty of colourful soft corals and a good diversity of reef-fish.

4 KOH MUK
★★★★★★★

Location: The island lies about 8km (4 n. miles) south west of Koh Ngai (Site 3). The site itself centres on the large rocky outcrop, rising 5m (16ft) from the water, off Koh Muk's northwest point.
Access: 90min by diveboat from Saladan Pier, about 5hr by live-aboard from Chalong Bay on Koh Phuket. Entry is off the western rock face.
Conditions: Generally moderate to strong currents.
Average depth: 5m (16ft)
Maximum depth: 10m (33ft)
The rock itself is covered in masses of splendid purple and red soft corals, with holes and cracks providing hiding-places for fish. You can head either south along the west coast or east along the north coast – both options offer overhangs, but the latter is more interesting.

More significant than the diving on offer, there's an interesting adventure for snorkellers – assuming they feel brave enough to navigate the winding cave/tunnel, 60m (200ft) long, which has been cut through the western rocky cliff. Known as Morukut ('Emerald Cave'), this penetrates the mountain and eventually emerges into a beautiful lagoon, about 60m (66yd) across, fringed by tropical forest, and with a superb beach. The tunnel affords the only access by water to this lagoon; the water at its entrance is only about 4m (13ft) deep and becomes shallower as the tunnel goes deeper into the mountain, while there is always at least 1m (40in) airspace and sometimes as much as 15m (50ft).

5 KOH KRADEN WRECK
★★★

Location: Off the southwest coast of Koh Kraden. No marine references mark the wreck's exact location. The wreck is in fact very difficult to find: operators without a GPS find it through luck rather than judgement.
Access: Just over 2hr by diveboat from Saladan Pier, over 5hr by live-aboard from Chalong Bay on Koh

Phuket. The site is unbuoyed.

Conditions: There is generally a thermocline at about 20m (66ft), and this reduces the visibility from 20m (66ft) to below 10m (33ft). Currents are moderate to strong.

Average depth: 24m (80ft)

Maximum depth: 28m (93ft)

The wreck is believed to be of a 60–70m (200–230ft) Japanese destroyer sunk by air attack in 1944. It sits in 28m (93ft) of water. As the visibility here worsens below 20m (66ft), the way to find the wreck is to follow the many fish that frequent what has become an artificial reef. Those experienced in wreck-diving can penetrate the bow sections, but it is not advisable to attempt entry to the stern section, which is draped with fishing nets and subject to much silting.

6 KOH ROK NAI
★★☆

Location: The northern of the two Koh Rok islands.

Access: Just over 4hr by diveboat from Saladan Pier. Five mooring buoys are in place, ranging from 50m to 200m (55–220yd) off the coast.

Conditions: Visibility is generally about 20m (66ft). The site has weak to moderate currents.

Average depth: 12m (40ft)

Maximum depth: 20m (66ft)

This is a good site at all depths. The diving is around the southern coast, heading slightly northeast. This is also a reasonable snorkelling site, and offers good night-diving, since conditions are almost always calm at night. The reef slopes gently and there are lots of hard corals, including brain and table staghorn, and many barrel sponges. The reef-fish are reasonably plenteous; they include bannerfish, large schools of Moorish Idols, and a good variety of clownfish. Out in the blue, large barracuda, tuna and jacks pass by, and turtles are often seen in this area.

7 KOH ROK NOK
★★★☆☆☆☆☆

Location: The southern of the two Koh Rok islands.

Access: Just over 4hr by diveboat from Saladan Pier. There is no mooring buoy. Access is by 'live-boat' dive.

Conditions: Visibility is quite good, averaging 20m (66ft). Currents are weak to moderate.

Average depth: 14m (46ft)

Maximum depth: 20m (66ft)

On the wall itself you may see enormous moray eels, lionfish, invertebrates and nudibranchs, plus Zigzag Oysters. Further around the headland you come across a

terrain of big boulders that extends all the way to the cliff face. This section is interesting in that a freshwater stream has, because of its high iron content, coloured the rocks bright orange; for the same reason, though, healthy coral growth is restricted. Whale Sharks can occasionally be seen here very close to the shore.

8 HIN MOUANG (PURPLE ROCK)
★★★★★

Location: 27km (15 n. miles) west of the Rok islands (Sites 6–7) and 500m (550yd) southwest of Hin Daeng (Site 9).

Access: Just over 5hr by diveboat from Saladan Pier. There is no mooring buoy. Access is by 'live-boat' dive or from a small serving tender.

Conditions: Currents can be very strong, and can rapidly change direction. Visibility depends on the current, ranging from 10m (33ft) in stronger currents to a staggering – and more common – 40m (130ft).

Average depth: 23m (76ft)

Maximum depth: 70m+ (235ft+)

This is one of the best dive sites in Thai waters. A series of six or more submerged pinnacles heads southwest, the shallowest being about 8m (26ft) beneath the surface. This site features the deepest dropoff in Thailand, exceeding 70m (235ft). Large pelagics often visit, including enormous barracuda and very large tuna. Whale Sharks often frequent these waters, as do other shark species and large stingrays.

9 HIN DAENG (RED ROCK)
★★★★★★☆☆☆

Location: 27km (15 n. miles) west of Koh Rok (Sites 6–7) and 500m (550yd) from Hin Mouang (Site 8).

Access: Just over 5hr by diveboat from Saladan Pier. There is no mooring buoy.

Conditions: Very similar to those at Site 8. Visibility ranges from 10m to 40m (33–130ft).

Average depth: 25m (83ft)

Maximum depth: 35m (116ft)

A series of wall dives, with intermittent shelves at varying depths. There are more soft corals than hard corals, but the main attraction is the great diversity of marine inhabitants, particularly pelagics: here and Hin Mouang (Site 8) are the only reef-type communities or feeding grounds within the area. This is one of the very few dive sites in Thailand where large schools of Grey Reef Sharks are sighted. Whale Sharks, too, often frequent these waters, as do Manta Rays. There are also large Nurse Sharks – particularly in a cave located in a depth of about 10m (33ft) on the south west wall.

There is a belief that these unusual creatures may have given rise to the mermaid myth - unlikely as it seems, they have been mistaken in the past for humans. This myth was underlined when in 1560 a group of Portugese explorers captured seven Dugongs and presented them to the viceroy's physician who commented that they were 'creatures comparable with humans in every respect'.

Adult Dugongs are mostly hairless apart from a few head hairs and bristles. The forelimbs are long and fin-like, ending with two hands featuring five fingers on each. Instead of hind legs they have a horizontal tail rudder and instead of having a neck, the head is separated from the body by a fold of skin. Female Dugongs have breasts which they use to nurture their young. They tend to inhabit shallow coastal seas generally in a depth range of between 1m (3ft) and 12m (40ft); preferred water temperatures range between 20 and 30 degrees. Dugongs rarely enter beyond the mouth of rivers and are never found in deep fresh water.

THREATENED SPECIES

In the past, heavy trawling in Thai waters has destroyed immense areas of seagrass forest. This is one, if not the prime, reason for the serious decline in their numbers as seagrass forest forms the staple diet of the Dugong. In Thailand however, Dugongs can still be spotted amongst the seagrass forests around a few of the offshore islands in Trang province, such as Koh Lipong. They are understandably nervous of snorkellers and divers so a close look is almost impossible.

Trang is now considered to be the last location in Thailand where herds of Dugongs can be seen. The high degree of public concern regarding the dwindling numbers of Dugongs makes it difficult for the authorities to ignore the problems associated with trawling so it continues, thankfully, to be regulated by the government. This means that there will still be enough marine life in the seas for the younger generations to continue to work as fishermen.

REPLENISHING SEAGRASS

An idea for replenishing the seagrass - and therefore the marine life - was that of the Yad Fon Association. Based in Trang Town, these volunteers have worked with seventeen fishing communities educating them in the importance and practise of seagrass planting. They started out by explaining that a single square metre of seagrass can contain over a million grasses and hundreds of thousands of small creatures such as crabs, fish and shrimp: all sources of food for the villagers. The three largest areas of seagrass now dominate an area of over one hundred and thirty three square kilometres.

If protected, this juvenile Dugong (Dugong Dugong) will live for around 75 years.

How to Get There

Koh Lanta can be reached by scheduled boat services from Krabi Town, Koh Phi Phi Don, Koh Phuket and Ban Baw Muang pier north west of Trang Town. To reach the island, transfer by minibus or private taxi to the pier at Ban Baw Muang which is around 40km (25 miles) north of the town. There are no direct routes, but Trang Town can be directly accessed by road, rail and air.

To Trang Town from Bangkok
By bus: VIP air-conditioned buses leave Bangkok's southern bus terminal twice daily at 18.00 and 18.30hrs - journey time is 17hrs. Each bus can carry 24 passengers on fully reclining seats. For further information regarding any bus services contact Bangkok southern bus terminal; tel (02) 434 55578.
By train: there are three types of train service running from Bangkok to Trang and as it is a 15hr journey it is advisable to travel sleeper class. Trains can be booked up to ninety days in advance – recommended as they fill up quickly. Express trains leave Bangkok Hua Lumphong railway station at 17.00hrs and arrive in Trang at 08.00hrs the following morning. All trains have a buffet car and bar. Travelling second class there is a choice between a fan sleeper and the slightly more expensive air conditioned sleeper. For further information about any of the train services contact Hua Lumphong railway station. Bangkok; tel (02) 223 7010. Trang Town railway station; tel (075) 218012.
By air to Trang: Flights are with Thai International - one flight daily from the domestic airport at 07.50hrs - flight time is around 2hrs. For further information contact Thai Airways International Limited, Bangkok; tel (02) 513 0121/fax (02) 513 0203. For bookings; tel (02) 233 3810, 280 0070, Trang airport office; tel (075) 218066
By car and taxis: It takes around 18hrs to reach Trang by road.

To Koh Lanta by Boat: From Krabi Town to Saladan Pier. Boats depart from Krabi Town to Saladan Pier daily at 13.30hrs - journey time two hours.

From Koh Phi Phi Don to Saladan Pier: Boats depart from the pier on Koh Phi Phi Don daily at 15.00hrs - journey time ninety minutes.

From Koh Phuket to Saladan Pier: This is via Koh Phi Phi Don - boats depart the southern bay of Ao Chalong at 08.00 daily - journey time ninety minutes.

From Ban Baw Muang Pier to Koh Lanta Amphoe Muang Pier: Boats depart the pier at 12.00hrs and 13.30hrs daily - journey time forty-five minutes.

All returning boats from both piers depart at 08.00 hrs.

For any information of bookings regarding further travel from Trang, the larger hotels in the town all have travel services and can make any necessary travel arrangements for you, as can the resorts listed on Koh Lanta. For any additional information on the Trang area contact **Tourism Authority of Thailand**, Phuket office; tel (076) 212213, 211036/fax (076) 213582.

Where to Stay

In Trang Town
There are a number of hotels in the town - three of which are listed below - but the vast majority cater for business guests rather than tourists. The rooms are clean but very basic. All the hotels listed here have their own restaurants: **Thumrin Hotel**, Thumrin Square, Trang; tel (075) 211011-30. Air-conditioned rooms. **Trang Hotel**, Clock Tower Intersection, Trang; tel (075) 218157. Fan-cooled and air-conditioned rooms. **Queen's Hotel**, Visertkul road, Trang; tel (075) 218229. Rooms are fan-cooled.

On Koh Lanta
Kaw Kwang Beach
This beach at the north west end of the island has the largest selection of accommodation on the island. There are no hotels on the island, all resorts are 'bungalow' type resorts.

Kaw Kwang Beach Bungalows; tel 01 722 0106. A selection of twenty bungalows spread along the beach in two rows. The resort has a restaurant and beach bar. There is a currency exchange service available. Major credit cards are accepted. Bungalows are fan-cooled and have their own individual bathrooms.

Lanta Royal Resort; tel 01 723 0876/fax (075) 210264. Twenty five beach front bungalows are equipped with electric fan and private bathroom. The restaurant has Thai and European menus. Motorbikes can be rented and there is a currency exchange. Major credit cards are accepted.

Lanta Villa, Kaw Kwang Beach, Koh Lanta - 27 fan-cooled rooms and an excellent restaurant.

On Koh Kradan/Koh Ngai
These islands are occasionally visited during diving trips allowing guests to stay at these quiet retreats. It is best to enquire at the dive centre prior to departure so arrangements can be made.

Kradan Island Resort, Koh Kradan; tel (075) 211367. This is a very comfortable and popular beach resort with its own swimming pool, restaurant, currency exchange and small friendly bar.

Koh Ngai Resort, Koh Ngai; tel (075) 211045. Sixty comfortable bungalows with fan cooled and air conditioned rooms are located between a mountainous terrain and the beach. The resort has its own restaurant and usual facilities.

Where to Eat

Trang Town
Kanok Restaurant; tel (075) 2110089. Recommended dishes include baked fish, sizzling prawns and large raw oysters with lemon, shallots and garlic.

Nammui Restaurant; tel (075) 218504. Specialities include Steamed Spicy Tuna and Baked Duck in Coffee.

Koh Lanta
There are as yet no independent restaurants of the island of Koh Lanta. However all the resorts on the island have their own restaurants which provide a wide selection of delicious food.

Dive Facilities

There are presently four operators on the island. The sites are visited as day trips with two different sites being dived in a day. However, the local sites are also visited by some of the operators on Koh Phuket and in Krabi as live-aboard excursions lasting several days. (For details see Live-aboards feature on page 32 and Krabi regional directory on page 93.)

Dive Trips
All trips depart from the northern fishing port of Saladan at around 08.00hrs and return during the late afternoon. Included in the price are refreshments, fruit, drinking water, lunch and Divemaster(s) services.

The cost of the day trips varies depending on the destination. Snorkellers and non divers are welcome to join any of the scheduled diving trips; snorkelling equipment is available. The larger dive boats will carry fresh water tanks for rinsing diving and photographic equipment, but the Longtail boats do not.

Dive Courses
All local instruction follows PADI diver training programmes. Single day Non certification Discover Scuba experience programmes are also available. PADI Open Water Diver Courses. Run over three to four days. PADI Advanced Open Water Diver Courses. Courses run over two to

three days. PADI Specialty Diver Courses. Courses run for an average of two days, with a range to choose from. PADI Rescue Diver Courses. The course time table is structured to suit both divers and dive centres.

Dive Operators
Diving Atlantis; tel 01 722 0106/fax 01 723 230868. PADI courses taught in German and English. Daily dive trips on board own boat, speedboat or rented Longtail. **Koh Lanta Diving Centre**, Saladan Amphoe, Koh Lanta, Krabi Province, 81150. PADI Courses taught in German and English. Daily dive trips on board own boat or rented Longtail. **The Dive Zone**, tel (01) 211 6938. PADI courses taught in German and English. Daily dive trips on board own boat and speedboat. **Aquarius Diving**: fax (01) 228 4346.

FILM PROCESSING

There are as yet no photographic services on the island of Koh Lanta, but there are several on the mainland in Trang Town and Krabi Town – see page 93.

HOSPITALS AND RECOMPRESSION CHAMBERS

There are no hospitals on the island. The nearest medical facilities are on the mainland in Trang Town which has five hospitals of which the main three are **Racha Damnern Hospital**; tel (075) 211203, **Watana Pat Hospital**; tel 218332 and **Trang Chatasongkroh Hospital**; tel 218060. The nearest **recompression chamber** is on Patong Beach, Koh Phuket - to get there takes 6hrs so divers should dive with extreme caution.

LOCAL HIGHLIGHTS

There are numerous beaches along the northern and western coastlines. The southern third of the island is designated as **National Park**. This area can only be visited with a Park Official acting as guide. The National Park Office is located at the southern tip of the island behind a long sandy beach which can only be accessed by boat. This southern section of the island is well worth visiting as the forested hills are home to a variety of wildlife including squirrels, reptiles, amphibians and many species of birds.

Island exploration is best done on a motorbike; available for rent at most resorts. The western side of the island features the best beaches, whereas the eastern coast has mostly been transformed into dead soil by the enormous amount of prawn farms, the majority of which are now disused.

The main **excursion** on the island is to a large cave with numerous giant bats clinging to the upper walls; the bulk of the other excursions involve snorkelling trips, most of which are day trips to the **Emerald Cave** at Koh Muk. Other trips venture to the seagrass rich waters around the island of Koh Libong in the hope of spotting the rare Dugong which still exist in these waters (see feature on page 99).

Car and Motorbike rental
Motorbikes can be rented from most resorts and are a good way to explore the island.

A Green turtle (Chelonio mydas) prepares for launch.

CHUMPHON

Chumphon Province, which has eight districts, is 500km (310 miles) south of Bangkok. Chumphon Town lies on the intersection of the main routes to the south and west. It was named over 600 years ago from the Thai word chumnumphon, meaning 'social meeting place'.

The Chumphon area is popular with Bangkok residents as it is the Gulf's nearest southern diving destination offering a wide selection of attractions, both natural and man-made, including spectacular beaches, over 30 permeable-limestone islands, picturesque landscapes – featuring waterfalls and caves – and holy shrines. The area is renowned throughout the country for its production of fruit, in particular its delicious red rambutans, finger bananas and pineapples.

Beyond the beaches of Chumphon Town are seven offshore islands, the largest and nearest being Koh Samet. Going southward, the others are Koh Sak, Koh Mattra, Koh Maphrao, Koh I Raet, Koh Lawa and Koh Ka. The outer islands, from north to south, are Koh Ngam Yai, Koh Ngam Noi and Koh Lak Ngam.

One thing to bear in mind when visiting this area is that the vast majority of signs still feature only Thai characters. Moreover, the vast majority of the local people speak only their native language.

DIVING IN THE CHUMPHON AREA

Local diving is concentrated around the outer islands and rocky outcrops in the area north and southeast of Chumphon Town. The nearer offshore islands are much affected by freshwater runoff and so have unhealthy corals and little marine life; they are not really suitable for diving.

Amenities aboard diveboats can be fairly basic: all lack galleys and freshwater showers and some have no toilets.

Local diving operators leave from one of three locations. If you are staying at either of the two beach resorts providing diving services, your boat will leave from the beach directly

Opposite: *Of all the offshore islands, boats are only permitted to land on Koh Mattra.*
Above: *A Striped surgeonfish (Acanthurus lineatus) hurries to catch up with its shoal.*

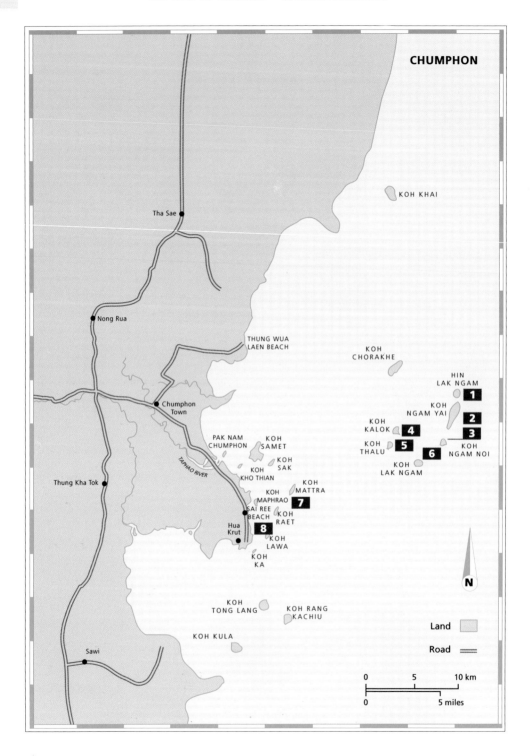

CHUMPHON

KOH KHAI

Tha Sae

Nong Rua

THUNG WUA
LAEN BEACH

KOH
CHORAKHE

HIN
LAK NGAM

1

KOH
NGAM YAI

2

Chumphon
Town

KOH
KALOK **4**

3

PAK NAM
CHUMPHON

KOH
SAMET

KOH
THALU **5**

6

KOH
NGAM NOI

Thung Kha Tok

TAPHAO RIVER

KOH
SAK

KOH
KHO THIAN

KOH
LAK NGAM

KOH
MATTRA

KOH
MAPHRAO **7**

SAI REE
BEACH

KOH
RAET

Hua
Krut **8**

KOH
LAWA

KOH
KA

N

KOH
TONG LANG

KOH RANG
KACHIU

Land

KOH KULA

Road

Sawi

0   5   10 km

0   5 miles

in front of the resort or – like divers not staying at these resorts – you can go from the Koh Tao passenger-ferry pier on the Taphao river just south of Chumphon Town; from both beaches Longtail boats are used to transfer divers and their equipment to the diveboats. When the departure point is the ferry pier, local dive operators will arrange transfers from their dive offices.

The plankton-rich waters attract a healthy diversity of marine life around the islands' fringing reefs. Populations are high and pelagics frequent. Gardens of fire, staghorns and small boulders of lesser star corals dominate the fringing reef-flats, with a range of black seafans and long sea whips being confined to the lower reef-slopes.

Visibility ranges from 3m (10ft) to over 20m (66ft) and currents are moderate enough for divers of any level.

In calm conditions night-diving around the islands can be very pleasant. The diving season is May to October.

KOH MATTRA

Koh Mattra, locally known as Koh Thung Kuay, is the only Chumphon offshore island where - if prior permission has been granted - visitors can land. You can stay overnight on the island, either in a tent or in one of the small beach shacks but there are no amenities, so you need to take basics like food and drinking water. The island is currently on the market; the only condition of sale being that the new owner must keep the present owner's three dogs.

Koh Mattra is also home to some unusual creatures: the land crabs - known as Chicken Crabs by the locals because they make a 'clucking' sound - and the large fruit bats which leave their caves after dark to swoop down in search of food.

---

1 HIN LAK NGAM (HIN PHAE)
★★★☆☆☆

Location: 21km (3.9 n. miles) west and slightly north of the mouth of the Taphao River. Twelve small rocky outcrops, running north–south, mark the site's location. They break the surface only at low tide. Two moorings are at the archipelago's northern and southern ends.

Access: 75min from Thung Wua Laen Beach, 1½hr from the southern locations. The best mooring and entry point for both divers and snorkellers is the northern buoy.

Conditions: This unprotected site is somewhat weather-dependent. In favourable conditions it can be enjoyed by snorkellers and divers of all levels. Visibility can be over 20m (66ft), but if a strong current is running it drops dramatically to below 5m (16ft).

Average depth: 15m (50ft)

Maximum depth: 24m (72ft)

The greatest variety of reef-life is between 10 and 15m (30–50ft) on the western side, and, 20m (66ft), along the eastern side.

The reef reaches up to and just below the surface, and consists mainly of staghorn, lettuce and vase corals mixed with numerous barrel sponges, covering the stacked rocks that form the western face.

Bullethead Parrotfish and Lunar Wrasse are always present around the corals, though generally there is little marine life present. But do look under the small overhangs immediately above the sand, as there are many moray eels, squirrelfish and soldierfish.

Around the rocks are many Dusky Batfish, Single-spot Snappers, Blue-striped Grunts, Moorish Idols, bannerfish and pairs of large Blue-ringed Angelfish. The plateaux are carpeted with sea anemones and small clusters of staghorns, both sheltering small creatures.

Rocks again form the main infrastructure of the eastern face of this site, their faces littered with large cowrie shells. There are many Honeycomb and Red Coral Groupers in this area. Large stingrays can be found resting on the sand beneath the rocks, and big groupers hide among them. The maximum depth before you go out over the sand is 20m (66ft). This site is an excellent location for sighting other large migratory pelagics, as this is their first encounter with substantial nourishment as they head south.

2 KOH NGAM YAI (EAST CLIFF ROCKS)
★★☆☆☆☆

Location: 800m (0.43 n. miles) southwest of Hin Lak Ngam (Site 1). The site spans the entire eastern length of this large rocky outcrop.

Access: 75min from Thung Wua Laen Beach, 90min from the other two departure locations. The entry point is 30m (100ft) off the northeast corner of the island. Boats moor to the large mooring buoy; if this is already in use, enter from the unmoored boat.

Conditions: Current is generally weak, so the site is ideal for all levels of divers. The current around the small sheltered inlet in the northern section of the eastern coast allows terrific snorkelling. Moderate to strong current can occasionally run north–south, transforming this into a good drift-dive site. Visibility in calmer seas

can be over 20m (66ft).
Average depth: 15m (49ft)
Maximum depth: 20m (66ft)
The dive follows the eastern wall southwards amongst scattered rocks, carpeted with fire, wonder, and zebra corals, reduce the depth to about 2m (6½ft).

Some rocks have small clusters of staghorn corals. As the corals are in good condition they entice a variety of reef-fish into the vicinity. Bearded Scorpionfish, Bluegreen Pullers and Three-spot Damselfish are in evidence.

At the southern tip is an impressive area of sea anemones, the endemic tenant of which is the Pink Anemonefish.

The northern section consists mainly of terraced staghorn, lettuce and vase corals interspersed with small mounds of lesser star coral and large rocks.

3 KOH NGAM NOI
★★★

Location: Koh Ngam Noi lies 500m (¼ n. miles) south of the larger Koh Ngam Yai (Site 2).
Access: 75min from Thung Wua Laen Beach, 90min from Sai Ree Beach or the passenger-ferry pier on the Taphao River. There is one mooring buoy, midway along the eastern coast.
Conditions: Visibility averages 15m (50ft). Moderate current, when present, flows north–south. There is a good area for snorkelling in the shallow waters around the island's northern apex.
Average depth: 15m (49ft)
Maximum depth: 20m (66ft)
The best diving is around the southern tip. Follow the gradient up to 12m (40ft); you find many small fallen rocks interspersed with black whip corals, which increase in size as you head east.

Marine life is scarce in this area, though there are schools of Humpback Snappers, juvenile Yellowtail Barracuda and jacks in the deeper waters.

Close inspection of the narrow inlets between the lower rocks and the sand often reveals small Blue-spotted Ribbontail Rays half-buried in the sand.

The most interesting section of the site is in the waters that fringe the southern face, with an average depth of 6m (20ft); In the south the terrain changes dramatically: the fallen rocks are no longer stacked, but more solitary, forming narrow swimthroughs seemingly bridged in places by gorgonian seafans.

A colourful variety of *Phyllidia* nudibranchs can be found on the broken coral fragments between the rocks. Mounds of lesser star corals are rich in colourful Christmas-tree Worms.

WHALE SHARK SIGHTING

The Whale Shark is by far the largest fish in the world. They have been sighted in this area sometimes measuring over ten metres in length, which is only four metres short of the largest examples ever seen anywhere. Because of its enormous size this particular species has been given the nickname of 'Gentle Giant'. On one occasion three of these giant fishes were spotted at Hin Phae (Site 1) in one dive, there were two adults and one juvenile. Although they are frequent visitors to Hin Phae this was an incredible experience for the divers present.

4 KOH KALOK
★

Location: 5km (2.7 n. miles) east of Koh Ngam Noi.
Access: Diveboats take 90min to reach this site from all the departure locations. There are no mooring buoys. The entry point is 20m (66ft) north of the outcrop in a depth of 17m (56ft).
Conditions: Visibility is 5–10m (16–33ft). Very strong north–south currents can run. In lesser currents you might be able to circumnavigate the island, but this is very rare and cannot be planned for.
Average depth: 8m (26ft)
Maximum depth: 20m (65ft)
A typical dive of the nearer offshore islands, with nothing really outstanding to see. Visibility and marine life are limited. The diving is, though, made more interesting by the presence of a small cave on the island's western side.

5 KOH THALU
★

Location: Of the outer island group, the nearest outcrop to the mainland.
Access: 90min from any of the usual departure locations. The entry point is 25m (83ft) off the north face in 16m (53ft) of water. There is no mooring buoy.
Conditions: Visibility is 5–10m (16–33ft). Very strong currents generally run north–south, making the site dangerous. Though the site is small, the conditions generally make circumnavigation of the island impossible.
Average depth: 8m (24ft)
Maximum depth: 16m (52ft)
Dive operators include this destination as a day excursion, but there is little to see in the way of marine life here. Freshwater runoff from the mainland limits the

Above: *A pair of Cleaner shrimps (Stenopus hispidus) off to work at the cleaning station.*
Below: *Masked pufferfish (Arothron nigripunctatus).*

growth of healthy corals, which in turn limits the marine life. The underwater landscape is typical of the area: many rocks are littered with bushy black corals and sea whips.

KOH LAK NGAM
★★★☆☆

Location: Two rocky outcrops, 50m (167ft) apart, 2.5km (1.4 n. miles) southwest of Koh Ngam Noi.
Access: 75min from any of the three usual locations. The entry point is off the southeast face in between the two outcrops. There is one mooring buoy.
Conditions: Visibility averages 15m (50ft). The current is generally moderate.
Average depth: 12m (36ft)
Maximum depth: 20m (66ft)
Descend at the rocks, turn right and follow the smaller ones due east for about 15m (50ft) until you come to a wide gully; swim left and up into it. On the right of this elevated shelf are large sea anemone beds leading you to one of the best diving spots in the area.

The gully is replaced at 11m (36ft), by a ledge featuring gardens of sea anemones. Here table staghorns shelter damselfish while parrotfish and wrasse peck among brain, cauliflower and black corals and Harlequin Sweetlips flutter between tiny rocks. (This area is also a very good site for snorkelling.)

Beyond this area, as you head southeast, the site becomes a wall-dive. The wall is encrusted with clams, oysters, Neptune Barrel Sponges and patches of orange and blue sponges. Halfway along the wall is a shallow 3m (10ft) cave, the back wall of which provides sanctuary for a diversity of shrimps.

7 KOH THONG KUAY (KOH MATTRA) – WEST BEACH REEF
★★★

Location: The southernmost site in the Chumphon area; 7km (3.7 n. miles) due east of Sai Ree Beach.
Access: 45min from Sai Ree Beach, 2hr from Thung Wua Laen Beach, and 1hr from the ferry pier on the Taphao River. A walk down the coral-substrate beach, which at a distance resembles white sand, takes you directly onto the shallow fringing reef.
Conditions: Moderate to strong current can run here; although this can limit visibility it does not render the site unsafe, as the water movement is commonly longshore and thus, if indirectly, towards the island.
Average depth: 6m (20ft)
Maximum depth: 12m (40ft)
Enter the water anywhere from the beach which

stretches along the island's west coast. The water here is still relatively shallow, so take care not to damage yourself or the corals.

The reef-flats abound with gardens of staghorn, cauliflower and, in patches, anemone corals. The reef-crest features boulders of lesser star corals pitted with bivalves and with Plume Worms adding colour.

Marine life is prominent around this shallow reef. The vibrant colours of the fish are displayed in their full, spectacular glory in the sunlit ocean.

8 KOH I RAET
★★

Location: The southernmost and nearest island to the mainland, just 4km (2 n. miles) due east of the southern end of Sai Ree Beach. The shallow reef runs along the western coast of this tiny island.
Access: 30min from Sai Ree Beach. From Thung Wua Laen Beach, go by road to join the diveboat at the passenger-ferry pier on the Taphao River, from where the journey takes 45min.
Conditions: Visibility is limited, averaging 5m (16ft). Strong currents are present.
Average depth: 8m (24ft)
Maximum depth: 16m (52ft)
The site can be disappointing due to poor weather conditions and the murky seas caused by freshwater runoff from the mainland also renders the corals in less than prime condition. Two prominent coral species here are black and zebra – the latter prefers turbid waters and is capable of surviving in areas of high sedimentation. There are many sea anemones and Giant Clams here, along with oysters and cowrie shells.

NUDIBRANCHS

Nudibranchs – or 'snails without shells' – are among the most colourful and interesting of the marine molluscs. The Chromodorididae nudibranchs on page 63 are a stunning example.

There are thought to be at least 2500 species of nudibranchs which are part of a large group commonly referred to as sea slugs. All nudibranchs are hermaphroditic (which means they can become both male and female) and carnivorous.

The many caves on the limestone outcrops of Koh Ngam Yai and Koh Ngam Noi are home to Edible Nest Swiftlets (*Aerodramus fuciphagus*). These small birds make their tiny white cup-shaped nests - out of hardened saliva and a few loosened down feathers - in the incredibly high crevices of the caves.

The nests are an extremely valuable commodity and provide a good source of income for the owners of these two privately owned islands. They have several uses such as making sweet isotonic beverages and as an ingredient in various savoury recipes, the most famous being Birds Nest Soup. The Chinese believe the nests have powerful medicinal qualities and use them for many different medicines.

Local people are employed on both islands to collect and protect the nests. They are armed with guns and have vicious guard dogs to ensure poachers stay away. The guards live in bamboo shacks, balanced precariously on narrow rocky ledges, supported by steel guylines to stop them being blown away in strong winds. Bamboo stilts of varying lengths ensure they remain horizontal.

The guards - or 'collectors' - gather the nests by scaling the crevice walls up long bamboo poles, bound together to increase the length rather than the width. These make-shift ladders consist of a thick central shaft with short thinner branches wedged in on either side serving as rungs. The collectors scurry barefoot up the long poles, which bend and sometimes snap under the weight. If the nests are too high and cannot be reached, another prepared trunk is simply carried to the top and lashed on to the existing one. Nests are then prised from the rock face with small pocket knifes and placed in hessian sacks which are lowered to the ground when full.

The guards will wave and smile at tourists as they sail past but they will not hesitate to shoot at trespassers or unleash the guard dogs. ***Do not under any circumstances attempt to land unless invited and accompanied by an official guide.***

Bamboo dwellings of the nest collectors on Koh Ngam Noi balance precariously on narrow rocky ledges.

HOW TO GET THERE

All the links to Chumphon are via land; there are no direct routes by sea or air from Bangkok.

By bus: VIP Air-conditioned buses from Bangkok are comfortable and spacious with fully reclining seats. Passengers are provided with a blanket as the air-conditioning can be quite cruel. Many travellers have been seen blocking the vents with toilet paper; an essential item anyway on any journey. Personal belongings are stored and locked away in one of the holds. The journey is broken at a bus station restaurant at around midnight, where you will be provided with a meal. The meal is included in the price of the ticket, as are the light refreshments you receive at the beginning of the trip. Buses leave the southern bus terminal in Bangkok daily at 21.00 and 21.40hrs. The journey lasts around eight hours and ends at the bus station in Chumphon Town. Air-conditioned buses from Surat Thani drive through the town and depart from various travel companies at around 09.50 and 13.00hrs. The journey takes two and a half hours. For further information ring Bangkok southern bus terminal; tel (02) 434 5557, Chumphon Town bus terminal; tel (077) 502725, Surat Thani bus terminal; tel (077) 272341.

By train: There are three types of train service running from Bangkok to Chumphon. The Rapid Train should be avoided; it is both slow and uncomfortable. Those listed below are much faster and can be booked 90 days in advance - they are very popular with both locals and travellers. The journey lasts between nine and ten hours. **Express Trains** leave Bangkok Hua Lumphong railway station every hour or so between 13.00 and 22.25hrs. There are four classes. All trains have a buffet car and bar. **The Sprinter** train leaves Bangkok Hua Lumphong railway station at 22.35hrs. This train consists solely of spacious air-conditioned carriages with reclining seats. There is a separate area to store your bags so corridors do not get cluttered. Blankets are provided and there is a buffet service available. The journey lasts six and a half hours. This is, in my opinion the most comfortable and enjoyable way to reach Chumphon. Chumphon can also be reached from Surat Thani in the south. There are six scheduled trains a day and the journey takes three and a half hours. For further information about any of the train services contact:- Hua Lumphong railway station; tel (02) 223 7010, Chumphon Town railway station; tel (077) 511103, Surat Thani railway station; tel (077) 311213.

By road: The journey from Bangkok takes anything from six hours upwards. The road follows route 4 out of Bangkok and heads south along the west coast of the Gulf of Thailand. Taking a taxi will be slightly quicker than driving yourself but it will also be very expensive. A cheaper option would be to hire an eleven-seater mini bus and driver. The best way of reaching the area is on scheduled public transport.

By boat: Chumphon can be accessed from Koh Tao by passenger ferry and speedboat which both arrive at the ferry pier on the Taphao River. Transfer from the ferry pier to the town is a further cost. The ferry boat leaves Mae Haad jetty daily at 10:00hrs, the journey takes six hours. The privately owned speedboat leaves Mae Haad jetty daily at 08.00, the journey takes ninety minutes.

For any additional information on the Chumphon area contact the **Tourism Authority of Thailand**; tel (077) 288 818-9/fax (077) 282 828.

WHERE TO STAY

The province has a good selection of accommodation but it really caters for the Thai nationals rather than foreign tourists so expect the service to be more relaxed than in other more 'westernised' locations. Bear in mind that international tourism has not been developed here and most tourists are just passing through so hotels and shops are not geared up to communicating with foreigners.

There are no camping amenities on the mainland but - if you ask permission - it is possible to stay overnight on the privately-owned island of Koh Mattra.

Chumphon Town
Tha Taphao Hotel; tel (077) 511479/fax (077) 502479 is conveniently located in the centre of Chumphon Town. Rooms are spacious, comfortable, clean with drinking water. The lively restaurant stays open until the early hours of the morning. Rooms catering for up to four people have either an electric cooling fan or the more expensive air-conditioning.

The type of accommodation on the beaches ranges from small fan-cooled rooms to luxurious air-conditioned beach-front bungalows. All the resorts have their own restaurants and sometimes breakfast is included in the price. Always check what you are paying for - rates are per room per night. There are two good resorts: **Chumphon Cabana Resort** on Thung Wua Laen beach and **Sai Ree Lodge** on Sai Ree beach. Both have friendly staff, clean rooms and their own restaurants. (The service in both is slow so allow plenty of time for meals.) As both resorts are out of town, arrange for a representative to meet you at your destination point prior to your arrival.

Thung Wua Laen Beach
Chumphon Cabana Resort and Diving Centre; tel (077) 501990/fax (077) 504442. This pleasant resort is right on the beach, 14km (9 miles) north of Chumphon Town. Air-conditioned rooms. There is a communal recreation area with a television which receives satellite. Two licensed restaurants serve Thai and European cuisine at reasonable prices. The resort maintains a full tourist information service.

Sai Ree Beach
Sai Ree Lodge; tel (077) 502023/fax (077) 502479. The first row of rooms at this resort are built right on the beach, the others follow up the steep hillside and are reached by walking along narrow elevated wooden walkways amongst banana trees. Fan-cooled and air-conditioned rooms are available and the resort has its own restaurant and small bar.

WHERE TO EAT

All the hotels and resorts have their own restaurants, mostly with reasonable prices and a good choice of Thai food and, on request, European. As the resorts are in remote locations it is best to use the facilities they provide. In Chumphon Town, another option is to try the restaurants in the other hotels.

DIVE FACILITIES

There are two diving operators serving the area which run in conjunction with beach resorts. The services of both are fairly basic and run on a skeleton, Thai-speaking staff. Both provide daily excursions to the local sites on their own dive boats and one offers the range of PADI diving courses. Spare dive equipment is limited so it is advisable to carry your own.

Chumphon Cabana Resort and Diving Centre, Thung Wua Laen Beach; tel 077 501990/fax 077 504442. The full range of PADI courses are available in English, German and Thai. This centre introduced diving to the area a decade ago and now has three dive boats of varying sizes. Food is prepared at the resort and taken on board. Boats leave from in front of the resort on Wua Laen beach or from the ferry pier on the Taphao River.

Sai Ree Lodge, Sai Ree Beach; tel 077 502023/fax 077 502479. This operator has one boat with a toilet and fresh water for rinsing equipment. Food is prepared at the resort and taken on board. The boat leaves from Sai Ree beach or the ferry pier on the Taphao River. There is no retail service.

Dive trips
All the local sites are accessed in under two hours and are offered in the form of daily dive trips. All the diveboats are owned and maintained by the beach

resorts. As yet none of the boats carry oxygen - but on a more positive note, they do have life vests. Transfer to and from the diveboats in on Longtail boats. Discounts of 15% are given for divers with all their own equipment (excluding tanks and weights). Snorkellers and non-divers are welcome to join any of the scheduled diving trips for a small fee. Mask and fins are available in different sizes.

Dive Courses
All courses require students to submit two passport-sized photographs for certification, which is included in the course costs. Courses available are Discover Scuba experience programmes, PADI Open Water Diver and PADI Advanced Open Water. More advanced courses are also available.

FILM PROCESSING

There are several photographic processing facilities in Chumphon Town - mostly along Prachautit Road - where the striking shop fronts resemble giant rolls of film. At the time of writing it is only possible to buy, develop and copy print film; E6 slide development must be either done in Bangkok or back in your country of residence. Slide film, however, is sold here.

HOSPITALS AND RECOMPRESSION CHAMBERS

There are two hospitals in Chumphon Town and it is advisable to be accompanied by an English speaking Thai who can translate for you as spoken English is extremely limited. **Provincial Hospital**; tel (077) 511180, **Virajsilp Private Hospital**; tel (077) 503238, 502694/fax (077) 501161.

The nearest **recompression chamber** is situated in Bangkok, in the **Department of Underwater and Aviation Medicine**, Bangkok; tel: (02) 468 6100 - or outside office hours; tel (02) 460 0000 ext. 341.

It takes six hours to reach by car. This is obviously not ideal but it is the quickest and nearest facility.

The local **Police Station** is located at Saladaeng Road; tel (077) 511505.

LOCAL HIGHLIGHTS

Of the many spectacular white sandy beaches in the area, the finest is probably **Thung Wua Laen Beach** in the Patiew district, located some 16km (10 miles) north of Chumphon Town. Thirteen km (8 miles) to the south is **Pharadorn Pharp** beach - the beach front road has many food stalls and restaurants.

Erected next to the monument is the **Shrine of Khromluang Chumphon Khet Udomsak**. The Shrine overlooks the sea and is one of the areas most popular tourist attractions with the local people.

Travel 1km south of the beach and climb to the top of **Chao Muang** hill where you can enjoy spectacular views of the islands . A further 6km (4 miles) take you to the picturesque bays of **Inner Thoug Makham** and **Outer Thoug Makham**.

There are several caves scattered throughout the province, two of which are well worth a visit: **Khao Kriab** cave in Lang Suan district and **Rap Ror** cave in the Sae district. Both contain mysterious Buddha images amongst impressive stalactites and stalagmites. Khao Kriab cave is located some 80km (50 miles) south of the town and is reached by route 41. The entrance to the cave is at the foot of a 370 step stairway. Inside is a large shrine housing a Buddha image. Legend has it that it emerged from the hilltop of it's own accord. Rub Ror is accessed from Chumphon Town by a journey of 9km (5 miles) north, along route 4, then a further 5km (3 miles) down a left hand turning sign posted to Thep Charoen Temple. The cave, situated on a high hill, is divided into two

chambers. Each chamber, according to local legend, contains mysterious secret treasure maps. The inner chamber, Phra cave, also contains an old enshrined Buddha effigy known locally as 'Luang Poo Luk Muang'.

One of the most spectacular waterfalls in the area is **Haew Loam Waterfall** some 126km (79 miles) south of Chumphon Town. Follow route 41 and turn right onto route 4006 at Lang Suan. Follow the road for 16km (10 miles) until you come to a signpost to the waterfalls. It is possible to raft this canal and the best time to visit is at both ends of the diving season.

There is one temple in the area worth visiting, the **Thammayuth sect Wat Phra Thart Thum Khwan Muang** is located 48km (30 miles) south of Chumphon Town. Follow route 41 until you reach the 37.5 km roadside demarcation, at this turn right. The Wat is built on top of a small hill and stands centrally on green lawns, shaded by rows of trees. Inside the Pagoda The Buddha's relics have been enshrined.

The town hosts the leading **Thai banks** which all provide a currency exchange service for customers with cash, travellers checks and major credit cards. Bangkok Bank; tel (077) 511446-7, Thai Farmers Bank; tel (077) 511380, Krungthai Bank; tel (077) 511050, Thai Military Bank; tel (077) 511890.

Car and Motorbike Rental
Car or motorbike rental agencies do not exist in the town, but this is not really a problem as there are plenty of local buses and taxis to take visitors to the variety of interesting tourist attractions on offer around Chumphon province.

Moorish idols (Zanclus canescens) can grow to 20cm.

KOH TAO

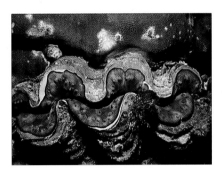

Koh Tao – or Turtle Island – is the northernmost and smallest in the chain of the three 'inhabited' islands in the Samui Archipelago with an area of 21 sq km (13 sq miles). The vast majority of the island's flora comprises coconut, mango and cashew-nut trees. The south and west coastlines are dotted with white sandy beaches; the north and east coasts have a couple of small sandy bays but are predominantly formed by large granite boulders stacked high above the water and rising to fringe the island's forests.

The island originally served as a holding place for political prisoners. Most fell victim to inefficient administration and were left to languish here, the majority dying of malaria, which in those earlier days was rife. Even today, you should take precautions before visiting the island as malaria still exists – albeit on a much smaller scale.

If you can, plan to spend a few days on Koh Tao, as it's not really worth coming all this way for less. Most tourists opt to spend a while relaxing and getting the feel of the place.

Transportation around the island comes in three, very different forms: you can sit in the back of an open pickup truck, ride on the back of a motorbike or, between the beach resorts, take a Longtail boat.

The island's only town, Mae Haad, is on the southern section of the west coast and amenities here are basic: a handful of general stores (selling only the barest essentials), a post office, and a small vegetable market.

DIVING AROUND KOH TAO

The diving around Koh Tao is the best anywhere in the Gulf of Thailand. The sites can become fairly crowded, although in recent years the situation has improved as the operators have formed an association to deal with this and other problems.

The diving is varied enough to suit all levels of divers. There are two main types of site around the island. Firstly, there are the deep sites around towering submerged pinnacles, with their craggy rock faces seemingly alive with various hard and soft coral species. These

Opposite: *Rocky Resort is situated right on the beach, Koh Tao.*
Above: *The bivalve Giant Clam (Tridaena gigas) is the largest of the living molluscs.*

sites are constantly visited by large pelagics. Secondly, there are dives along gentle sloping coral reefs. These are good places to see many diferent species of laminate and foliaceous corals and a rich diversity of marine life.

Apart from those in the bay at Nang Yuan, which were mostly destroyed in 1988 when the Gulf of Thailand was hit by Typhoon Gay, the corals around Koh Tao are generally in reasonable condition. There is evidence of slight anchor damage in the area, but none of it recent.

Since 1992 a project has been underway which involves the installation and maintenance of mooring buoys at the sites and the education of the local captains and boatmen regarding their use.

Good snorkelling sites around the shallow reefs and rocks of the sandy bays can be reached by a short swim from the beach. Further afield snorkellers often join diveboats to visit the shallower parts of the fringing reefs, where hosts of colourful reef fish, a diversity of crustaceans and beds of sea anemones await the intrepid visitor.

> ## THE JINXED ANCHOR
>
> Legend has it that the island of Samui appeared on ancient Chinese maps dating back to the 16th Century.
>
> The island was one of many destinations in the area being supplied with ceramics. One particular voyage ended in tragedy when the vessel became disorientated en route to Samui and the over-laden vessel bottomed on Hin Tung Gu (Site 9), causing it to sink.
>
> The ship's anchor still rests semi-buried in the sand where it dropped all those hundreds of years ago.
>
> Several attempts have been made over the years to retrieve this valuable brass artifact but rumour has it that those people who have attempted to retrieve it have apparently died in mysterious circumstances.

Koh Tao's local sites can all be reached in a 1 hour journey from the island. Sail Rock and the Samran Pinnacles in the south are 90 mins away.

As yet, operators on Koh Tao do not schedule trips to the Ang Thong Marine National Park as they consider the local sites to be superior.

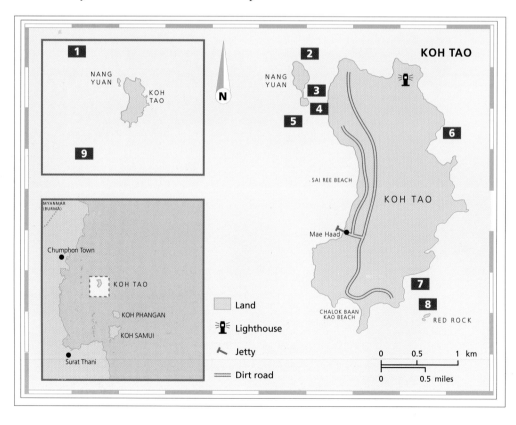

1 CHUMPHON PINNACLES
★★★★

Location: About 5km (2.7 n. miles) northwest of Nang Yuan.
Access: 50min from Mae Haad. There are no obvious above-water signs of this site, as it has no mooring buoy and is out in the open sea. Local dive-shops repeatedly buoy the site, only to have the local fishermen cut the mooring lines and discard the buoys.
Conditions: If the mooring buoy is there, its line serves as the descent line – sometimes very important, as the current can be extremely strong and dangerous. Only when the current is slack is this site suitable for novice divers. Visibility can be excellent – often over 30m (100ft).
Average depth: 20m (66ft)
Maximum depth: 36m (120ft)
Probably Koh Tao's most impressive site. Divers revisiting the island enquire at every dive-shop to find the earliest scheduled trip to Chumphon Pinnacles!

The site consists of four underwater pinnacles which tower up from around 34m (112ft); the highest peaks are 16m (53ft) below the surface. This is an ideal place to spot many pelagics. Large schools of Great Barracuda, Big-eyed Jacks, tuna, mackerel, Goldbody and Giant Trevally are all frequent visitors. Whale Sharks, with accompanying Striped Remoras, are often sighted here during the season's later months.

Leaving the descent line, head northeast and pass between two small pinnacles. On the far side of the bigger rock, at a depth of 21m (70ft), is a large overhang which shelters several enormous groupers; the largest must be over 2m (6½ft) long.

As you head west there appears on your left a narrow gorge. Here you find a large school of inquisitive batfish, which will swim up to you; just hover and the fish will come to you.

The terrain changes in the southeast section, where a number of ledges are completely covered in sea anemones. Pink Anemonefish dart about, attending to their hosts.

2 GREEN ROCK (HIN KEE-OH)
★★★★★

Location: The large submerged rock some 50m (55yd) off the northern shore of Nang Yuan marks the centre of this dive.
Access: About 30min by diveboat from the jetty in Mae Haad. There are two mooring buoys, one at each of the rock's eastern and western ends.
Conditions: In the high seas access to the site is not

VALUE FOR MONEY

Not all courses include everything in their quoted price and hidden extras or non-inclusions sometimes arise. Find out exactly what you are paying for by asking these questions:

- Can you keep the manual on completion of the course or is it just on loan?
- Does the course cost include the certification fee?
- Are all the boat trips included?
- What about refreshments?
- Is full equipment included for ALL the water training sessions?

attempted. Unless you visit immediately after a storm, visibility is high, ranging between 10m and 30m (33–100ft), generally in the higher range. Currents are weak to moderate.
Average depth: 12m (40ft)
Maximum depth: 25m (83ft)
Divers come here for the tremendous selection of adventurous swimthroughs provided by large archways, caverns, caves and crevices which cut through Green Rock. There are many Groupers, Blue-spotted Ribbontail Rays and Titan Triggerfish, which can be aggressive – especially if protecting their nests during the spawning season. This is a good place to see Green and Hawksbill Turtles.

Green Rock makes an interesting night-dive. The triggerfish secure themselves in the smaller crevices for the night and the parrotfish sleep in their cocoons while the nocturnal community comes to life.

3 NANG YUAN (NORTHWEST BAY)
★★★★

Location: There are two small divable bays at the southern end of Nang Yuan. This site follows the coastline of the north west bay.

PLANKTONIC CREATURES

Zooplankton comprises millions of tiny animals drifting in almost all the oceans of the world. It is the foundation of the entire marine food chain and virtually every sea creature depends both directly or indirectly on this food source.

Many of the sea's habitants, during the early stages of their development, start life as a free floating planktonic creature, covering enormous distances whilst drifting along with currents. As they develop, corals, crustaceans and reef fishes will eventually settle down in a particular area which is capable of supplying their nutritional requirements. Other planktonic creatures develop into pelagics, or open-water species, such as tuna, manta rays, or jacks. These species do the opposite, becoming ocean nomads for the rest of their lives.

Access: 25min from Mae Haad
Conditions: Visibility is between 5m (16ft) and 25m (83ft). The dive's first section is very well sheltered, with little current. As you go along the reef to the point, the current's strength increases to moderate, and visibility can drop. This shallow dive in a sheltered bay is ideal for diver training.
Average depth: 6m (20ft)
Maximum depth: 12m (40ft)
Descend and proceed north until you hit large rocks in a depth of 9m (30ft).

Black sea cucumbers occur in large numbers, but are part of a more interesting community scattered around rocks and lesser star boulder corals, which are rich with multicoloured plume worms and bivalves.

The larger rocks, rich in foliaceous and soft corals, provide small-scale wall-dives and swim-arounds. Neptune Barrel Sponges are covered in long white Alabaster Tubeworms. The rocks are interspersed with small elevated sections hosting gardens of sea anemones.

Around and beyond the rocks the fish life becomes prolific. There are lots of Bullethead Parrotfish, Checkerboard Wrasse, Red-tailed Butterflyfish and Emperor Angelfish, and Large White Snappers, trevallies, cuttlefish and jacks.

▌4▐ NANG YUAN (JAPANESE GARDENS)
★★☆☆

Location: This site follows the coastline of Nang Yuan's southeastern bay.
Access: 25min by diveboat from Mae Haad. Dive operators secure their boats to any one of the several mooring buoys in the bay.
Conditions: General conditions are the same as in the northwest bay (Site 3).
Average depth: 6m (20ft)
Maximum depth: 12m (40ft)
Although the general conditions may be the same, this site is not a replica of Site 3. There is sand beneath the entry buoy and the dead coral is less evident. As you head south towards the rocks, the sand is slowly replaced by boulder corals rich in small bivalves and Plume Worms.

Beyond the boulder corals is a shallow sloping reef formed of table staghorns and various leaf corals; Black-banded Sea Snakes intertwine around the branches, while pufferfish and damselfish create their own blankets of colour.

Following the reef east, you approach a number of small caves and overhangs; these serve as shelters for many Blue-spotted Ribbontail Rays. A good selection of *Phyllidia* Nudibranchs feed on the rock-encrusting sponges. This is a good site for observing passing turtles.

WHITE ROCK SITE

The Titan Triggerfish (*Balistoides Viridescens*) is renowned for being territorial during the spawning season. However, White Rock has one rather large specimen which has achieved worldwide fame amongst the diving fraternity by being territorial all year round - and the territory of this particular fish seems to extend over the entire site, right up to the surface!

Local instructor, Ryan Dowling, lovingly named this armoured aggressor 'Trevor' over three years ago and the name has stuck. Trevor's favourite colour seems to be fluorescent green and his biggest dislike is diving humans. He enjoys a diet of sea urchins, Lycra and skin so be careful down there!

▌5▐ WHITE ROCK (HIN KHAO)
★★★

Location: About 1km (½ n. miles) south of Nang Yuan and the same distance off the west coast of Koh Tao.
Access: 15min by diveboat or 30min by Longtail from the jetty in Mae Haad. The site's mooring buoy is anchored in 14m (46ft) of water.
Conditions: Visibility is usually good, averaging about 15m (50ft); in slack current it can exceed 30m (100ft). Current varies, but is usually weak; this unsheltered site cannot be accessed in poor conditions.
Average depth: 9m (30ft)
Maximum depth: 22m (73ft)
This is a very enjoyable dive, suitable for both novice and experienced divers. The site consists of two submerged pinnacles, the higher of which is covered by only 2m (6ft) of water.

The pinnacles are broken by a number of elevated shelves graced with a host of Honeycomb Groupers, Long-spined Black Sea Urchins, *Phyllidia* Nudibranchs and various sea anemones. Radiant trees of soft corals mix with knob and pore corals, and are rich with colourful plumeworms. Small moray eels, crabs and shrimps have taken up residence in the many cracks and crannies of the rock faces.

White Rock is the area's most popular night-diving destination. You can see turtles, Hermit Crabs and large barracuda, attracted to the rock by smaller fish.

▌6▐ HIN WONG
★★

Location: About 100m (110yd) off Hin Wong Bay, on the island's eastern coast.
Access: 20min by diveboat from Mae Haad. The site's mooring serves also as a descent line.
Conditions: The site is easily accessible except during

Above: *A Red saddle-back anemonefish (Amphiprion ephippium).*
Below: *Longnosed Hawkfish (Oxycirrhites typus) are only seen at deep sites.*

the northeast monsoon, when high seas and rolling waves render it unapproachable. Generally currents are moderate, but they can change very quickly to strong. Visibility ranges from 5m (16ft) to 30m (100ft).

Average depth: 12m (40ft)

Maximum depth: 26m (86ft)

The site consists mainly of a large tabletop rock formation with an array of soft corals scattered over the surrounding area. The rock's plateau is almost completely obscured by fire corals. East of it, the sandy bottom slopes steeply down to the site's maximum depth past other, slightly smaller granite structures.

The resident fish are dominated by Blue-spotted and Red Coral Groupers, bannerfish and Moorish Idols. Fusiliers and snappers are found in small groups in the deeper waters. This is a fairly reliable place to see Green and Hawksbill Turtles.

7 AO LEUK
★★☆☆☆

Location: Around the rocky western shoreline of the small bay, Ao Leuk, on Koh Tao's southeast coast.

Access: 20min by diveboat from Mae Haad. There are two mooring buoys, both off the western shore; either can be used as moorings and then act as a reference on descent.

Conditions: The bay is very well sheltered and current is minimal. Visibility averages about 10m (33ft) and peaks at 30m (100ft).

Average depth: 6m (20ft)

Maximum depth: 12m (40ft)

This is really a diver-training site, and provides an excellent alternative to the Nang Yuan site (Site 3): if weather makes one inaccessible, the other will not be.

Entering at one of the mooring buoys, head west over the sand, which is broken by small mounds of staghorn corals and numerous patches of Long-spined Black Sea Urchins. Mushroom corals lie individually scattered, as do small sponge-encrusted rocks. These rocks increase in size until they block your passage; at this point bear north or south.

The dominating species among the many fish around these undulating rocks are parrotfish, wrasse, juvenile snappers, squirrelfish and soldierfish. Away from the rocks, numbers of Yellowfin Goatfish and Schooling Bannerfish pass by.

8 RED ROCK (HIN DAENG)
★★★☆☆☆

Location: 1km (½ n. mile) off the southern tip of Koh Tao. Two large rocky outcrops – the larger standing 10m

(33ft) proud of the water – mark the site, which spans the rock's entire eastern face and fringes its northern apex.

Access: 20min by diveboat from Mae Haad. There are two mooring buoys, one at the north end of the outcrop and the other off its southeast end; divemasters will assess the conditions on arrival and decide which would make the better entry point.

Conditions: There are always north–south currents. They are generally weak, and in such conditions the site is suitable for all levels of divers. When they are moderate to strong, this offers a good drift-dive. Visibility varies quite dramatically with the amount of current present, between 5m (16ft) and 30m (100ft). When the northwesterly winds gust in Mae Haad, sea conditions around the island's southern area are generally too harsh for the dive operators to be willing to come here.

Average depth: 15m (50ft)

Maximum depth: 28m (93ft)

The good thing about this site, provided access is possible, is that you can virtually always have a pleasant dive; it also offers very good night-diving. It consists of a steeply sloping reef. The shallower part, around the northeast section, varies from 4m (13ft) to 2m (6½ft) and is an excellent place to snorkel. Lavish sea-anemone gardens and table corals are interspersed with large flat-topped rocks, providing a playground for a multitude of reef-fish.

Starting the dive off the southeast face, follow the reef north; it is constructed mainly of foliaceous rather than laminated corals, in reasonable condition. There are many different species of fish along the reef: Titan Triggerfish, pairs of Blue-ringed Angelfish, Lunar and Bicolour Wrasse, large parrotfish, fusiliers all abound. There have been numerous sightings here of Hawksbill and Green Turtles.

In the deeper waters, elongated coral boulders and bushy black corals change the appearance of the seascape.

9 SOUTHWEST PINNACLES (HIN TUNG GU)
★★★

Location: About 7km (4 n. miles) south west of Koh Tao.

Access: About 30min by diveboat from Mae Haad. The three pinnacles have a single mooring buoy. The highest pinnacle peaks 10m (33ft) below the surface.

Conditions: As the pinnacles are in the open sea, very strong currents can run around them; these can change fairly rapidly. Visibility can drop from as much as 30m (100ft) to nonexistent.

Average depth: 17m (56ft)

Maximum depth: 28m (93ft)

These three submerged pinnacles represent a series of short wall-dives. The surrounding reef-life is fairly minimal, the more noticeable species being groupers, Schooling Bannerfish, Moorish Idols and Humpback Snappers. Between the rocks are many bushy black corals, sea whips and gorgonian seafans, all in relatively good health. Butterflyfish, including Raccoon and Threadfin, share these waters. The walls of the pinnacles have many Neptune Barrel Sponges, which increase in size the deeper they are below the surface.

Away from the rocks there are many pelagics of all sizes. Great Barracuda and juvenile Yellowtails, mackerel, trevallies, Dog-faced Tuna and Big-eye Jacks all patrol these waters.

A Pin cushion starfish (Culcita novaguineae) and two crinoids (Oxycomanthus bennetti).

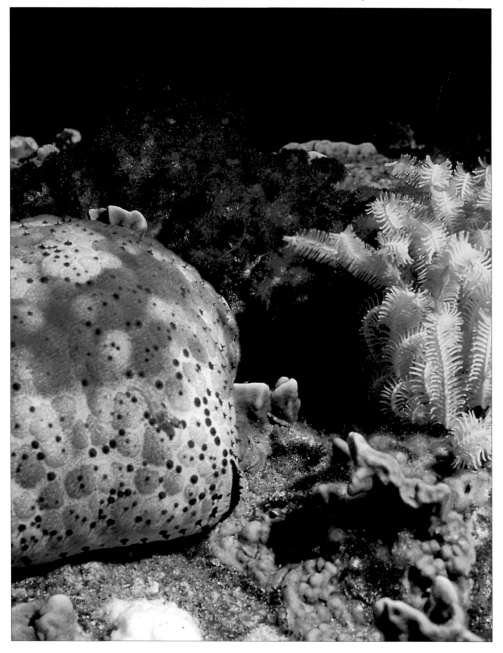

HOW TO GET THERE

By air and boat

There are no airports on Koh Tao but planes fly to the neighbouring island of Koh Samui, providing a relatively comfortable though indirect means of accessing Koh Tao. Bangkok Airways exclusively serve Koh Samui with flights departing Bangkok domestic airport thirteen times a day. The company also schedules daily flights directly to and from Singapore. Flight times are 1 hour 20 minutes and 2 hours 20 minutes respectively. There are also daily domestic flights between the islands of Phuket and Samui for those wishing to skip coasts. For bookings and current air fares contact Bangkok Airways, tel (02) 229 3456/fax (02) 229 3450.

The second leg of this journey is via air-conditioned minibus from the airport on Koh Samui to the boat departure point. Speedboats depart from the northern fishing village of Bophut at around 8.30am, taking 90 min for the crossing. If this departure is too early, Songserm Travel offer an Express boat service from the Nathon on the western coast which departs the pier at 11am, taking 2 hours. Both boats drop off passengers on the island of Koh Phangan en route, so make sure that the crew is aware of your intended destination.

By bus and boat

VIP air-conditioned buses travel from Bangkok to this part of Thailand. There are two possible routes to Koh Tao. Both leave the southern bus terminal in Bangkok daily at 21.00 and 21.30hrs. Direct tickets to Koh Tao via Chumphon cannot be purchased, new tickets for the ferry have to be bought in Chumphon Town or at the ferry pier.

Via Chumphon Town: The first leg of the journey lasts around eight hours and ends at the bus station in Chumphon town. The passenger ferry pier on the Taphao River is reached in thirty minutes by local bus - taxis are slightly more expensive. The passenger ferry departs at midnight and takes six hours to reach Koh Tao. Connection can also be made aboard a privately run speedboat in ninety minutes. It departs from the Taphao at 08:00hrs daily.

Via Surat Thani: The bus journey to Surat Thani takes twelve hours, arriving at around 7am. Buses connect with the Express Boat in Surat Thani. Boats depart five times daily and take two and a half hours to reach Koh Phangan. The ferry

takes ninety minutes. Both boats arrive at Thong Sala jetty at 10.40am. Buy joint tickets for bus and boat. The final stage of the journey is by speedboat or onboard the Koh Tao passenger ferry. This is joined on arriving at Thong Sala. A further three and a half hours are required to reach Mae Haad by ferry, or 1hr by speedboat. For further information regarding bus services ring Bangkok southern bus terminal; tel (02) 434 5557, Chumphon Town bus terminal; tel (077) 502725, Surat Thani bus terminal; tel (077) 272341.

By train and boat

Both Chumphon and Surat Thani can be accessed directly from Bangkok. There are three types of trains available. Two are listed below but the third - termed a Rapid Train - is in fact slow and uncomfortable. Express trains leave Bangkok Hua Lumphong railway station regularly - the journey to Surat Thani lasts around twelve hours. The Sprinter train leaves Bangkok Hua Lumphong railway station daily at 22.35hrs. Refreshments are available until midnight and the journey to Surat Thani lasts nine hours. For further information about any of the train services contact Hua Lumphong railway station, Bangkok; tel (02) 223 7010, Surat Thani railway station; tel (077) 311213.

For any additional information on Koh Tao contact **Tourism Authority of Thailand**; tel (077) 281 828/fax (077) 282 828.

WHERE TO STAY

Some 700 units on Koh Tao are grouped into what are termed as 'resorts' but what are really collectives of bungalows in a variety of sizes and condition. At the top of the range, **Sunset Buri Resort**, tel (077) 377171 offers luxury air-conditioned rooms. Further along the beach, **Sensi Paradise Resort**, fax (077) 377196 (Attn: Sensi Paradise Resort) has a great selection of accommodation. Most of the resorts have their own restaurant serving Thai and European menus. There is also extremely basic, inexpensive accommodation to be found on Koh Tao, but don't expect much. Amenities follow the theme of bamboo shacks with only a mosquito net for protection, communal showers and toilets. Electricity shuts down at midnight.

There was a time when obtaining accommodation on the island was reasonably straightforward, but nowadays the majority of bungalow collectives have extended their name from 'Resort' to 'Diving Resort' and some have changed policy to suit. For instance, one particular

establishment bans holidaymakers from utilising the accommodation on the premises unless they make use of the available Scuba Diving services. On a brighter note, two set-ups presently continue to extend a cheery welcome beyond the realm of scuba diving. They are:

Buddha View Dive Resort, Chalok Baan Kao Beach, Koh Tao, Surat Thani, 84280, tel/fax (01) 725 0948, (01) 229 4466. PADI 5-star Dive Resort. Economically priced rooms and good restaurants selection. Scuba instruction takes place in the only air conditioned classroom on the island.

Nang Yuan Dive Resort, Nang Yuan Island, Post Office, Koh Tao, Surat Thani, 84280, tel (01) 726 0085/fax (01) 726 0212. Highly recommended. Bungalows with splendid views of the three interconnected islets on which they are located. Not all rooms share the comfort of air conditioning; fan cooled rooms are nevertheless available.

WHERE TO EAT

All resorts have their own restaurants with a good selection on their menus - however most have a rather unwelcoming rule stating that every guest must eat in their restaurant at least once every two days or they will have to leave the resort! The only independent restaurants are in Mae Haad. They serve all types of cuisine which is good and very reasonably priced, but unless you are staying within walking distance it can be both difficult and expensive to travel back to your resort, especially in the later hours of the evening.

Neptune Restaurant is a beach front restaurant serving dishes from over the world. It is reasonably priced and the service is polite and friendly. Many diving students come here to watch the glorious Koh Tao sunsets - and revise the day's lessons!

The Far Out Café is a very popular destination for pre-dive nourishment. Breakfast lovers wait for their dive boats and ferries here exchanging the previous days experiences. This is a good a good place to meet, or to find a dive buddy.

DIVE FACILITIES

The diving operations on the island range from one-man operations to prestigious PADI 5 star IDC facilities. Most operators have established themselves in Mae Haad. On leaving the ferry, visitors to the island are literally swamped by operators touting for business. My advice is to ignore the onslaught from the operators and sort out your accommodation instead - rooms can be in short supply as the dive facilities outnumber the accommodation on the island. You can then return later - when the crowds have dispersed - and sort out your diving options. There are more than enough diving services for everyone and the first-come-first-served rule does not apply here.

Dive trips

Most of the larger diving facilities have their own dive boats. These access the sites quicker and more comfortably than by Longtails, which are still used by some of the smaller operations. Check what type of boat is being used when you are asking about trips. Also find out what is actually included in the price of the trip; some will include fruit, a meal and soft beverages whereas some will only provide drinking water. If you are new to the area check that you will either get a pre-dive briefing or that the dive will be led by a diver who is qualified to do so. Weather permitting, dive trips run on a daily basis. None of the operators provide an independent equipment rental service and divers have to join the scheduled trips. A handful of operators, however, will rent snorkelling gear.

Courses

All the instruction on the island is taught by qualified instructors following PADI diver training programmes. I strongly recommend that you avoid any local courses on offer that do not carry international recognition, no matter how irresistible their prices are.

Dive Operators

There are over twenty dive facilities on Koh Tao, mostly situated in the hamlet of Mae Haad or strung along the beaches of Sai Ree and Chalok Baan Kao. These are some of the recommended ones:

Planet Scuba, Head Office, PO Box 40, Koh Samui, Surat Thani, tel/fax (077) 231242, 422386, email: planet@mozart.inet.co.th PADI 5-star IDC Dive Centre. This is the most established of the islands operators, located 50 metres left of the landing jetty. The complete range of PADI courses, including Instructor are available in English, French, German, Italian, Swedish and Thai. Daily dive excursions aboard the centres own boats. Snorkelling equipment for hire. Tanks are filled at the centre, keeping noise on the boat to a minimum.

Big Blue Diving, 20/1 Moo 1, Koh Tao, Surat Thani, , tel/fax (01) 213 9440. PADI 5-star IDC Dive Centre. Situated at the left hand end of the landing jetty in Mae Haad. PADI courses available in English, French, German, Japanese and Swedish. Daily dive excursions aboard the centre's own spacious boat.

Master Scuba Divers, Post Office, Koh Tao, Surat Thani, 84280 Thailand, tel (01) 210 1808. The shop is in Mae Haad adjacent to the landing jetty. PADI courses are available in English and German. Daily dive excursions aboard rented boat. Excellent associated retail outlet. Snorkelling equipment for hire.

Bans Diving Resort, PADI 5-star facility; tel 01 725 0828. PADI courses are available in English. Daily dive excursions aboard the centres own boat.

Scuba Junction, Sai Ree beach, Koh Tao, Surat Thani, 84280 Thailand, tel/fax (077) 377 196, (01) 726 0112 (Attn: Scuba Junction). This well stocked diving centre is at the northern end of the beach, just before the Koh Tao Cabana Resort. PADI courses are available in English, French, German and Swedish. Daily diving excursions aboard the centre's own boat.

FILM PROCESSING

Print film and batteries can be bought in one of the general stores in Mae Haad. There is one photographic processing facility on Koh Tao, in the town.

HOSPITAL AND RECOMPRESSION CHAMBERS

As yet hospitals and indeed practising doctors do not exist on Koh Tao, however there is one small clinic in Mae Haad. The nearest hospitals are on Koh Samui but there are no pre-arranged emergency transfer services available, so the patients have to either travel by their own, or request that a member of the diving operators staff assist or accompany them on the journeys to Koh Samui.

The hospitals should only be visited in extreme emergencies as it can take around 2hrs to reach them. Hospitals can be contacted by one of the telephones available in Mae Haad or at some of the larger resorts around the island 24 hours a day. See Koh Samui regional directory for further information on page 139.

The nearest **recompression chamber** is in Bangkok, in the **Department of Underwater and Aviation Medicine**, Bangkok; tel: (02) 468 6100 - or outside office hours; tel (02) 460 0000 ext. 341. The chamber can be reached in around 4hrs from call-out. Victims of, or suspected victims of, DCS are evacuated via helicopter from the boat or the island depending on the situation, then flown at low altitude to the department.

LOCAL HIGHLIGHTS

The main reason people come here - apart from possibly the best diving in the Gulf of Thailand - is to relax. Basking in the sun and sipping cool drinks is the order of the day. For the more energetic there is an interesting and varied **nature trail** which passes through beautiful areas of flora and over undulating hills dense with semi-evergreen forest. If a walk is too exhausting you can enjoy the island from the water onboard one of the privately owned **Longtail boats** which come complete with umbrella for shade. All you have to provide are your refreshments and some suntan oil. Boats can easily be chartered and are inexpensive.

The neighbouring islets of **Nang Yuan** can be accessed by Longtail boat from Mae Haad. Scheduled boats leave the town at 10.00hrs and return in the afternoons at 16.30hrs. If you want to get away from it all this is the place for you and the islets provide some very enjoyable snorkelling.

There are no **banks** on the island but money can be exchanged at the larger resorts and in the town.

KEEP IT CLEAN

The stunningly beautiful islets of Nang Yuan probably feature in more photographs than any other location in Thailand - with splendid aerial views depicting the three islets covered in lush vegetation and interconnected by a clean white beach.

Imagine how the picture would differ if the beaches became littered? Well, the local people already have and strict regulations have been enforced to maintain Nang Yuan's beauty. For instance, tourists are warned in advance that plastic water bottles are banned on the island and anyone attempting to land with them will instantly be deported back to Koh Tao. (Anyway, bottles of water become warm in next to no time, and cold drinking water is available all day at the restaurant.) A good rule to remember is ... don't leave anything behind on the islets other than footprints!

KOH PHANGAN

As Koh Samui has gradually succumbed to mainstream tourism, Koh Phangan remains the most popular backpackers' island in the Gulf of Thailand. Covering an area of around 190 sq km (74 sq miles), its mountainous terrain is covered in dense jungle, with granitic outcrops scattered around the coast. There are plenty of beaches – although they tend to be small, secluded bays rather than the long, sweeping white beaches which characterise Koh Samui.

Most of the island's 8000 residents live in and around the main port of Thong Sala. For most visitors Thong Sala is a transit point to elsewhere on the island. On arrival, you'll find a large number of Longtail boats waiting to transport visitors to the various beach resorts.

Longtails are the way to travel around Koh Phangan for the simple reason that the road system is appalling, consisting as it does largely of deeply rutted dirt tracks which are hazardous at the best of times and positively lethal after rainfall.

It was not until the inauguration of the island's famous Full Moon parties in the 1980s that travellers began arriving in large numbers. Clubbers and ravers stayed on, earning Koh Phangan its reputation as the 'Ibiza of the Orient' but there is also a well established alternative scene, with Tai Chi, meditation, open-air yoga and other New Age pursuits. Most of these activities are centred on the two Haad Rin beaches on the southeast coast.

DIVING AROUND KOH PHANGAN
Koh Phangan, like Koh Samui, is a good departure point for the sites at the northern end of the Ang Thong Marine National Park. Two-day excursions run to the local sites around Koh Tao. It takes about 3hrs to reach Koh Tao's southern sites.

Visibility around the island averages only 4m (13ft), with the highest expectancy being 25m (83ft). Visibility tends to be better between the months of May and October.

Marine life around the reefs is fair, but the sites are seldom visited by pelagics. There are occasional sightings of small juvenile reef sharks, turtles and rays. Only small coral colonies and boulders are found.

Opposite: *Beach cottages, Haad Rin Beach, Koh Phangan.*
Above: *Hawksbill turtle (Eretmochelys imbricata).*

1 KOH MA

★★☆☆

Location: The shallow fringing reef around the southern shoreline of the small islet some 500m (550yd) off the northwest coast of Koh Phangan.

Access: Boats take 45min from Haad Rin Beach and 10min from Ao Cholok Lam. There are no mooring buoys.

Conditions: Currents run north–south and are generally weak to moderate. Stronger currents allow good drift-dives along the rocky reef-slopes. Visibility ranges from 4m (13ft) to an impressive 25m (83ft).

Average depth: 9m (30ft)

Maximum depth: 30m (100ft)

This is considered the most interesting of the Koh Phangan sites. The marine life is good and the corals reasonably healthy. Away from the reef are schools of fusiliers, Red Snappers and Blue-striped Grunts; groups of cuttlefish occasionally mingle with pairs of Imperial and Blue-ringed Emperor Angelfish. Honeycomb Groupers, parrotfish, wrasse and butterflyfish stay closer to the reefs, and anemones and sponges encrust it. The reef itself consists mainly of numerous boulders of lesser star, double star and brain corals of varying sizes; the deeper waters have black corals dividing up the rocky

borderline. There are many small crevices worth peering inside as you can find a host of invertebrates.

2 KOH TAE NOK

★★☆☆

Location: The outer of the two islands off Koh Phangan's west coast. The site is around the reef that fringes the northern bay of this island. There are no mooring buoys; boats drop anchor in the bay.

Access: 45min from Haad Rin Beach, slightly longer from Ao Cholok Lam.

Conditions: Visibility is limited by freshwater runoff to 3–8m (10–26ft).

Average depth: 16m (53ft)

Maximum depth: 25m (83ft)

When the visibility is good this rarely dived site can be very enjoyable. There is little coral damage, and the specimens are reasonably healthy.

The reef-flat consists of various table corals and small boulders of star corals. The waters provide interesting snorkelling, a rainbow of colours being added by wrasse, parrotfish and various chromis and damselfish. The steep, sometimes sheer reef here consists mainly of gorgonian seafans and encrusting coralline.

On the wall-like reef-slope are many barrel sponges

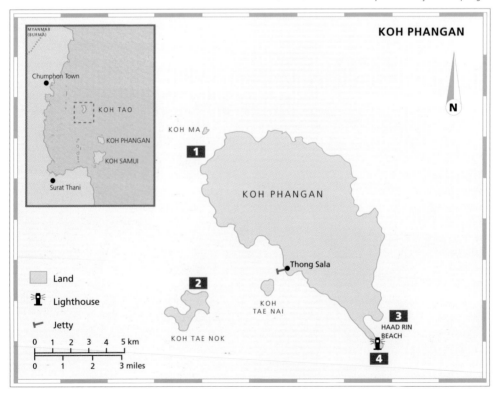

covered in tubeworms and these continue right down to the sea-bed, which they share with Black Sea Cucumbers and patches of sea urchins. Fusiliers, rabbitfish and snappers hang in midwater and Blacktip Reef Sharks occasionally sweep past.

3 HAAD YUAN
★★★★

Location: From the northern end of Haad Rin northwards around the headland. There are no mooring buoys.
Access: 5min from Haad Rin, 30min from Ao Cholok Lam.
Conditions: Visibility is restricted to an average of about 4m (13ft). Currents are weak to moderate.
Average depth: 6m (20ft)
Maximum depth: 12m (40ft)
Primarily used as a diver-training site, this is in fact quite an acceptable dive around a wide, shallow undulating reef. It is broken by many large domed rocks that lie in forests of Black Sea Whips. Many of the rocks are, in addition, highlighted by small trees of soft coral. This makes a suitable area for snorkellers, who will also enjoy its array of colourful reef-fish and diverse invertebrates, including featherstars, nudibranchs and several species of cowrie shells. The reef's hard corals are mostly laminates, with Black Sea Whips and small fans sharing the deeper portions of the site. The usual reef-fish, like parrotfish and wrasse, are present but in small numbers. Nurse Sharks and Blue-spotted Ribbontail Stingrays are sometimes spotted away from the reef.

An interesting feature of this dive site is a narrow dog-legged cave, 15m (50ft) long. Entry should be attempted only if you are trained in cave diving.

4 KOH KON RIN
★

Location: Slightly south of Koh Phangan's southeastern cape. A single rocky outcrop marks the eastern half of the site. The reef fringes this and the group of large submerged rocks to its west.
Access: 5min from Haad Rin Beach, 30min from Ao Cholok Lam.
Conditions: Currents are generally strong. Visibility averages only 4m (13ft) but is occasionally 10m (33ft).
Average depth: 15m (50ft)
Maximum depth: 27m (90ft)
The eastern half of this dive circumnavigates the large rocky outcrop; the rock's northern side has an average depth of 12m (40ft) while the southern face drops off to the site's maximum depth. This, the best section of the site, is a wall with numerous barrel sponges, oysters and clams on the rock face. Spiny Lobsters and moray eels can often be seen concealing themselves in the nooks and crannies. As you head east the wall disappears and you find instead, at about 15m (50ft), an area of large rocks intermixed with sea whips. Blacktip Reef Sharks have been spotted along the site's southern perimeter, but otherwise fish life is poor.

This school of Glassfish and the soft coral are both feeding on the plankton.

How to Get There

Koh Phangan can be reached by road, air and directly by sea.

By bus: VIP air-conditioned buses leave Bangkok's southern bus terminal daily at 21.00 and 21.30hrs. Joint tickets including all travel by bus and boat to Koh Phangan can be bought in Bangkok. The bus journey to Surat Thani takes twelve hours. Buses then connect with either the Express Boat in Surat Thani, or continue for an extra hour's journey to join the ferry boat in Donsak.

By boat: Express boats depart five times daily from the pier in Surat Thani and take two and a half hours to reach Koh Phangan. The passenger ferry takes two and a half hours from Donsak – in high season there are five scheduled daily departures. Both boats arrive at Thong Sala jetty. Buy joint tickets for bus and boat.

By night ferry: There is also a slow night ferry which departs Donsak pier daily at 23.00hrs, arriving at Thong Sala at 06.00 hrs the following morning. This journey will save you one night's accommodation but the sleeping arrangements are very basic, the most luxurious class consists of only a pillow and a thin mattress on the upper deck.

By boat from Koh Samui: There are two direct links from Koh Samui to Koh Phangan. Express Boats leave Nathon pier regularly between 7.00hrs and 17.00hrs and arrive at Thong Sala forty five minutes later. Boats also depart from the pier in Bophut twice daily at 10.30 and 15.00hrs for the trip to Haad Rin beach.

NB: Timetables do vary with demand and season. There is also an irregular speedboat service which operates from Nathon.

Up-to-date information should be obtained near date of travelling. Information and tickets available from Island Jet Co. Ltd; tel Surat Thani (077) 281021, 281769, Songserm Travel Centre; tel Surat Thani (077) 285124, Songserm Travel Centre; tel Bangkok (02) 281 1463-5. For further information regarding buses ring Bangkok southern bus terminal; tel (02) 434 5557, Surat Thani bus terminal; tel (077) 272341.

By train from Bangkok: There are three types of train serving Surat Thani. The better two are listed below - the third is termed a rapid train but it is both slow and uncomfortable.

Express Train

Trains leave Bangkok Hua Lumphong railway station at 13.00, 14.00, 15.15, 15.50, 17.05, 18.30, 19.20, 19.45 and 22.25hrs.

There are four classes. All trains have a buffet car and bar. 1st class with private air-conditioned cabin, 2nd class with air-conditioned cabin sleeper, 2nd class cabin seat with fan and 3rd class seat only. The journey to Surat Thani from Bangkok lasts around twelve hours.

Sprinter train

The Sprinter train leaves Bangkok Hua Lumphong railway station daily at 22.35hrs. Refreshments are available until midnight. For further information about any of the train services contact Hua Lumphong railway station. Bangkok; tel (02) 223 7010, Surat Thani railway station; tel (077) 311213.

By air: There are no airports on Koh Phangan. Planes can however access the neighbouring island of Koh Samui. For details of flights see Koh Samui's Regional Directory see p.138.

By car and taxis: This would take around eleven hours upwards and is inadvisable. For any additional information on Koh Phangan contact **Tourism Authority of Thailand**. Southern office, 5 Talad Mai Road, Muang, Surat Thani, 84000; tel (077) 281 828/fax (077) 282 828.

Where to Stay

There are various types of accommodation on the islands, mostly on and around the many beaches; at the time of writing there are over 130 bungalow facilities, with accommodation for around 3000 people. The majority of the island's guests are dispersed to these resorts from Thong Sala by Longtail boat. As most visitors are backpackers, most of the accommodation is very basic but there are still plenty of bungalow resorts which provide more than just a roof over your head and communal showers and toilets. There is no electricity on the island - the better-equipped resorts have their own generators which shut down in the early hours of the morning. Rooms without fans are kept cool by refreshing sea breezes through open windows. Thong Nai Pan bay on the island's north east coast has one beach resort with air-conditioning but it is very expensive.

It is advisable to choose accommodation near to the diving facility. If you are staying some distance away, you will need to transfer by Longtail boat which can be both uncomfortable (most of the boats have no shade) and time-consuming. It is therefore more relaxing and hassle-free to use the amenities on Haad Rin.

Haad Rin consists of two beaches: Haad Rin Nai (inner rin beach) and Haad Rin Nok (outer Rin beach), usually referred to as 'Sunrise' and 'Sunset' beach respectively. They are joined together to form one beach which covers both the east and west shores of Haad Rin Cape. There is a larger selection and better range of accommodation on Haad Rin Nai. The more comfortable bungalows are located towards the western end of the main beach. There is a small group of shops in the village which sell basic provisions.

Accommodation on the island is generally sufficient to meet demand. However, it is worth remembering to avoid arriving on the island just before a full moon when thousands of visitors flock to the now legendary Koh Phangan 'Full Moon' parties held on Haad Rin Nok beach (see box p.127). When this party takes place accommodation on the island is scarce.

Haad Rin Nai (Sunrise Beach)

Sun Cliff Resort; tel (01) 725 0016. This resort has 19 rooms with mosquito nets or fans and is located towards the southern end of the beach next to the diving centre. Good family restaurant with good European and Thai selections.

Light House. There are 30 rooms, some with mosquito nets or electric fans. Located on Haad Rin Cape, this resort has splendid panoramic views of northern Koh Samui. The resort has a good restaurant.

Haad Rin Nok beach (Sunset Beach)

Phangan Bay Shore Resort; tel (01) 725 0430. This resort has 22 basic rooms with mosquito nets, others come with electric roof fans. Restaurant has a reasonable Thai and European menu.

Thong Nai Pan Bay

Panviman Resort has 49 rooms, some with fans and some with air-conditioning. This resort is for the tired traveller in need of luxury for a couple of nights - it is really out of character and budget for Koh Phangan's visitors although the price for a basic room is not unreasonable. The resort has an excellent restaurant serving International and Thai cuisine.

Where to Eat

The laid-back life style here means there is no necessity for independent restaurants although the nearest thing is an excellent bakery on Haad Rin beach.

Most resorts have their own restaurants (which you are not obliged to use - unlike the resorts on Koh Tao). In fact, the resorts are much more easy going here and allow you to eat when and where you want. Most have a good selection of vegetarian and European dishes and of course the delicious local seafood.

DIVE FACILITIES

There is one operator on Koh Phangan, at Haad Rin beach. Due to the lack of competition from other dive operators on the island the price structures are fairly rigid. On the whole, course prices are typical of the area and there are good deals available for group and multiple bookings.

Dive trips
Price per diver for diving the local sites is inclusive of all equipment, boat, Divemaster, fruit and soft drinks. Day trips to the further destinations of the Marine National Park, Samran pinnacles or Sail rock are also all-inclusive and you even get lunch. A discount of 15% is given for divers with all their own equipment.

Courses
There is a wide selection available at the dive centre and course duration and price depends on which kind of course is chosen.

Dive Operators
Koh Phangan Divers, tel (01) 958 4857. Located on west Haad Rin beach. The complete range of PADI courses are available in English and German. Daily and overnight diving excursions available to Koh Tao and all the local sites, on the centre's own boat.

FILM PROCESSING

Print film and batteries can be bought in one of the general stores in Thong Sala. But it is a much better idea to purchase them before arrival as they are both limited in supply and variety. There are no photographic processing facilities on Koh Phangan, the easiest accessed ones from Thong Sala are in Nathon Town on Koh Samui (see p. 139). If you are travelling directly from Haad Rin to Bophut the most convenient ones are around the Chaweng beach area.

HOSPITALS AND RECOMPRESSION CHAMBERS

The nearest hospitals are the two on the neighbouring island of Koh Samui (see p.139). Patients transfer on one of the boats, either to Nathon from Thong Sala

or Bophut from Haad Rin and then continue the journey by local bus or taxi. In the event of an emergency the hospitals can be contacted on one of the radio telephones in the larger resorts on the island.

The provincial hospital is ten minutes outside Nathon and is well signposted. There is a minimal charge for seeing the doctor. The hospital is clean and staff will arrange for you to see an English speaking doctor if possible.
Koh Samui Provincial Hospital; tel (077) 421399, 421230-2.

The private hospital is located on the main road between Bophut and Ban Chaweng. The hospital is clean and more expensive than the provincial one.
Bandon International Hospital; tel (077) 425382-3/fax (077) 425342.

The **recompression chamber** at The Department of Underwater and Aviation Medicine in Bangkok best serves this island; it can be reached in around four hours from call-out to chamber. If an accident occurs, boats will head north towards Koh Tao and helicopters will lift the victims from the boat en route. This interception is vital as it shortens the journey-time to the chamber. In emergency situations every second counts.

The Department of Underwater and Aviation Medicine, Bangkok Office; tel (02) 468 6100, 24 hours; tel (02) 460 0000 ext. 341.

Koh Phangan's only **police station** is located slightly north of Thong Sala. There is also a police box on Haad Rin Nok.

LOCAL HIGHLIGHTS

The atmosphere on the island is laid-back. Tourist development is a long way behind Koh Samui and there are no cities or high-rise buildings. The island seems to be fixed in a transient state between its two neighbours. Guests of the island tend not to need to be lured away on day excursions or trips. There are many natural and man-made attractions to enjoy on the island and there are always the terrific beaches.

A famous cave temple, **Wat Khao Thamon** can be found after a steep climb up the hills north east of the southern village of Ban Tai. Buddhist monks arrange ten-day meditation retreats here and anybody with strict self-discipline is welcome to join the classes, or simply stay overnight.

Two waterfalls worth visiting are the **Phaeng Waterfall Forest Park** in the centre of the island and

Than Sadet, which is slightly inland from the east coast and is actually a series of waterfalls. This sight has become famous because many royal personages have visited and left their initials carved into the surrounding rocks.

There are many beautiful **beaches** around the island, the majority of which remain undeveloped. The west coast is virtually one long beach whereas the eastern shore features beaches in picturesque bays and coves. They are all easily accessed from Thong Sala via Longtail.

The most developed beach is Haad Rin, the white sandy beaches of which cut through the southeast cape. Transfer by Longtail boat to the inner beach, Haad Rin Nai, takes around forty minutes from Thong Sala. The beach hosts a wide selection of accommodation, restaurants and souvenir stalls as does the outer beach, Haad Rin Nok. The beach also has a small number of **watersports** facilities available for rental such as dinghy, catamaran and wind-surfer boards.

There are a number of beautiful beaches and coves in this area, all are worth a leasurely stroll and you may find yourself the only person on the beach.

Heading north along the east coast from Haad Rin, **Haad Yuan** is the first beach encountered after 3 km (1.8 miles), then **Haad Yai Nam, Haad Yao, Haad Yang** and lastly **Haad Nam Tok** after 7km (4.4 miles).

Thong Nai Pan Bay is a cove located at the northern end of the eastern coast which features two beautiful beaches with bungalows and a restaurant. In good conditions this bay can be accessed by jeep.

The largest bay on the northern coast is **Cholok Lam Bay** on the northern shoreline and is also recommended. There are a few pleasant beaches with resorts and refreshments.

FULL MOON PARTY

Every month literally thousands of people descend from all over the country to attend the now legendary 'Koh Phangan full moon party'.

This tremendously popular social event takes place on Haad Rin Nok beach and lasts from dusk until dawn. A line of bonfires span the beach, loud music plays, people dance and generally have a great time.

ANG THONG MARINE NATIONAL PARK

Ang Thong Marine National Park, so designated in 1980, was the second of Thailand's Marine National Parks; the first, Koh Tarutao, had been established in 1974. The Marine Park lies some 30km (16 n. miles) northwest of Koh Samui, and covers an area of 102 sq km (40 sq miles). It comprises an archipelago of over 41 forest-covered, eroded-limestone formations, ranging in size from small rocky outcrops to towering islets.

Above water the Park is in a relatively healthy condition. A contributory reason for this is that the Royal Thai Navy was once responsible for the area's upkeep. Indeed, it still has rights to return and make use of it for military operations.

The flora of the larger islands can be divided into two categories. The lower elevations are covered with lush semi-evergreen deciduous trees while the higher levels feature hardier scrub forests.

DIVING IN THE ANG THONG MARINE NATIONAL PARK

Coral growth is restricted by high sedimentation, most of it caused by the Tapi Phumduang River. However, the strong porite species of corals have survived and continue to flourish, but the weaker branch corals are severely restricted.

The Marine National Park designation has undoubtedly reduced the rate of further deterioration of the underwater environment, but there is no escaping the fact that the Park has been overfished. The corals show some evidence of dynamite fishing and bottom trawling and large anchors of cruise ships have caused some additional damage, even though at first sight this does not seem to be directly to the corals. The huge anchors of these vessels are embedded in the sand and other loose particles so that when they are hauled up, the flowing waters distribute the particles over a wide area, up to a kilometre (1100yd) away.

The best diving in the Park is around the northern outcrops of Koh Wao Yai and Hin Nippon, where the corals flourish more abundantly, as they are less affected by freshwater runoff. The best time to visit the Park is between February and May.

Opposite: *These limestone outcrops are collectively referred to as Ang Thong Marine National Park.*
Above: *Plume worm (Spirobranchus giganteus) is also referred to as the Christmas Tree Worm.*

1 HIN NIPPON (JAPANESE ROCK)

★★★☆

Location: Around the larger and more northerly of two rocky outcrops, at the northernmost point of the Ang Thong National Park.

Access: About 2hr by boat from Koh Samui or Koh Phangan. Entry to the site is off the southeastern apex. The site is unbuoyed; anchors, dropped away from the reef, secure themselves firmly among the rocks.

Conditions: Visibility ranges from 10m (33ft) to 25m (83ft). Currents, are weak to moderate.

Average depth: 12m (40ft)

Maximum depth: 30m (100ft)

On entering the water, descend and simply follow the reef. Beneath the boat are many large fallen rocks and boulders forming alleyways for adventurous swimthroughs. On the rocks are Neptune Barrel Sponges, slightly obscured by Alabaster Tubeworms. Closer inspection reveals a diversity of invertebrates and crustaceans.

Most of the corals on the reef are foliaceous. This changes as you head round to the site's northwest face. The rocks are now dominated by a gradually sloping reef of healthy coral laminates. Jacks, tuna and juvenile Yellowtail Barracuda are familiar passers-by.

2 KOH WAO

★★★☆☆☆

Location: 30m (100ft) from the beach in sheltered bay on the western shore of the Marine Park's northernmost island, and continues north around the headland.

Access: About 2hr by boat from either Koh Samui or Koh Phangan. The mooring buoy is the entry point.

Conditions: Currents are minimal. Visibility averages about 12m (40ft).

Average depth: 6m (20ft)

Maximum depth: 20m (66ft)

As you follow the incline northeast, the bottom composition slowly changes to become punctuated with small mounds of lesser star boulder corals: there are mixed table staghorns and good examples of cauliflower, lettuce and vase corals. Into the deeper waters, the reef becomes steeper. There are many sea anemones, and Pink Anemonefish. Among the selection of colourful butterflyfish are Raccoon, Red-tailed and Copperband. Around the island's northern tip are schools of snappers and fusiliers, and you may be able to watch Great Barracuda, jacks and trevallies patrolling the depths. During January and February this is a good place to hover motionless in the waters and observe cuttlefish as they come to find mates.

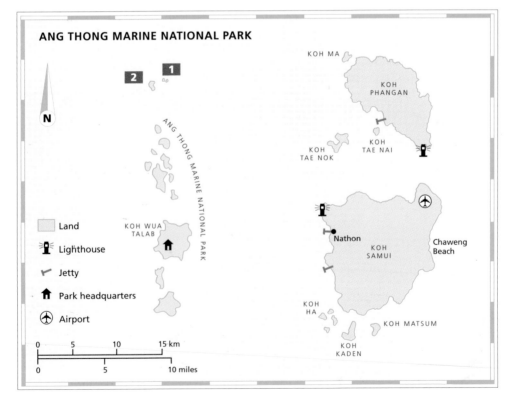

ANG THONG MARINE NATIONAL PARK

HOW TO GET THERE

Daily trips are arranged by Songserm Travel departing from Nathon Town at 0830 and returning at 1700. Private excursions can also be arranged through any of the larger resorts or hotels.

WHERE TO STAY

It is possible to stay on the largest island, Koh Wua Talab. There are five government-run dormitories, each accommodating between ten and twenty guests in reasonable comfort; they are rented as complete units. Visitors are allowed to camp on the island but only with permission from the Park Headquarters office on the island. To book accommodation or to camp, contact: Ang Thong Marine National Park Headquarters, PO Box 29, Surat Thani, 8400; tel (077) 286052.

DIVE FACILITIES

Dive trips can be arranged through most of the operators on Koh Samui or by contacting Divelink Thailand (p.21) in Bangkok.

FILM PROCESSING

Refer to Koh Samui regional directory on page 139.

HOSPITALS AND RECOMPRESSION CHAMBERS

Refer to Koh Samui regional directory on page 139.

LOCAL HIGHLIGHTS

The park's name, Ang Thong, translates as 'Golden Bowl' and refers to a landlocked lake on Koh Mae Koh to the north of Koh Wua Talab. This 250m diameter lake can be reached along a well marked track from the beach, with superb views across its waters to the islands beyond.

The National Park Headquarters are based on **Koh Wua Talab**, the largest of the islands. There is an incredible view from the island peak (400m) of the surrounding islands with Koh Samui and Koh Phangan visible in the distance. A cave in the cliff face, **Tham Buabok**, has numerous stalactites and stalagmites.

Bird watchers will find Koh Wua Talab particularly interesting as there have been confirmed sightings of over 40 species, including several kingfishers. A small population of edible nest swiftlets live in the caves on this island and on Koh Wua Jil, Koh Phluai and Koh Mae Koh.

Ember parrotfish (Scarus rubroviolaceus) on a reef shelf.

KOH SAMUI

The fabulous beaches of Koh Samui have been attracting backpackers for decades. The island – the third largest in Thailand – is now firmly on the international tourist map, with an ever-increasing range of facilities springing up to meet demand. Fortunately planning laws have ensured that development has not been allowed to spoil this popular destination and, although much of the backpacker trade has moved on to neighbouring Koh Phangan (see page 123), Koh Samui is still a highly appealing, laid-back place to visit. Koh Samui has escaped being totally swamped by tourism mainly because it is a long way from any large town or city – Bangkok is over 700km (437 miles) away.

Covering 247 sq km (96 sq miles), the island of Koh Samui lies 35km (22 miles) off the coast of Surat Thani.

The central region, comprising almost two-thirds of the island, consists of thickly wooded mountainous terrain, with coconut palms interspersed by gushing streams and waterfalls. The island's single main road circumnavigates these highlands and links together the various beach resorts on the coastal plains.

The island's 35,000 inhabitants make their living mostly from fishing and tourism, with the export of coconuts still an important part of the island economy.

DIVING AROUND KOH SAMUI

There are several enjoyable dives to be had around Koh Samui itself, all but one of which are reached by boat. On these local sites visibility is generally low, averaging about 5m (17ft) for most of the year; although this improves during the months May to October, when it increases to an acceptable average of 15m (50ft). The local sites are accessed by boat rides taking 10–90min.

The best sites in the vicinity are much further north, and require long boat trips to reach. More experienced divers can enjoy exciting and exhilarating deep wall-dives around the Samran Pinnacles and Sail Rock.

Opposite: *Every traveller's dream, the unspoilt Chaweng Beach, Koh Samui.*
Above: *The Three spot angelfish (Apolemichthys trimaculatus) is beautiful but very shy.*

The low cost of living makes Koh Samui a good place for diver education, whether you want to gain basic certification or continue to a professional level. Few operators have a retail service, so you should carry a good selection of spares and other small necessities.

1 SAMRAN PINNACLES (HIN SAMRAN)

★★★★

Location: About 19km (11 n. miles) north of Koh Phangan, and 18km (10 n. miles) southeast of Koh Tao.

Access: By diveboat, just over 1hr from Koh Tao, about 90min from Koh Phangan and about 2¹/₂hr from Koh Samui. No mooring buoys indicate the position of this completely submerged site, so finding it requires GPS.

Conditions: This site can be dived only in the kinder weather conditions of the southwest monsoon, between early May and late September, when the visibility ranges between 5m (16ft) and an impressive 40m (130ft). Currents can be strong, as the site is in unprotected open ocean. It is suitable for supervised and experienced divers only.

Average depth: 18m (60ft)

Maximum depth: 28m (93ft)

Pelagics enthusiasts will find this site terrific, as you encounter school after school of Great Barracuda, Threadfin Trevally, Big-eyed Jacks, Spanish Mackerel and Dog-faced Tuna – indeed, they appear with such regularity they could almost be considered reef inhabitants.

There are three main pinnacles – the top of the tallest is 12m (40ft) below the surface – plus a mountainous terrain of scattered rocks large enough to swim around and explore. The larger of these rocks are obscured by healthy masses of soft corals, featuring shimmering whites, reds, oranges and yellows. Marine life around the pinnacles consists mainly of Honeycomb Groupers, juvenile moray eels and Schooling Bannerfish. Large Red and White Snappers and fusiliers wander in the deeper waters.

2 SAIL ROCK (HIN BAI)

★★★★

Location: 8km (4.3 n. miles) east of the Samran Pinnacles (Site 1). The rock stands 15m (50ft) proud of the surface.

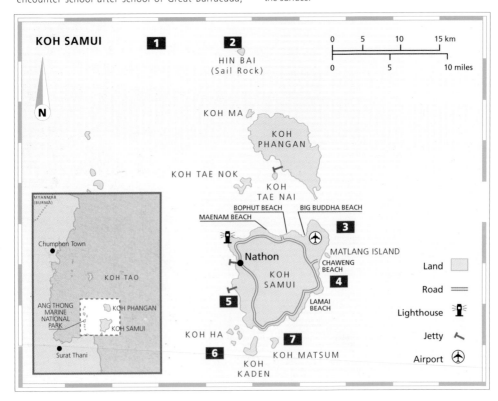

Access: By diveboat from Koh Tao (just over 1hr), Koh Samui (about 2¹/₂hr) or Koh Phangan (about 1¹/₂ hr). There is no mooring buoy.

Conditions: Currents are common, but on the leeward side they are always weak, with good visibility.

Average depth: 22m (73ft)

Maximum depth: 34m (113ft)

This site is probably the finest in the Gulf of Thailand. It is a wall-dive surrounded by a number of smaller but still impressive pinnacles.

On the northern wall at a depth of 16m (53ft), is one of the finest examples of a Barrel Neptune Sponge you are ever likely to see.

This impressive section of the wall is heavily encrusted with orange sponges; many oysters and clams cling to the craggy surface. The southeast face has a natural chimney eroded into the rock. You enter a wide orifice at 18m (60ft) and ascend the chimney to come out at 10m (33ft). Poisonous Bearded Scorpionfish and sea urchins abound, so dive slowly and carefully, and pay special attention to your buoyancy.

Beyond the chimney lies an elevated plateau busy with many forms of marine life. There are gardens of sea anemones tenanted by Pink Anemonefish. Winding Yellow-edged Moray Eels explore the holes and crevices, while Cleaner and Painted Shrimp, along with medium-sized Edible Crabs, remain in their shelters.

At the eastern end of the wall you can often see Great Barracuda – occasionally 3m (10ft) long – patrolling the depths. Schools of Big-eye Jacks, tuna and rainbow runners mingle with Threadfin Trevally in the shallower waters. Whale Sharks are often spotted here.

3 MATLANG ISLAND

★★☆☆☆☆

Location: Following the shallow reef that fringes the southern shoreline of Matlang Island, immediately off Chaweng Beach's north end.

Access: There are two ways of accessing this site: you can‑wade, then swim along the island's southern shoreline and follow the reef east; or you can go by diveboat.

Conditions: Currents increase at the island's eastern tip, and divers should remain alert and close to the reef. Strong currents often flow, turning what is generally a training site for new divers into a reasonable location for drift-diving. Visibility is generally about 5m (16ft).

Average depth: 8m (26ft)

Maximum depth: 9m (30ft)

The reef-flat is built up mainly of table staghorns, interspersed with gardens of sea anemones. The waters above these structures provide some of the area's best snorkelling, the sunlight that penetrates the shallows enhancing the reef creatures' glorious colours.

The dive continues along a shallow, sloping reef consisting mainly of elkhorn, vase and foliaceous corals. Small rocks play both anchor and host to numerous gorgonian seafans and whips, which grow sideways

---

Blue ringed angelfish (Pomacanthus annularis) usually swim in pairs and are approachable.

rather than vertically, having been bent over by prevalent rushing currents.

The marine life is sporadic. At the eastern point you can occasionally see Blacktip Reef Sharks.

4 CHAWENG REEF

★★☆☆

Location: Along the northern end of Chaweng Beach, following the outer side of the rocks that run parallel to the beach.

Access: Either by boat or directly from the beach. You should use a Surface Marker Buoy to warn jet skiers and other water traffic that you are there.

Conditions: Currents are weak to moderate when present at all. Visibility usually about 5m (16ft).

You can snorkel here except when an onshore wind is blowing, as it tends to push snorkellers and swimmers over the sharp craggy rocks and corals, where many stonefish lie camouflaged.

Average depth:: 5m (16ft)

Maximum depth: 7m (23ft)

A very simple, shallow dive. The shallow reef-flat is very popular with snorkellers as there is plenty to see.

The corals are not in pristine condition: they have sustained damage from boats and siltation, as well as human carelessness and littering.

The marine life is scanty all over the site. Parrotfish, wrasse and groupers are all common residents, with the larger specimens being more apparent towards the northern end of the reef.

5 CAR FERRY REEF (BAN NA SAI)

★

Location: On the island's west coast, starting at the southern end of the beach south of the car-ferry jetty and following the headland for about 400m (440yd).

Access: There are two ways of locating this site. The easier is by diveboat: these leave the pier in Nathon and arrive at the northern end of Car Ferry Reef in about 30min. If you choose to come by road, it's best to be accompanied by someone from one of the island's dive operators who knows both the route and the site.

Conditions: Poor. Visibility is extremely limited – below 5m (16ft). Currents are weak to moderate.

Average depth: 4m (13ft)

Maximum depth: 7m (23ft)

Despite the conditions described above, do try to take time to visit, experience and judge this site for yourself.

The lifeforms and corals here were once rich, with a good diversity of associated marine life. Human activities in the area have almost completely destroyed them.

> **BUTTERFLY FISH**
>
> The appealing colours and splendid patterns of the Butterflyfish have an important function. The dark spots on the tail resemble the eyes of the fish which confuses predators. The eyes are concealed even further in many species by the presence of a dark vertical bar running through the eye. Some butterflyfish even swim backwards when pursued which enables them to keep watch over their predators and then bewilder them by darting forward when attacked.

6 FIVE ISLANDS (KOH HA)

★★

Location: Around the south-western apexes of the five small islets off the south west coast of Koh Samui.

Access: 1hr by diveboat from the pier in Nathon Town.

Conditions: The various sites around these islands share the same basic characteristics and conditions. Due to freshwater runoff from the mainland, maximum visibility is generally only about 5m (16ft). Currents range from moderate to strong.

Average depth: 9m (30ft)

Maximum depth: 24m (80ft)

Though interesting and worth a visit, these sites suffer from their location, and during inclement weather (Jun–Oct) are unsuitable for diving and anyway cannot be reliably accessed; furthermore, they bear the brunt of any strong winds coming over the mainland and receive a considerable amount of freshwater runoff from Khao Chai Son (Chai Son Mountain). The area comprises steep coral reefs and drop-offs, with the shallower waters hosting the more interesting diving – there is little to see in deeper waters.

7 KOH MATSUM

★★★☆

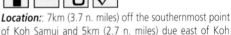

Location:: 7km (3.7 n. miles) off the southernmost point of Koh Samui and 5km (2.7 n. miles) due east of Koh Kaden; the site spans the island's eastern coastline.

Access: About 50min by diveboat from Nathon Pier. The site is unbuoyed.

Conditions: Currents range from very weak to moderate. Average visibility is 6m (20ft).

Average depth: 8m (26ft)

Maximum depth:: 14m (46ft)

Primarily a training site, this is nevertheless a reasonable dive. You may see fine examples of Giant Clams and Blacktip Reef Sharks, as well as schools of squid and barracuda.

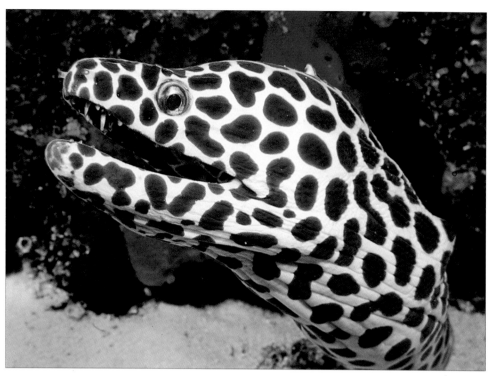

Above: *The distinctive Honeycomb moray (Gymnothorax favagineus) can grow up to 2m.*
Below: *A closer look at one of the many Gorgonian seafans at Sail Rock.*

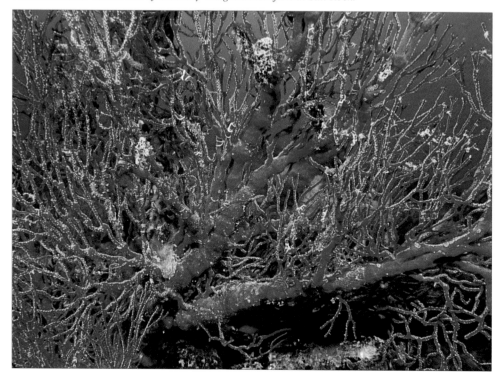

How to Get There

Koh Samui can be reached by road, rail, air and sea.

By bus: VIP Air Conditioned Buses from Bangkok leave Bangkok's southern bus terminal daily at 21.00 and 21.30hrs. Joint tickets including all travel by bus and boat to Koh Samui can be bought in Bangkok. The bus journey to Surat Thani takes twelve hours. Buses then connect with either the Express Boat in Surat Thani, or continue for an extra hour's journey to join the ferry boat in Donsak.

By boat: Express boats depart five times daily from the pier in Surat Thani and take two and a half hours to reach Koh Samui. The passenger ferry takes one and a half hours from Donsak, in high season there are five scheduled daily departures. Express boats arrive at the pier in Nathon Town. Ferry boats arrive at the ferry pier at Ban Na Sai and are met by the local bus services - passengers are transferred directly to their resorts on any of the beaches. There is also a slow night ferry which departs Donsak pier daily at 23.00hrs, arriving at Ban Chon Khram at 04.00hrs the following morning. This journey will save you one night's accommodation but the sleeping arrangements are very basic, the most luxurious class consists of only a pillow and a thin mattress on the upper deck.

There are two routes from Koh Phangan to Koh Samui via Express Boat and a speedboat service from Koh Phangan. One leaves Thong Sala pier regularly between 7.00hrs and 17.00hrs and arrives at Nathon forty five minutes later - the other is via boats which depart from Haad Rin beach twice daily for the 30 minute trip to the pier in Bophut. Both journeys cost the same amount. Information and Tickets available from: Island Jet co. Ltd; tel Surat Thani (077) 281021, 281769, Songserm Travel Centre; tel Surat Thani (077) 285124, Songserm Travel Centre; tel Bangkok (02) 281 1463-5. For further information regarding buses ring: Bangkok southern bus terminal; tel (02) 434 5557, Surat Thani bus terminal; tel (077) 272341.

By train: There are three types of train serving Surat Thani from Bangkok. The better two are listed below - the third is termed a rapid train but it is both slow and uncomfortable!

Express trains leave Bangkok Hua Lumphong railway station - the journey to Surat Thani from Bangkok lasts around twelve hours. All trains have a buffet car and bar. The Sprinter train leaves Bangkok Hua Lumphong railway station - the journey to Surat Thani lasts nine hours. For further information about any of the train services

contact: Hua Lumphong railway station, Bangkok; tel (02) 223 7010, Surat Thani railway station; tel (077) 311213.

By air: Direct flights are with Bangkok Airways and leave Bangkok Domestic Airport five times daily. Be sure to confirm flights as they are prone to last minute re-scheduling and cancellations, mainly due to weather conditions. The flight time is 70 minutes. For further information contact: Bangkok Airways; tel (02) 229 3434. Flights via Surat Thani are with Thai International and depart Bangkok Domestic Airport three times daily. Connections are easily made from any international flight - flight time is sixty five minutes. On arrival at Surat Thani airport a Thai International courtesy bus transfers passengers to the town centre. For further information contact: **Thai Airways International Limited**; tel (02) 513 0121/fax (02) 513 0203.

By car and taxi: This would take over eleven hours and is inadvisable.

For any additional information on Koh Samui contact: **Tourism Authority of Thailand**; tel (077) 281 828/fax (077) 282 828.

Where to Stay

Divers can stay anywhere on the island as the diving operators will collect and return their guests to and from their resort, free of charge, as part of diving courses and excursions. This allows much greater freedom of choice in selecting accommodation. Many of the resorts cater for families and provide baby sitting services and child-minders. Services are generally good and reasonably priced.

Nathon Town

Visitors arriving on the last ferry from Donsak should transfer from the pier directly to a beach resort by one of the local buses, and avoid Nathon as accommodation there is limited. If you do get stranded the **Win Hotel**; tel (077) 421500, 421501 is reasonable.

Chaweng Beach

Fair House; tel (077) 422256, 422373/fax (077) 422373. This bungalow resort is located, in my opinion, on the best beach on the island. The resort's restaurant is one of the best on the island.

Malibu Resort; tel (077) 422386. Situated on the beach with basic accommodation. There is also an excellent restaurant and on-site dive facility.

Lamai Beach

Galaxy Resort has comfortable rooms and is situated on the beach. There is a good restaurant and bar on the beach.

Best Resort is ideally located for easy access for both the beach and the cosmopolitan night life of Lamai. The resort has over 30 rooms.

Maenam Beach

Home Bay is accessed by a trek to the furthest point of a long track at the western end of Maenam. A good restaurant serves both European and Thai meals. Rooms have private bathrooms. **Shady Shack** is one of the secret treasures of the beach, as it remains hidden under the shade of beach fringing coconut trees. There is a large restaurant with a good menu.

Bangrak Beach (Big Buddha Beach)

Nara Lodge; tel (077) 421364/fax (077) 421364. There is a swimming pool by the beach. A good restaurant serves a varied selection or European and Thai food.

Bophut

World Resort; tel (077) 421355-6. Located on the main road between MaeNam and Bophut this resort has a swimming pool, poolside bar, restaurant and coffee shop. There is also a good car and motorbike rental service. **Samui Euphoria Hotel**; tel (077) 286948/fax (077) 286949. The air-conditioned rooms and suites are spread over a very large area with a swimming pool, restaurant and a selection of sports facilities, including tennis courts.

Where to Eat

There are hundreds of restaurants on the island, mostly around the beaches. Chaweng beach has a selection of International restaurants as does Lamai. Service is slow but the food is good and reasonably priced. Koh Samui is particularly noted for its delicious seafood and coconut dishes. The resorts also have their own eating facilities and the majority are worthy of a visit.

Dive Facilities

There is a vast selection of dive operators on Koh Samui and most provide diving education in some form or another. (NB: Watch out for small operators who advertise a full diving schedule which is in fact dependant on combining forces with a larger operator.)

Dive trips

Dive trips run on a daily basis and two day one night excursions to Koh Tao are available. All trips come complete with transfers to and from the dive boat from the resort, light refreshments, fruit and beverages throughout the trip, lunch, divemaster(s) services, all equipment and two full tanks of air. Included in the

Koh Tao trip are all the meals and accommodation on the island. Discounts of 15% are given for divers with all their own equipment (excluding tank and weights). Snorkellers and non-divers are welcome to join any of the scheduled diving trips - equipment and instruction available. Many of the dive boats will carry fresh water tanks for rinsing diving and photographic equipment. The majority have toilets and a shaded area away from the sun or rain.

Dive courses
Courses for the complete beginner are very popular here and there is a good selection of suitable locations for that first experience of breathing underwater. Courses are available right up to professional qualifications. All the instruction on the island is taught by qualified instructors following PADI diver training programmes. Courses run that do not carry the PADI insignia should be avoided.

On the whole course prices on the island remain relatively stable. Due to the location of the better dive sites, courses are slightly more expensive here than they are on the two neighbouring islands, but the majority of people are happy to pay extra to stay on the more comfortable and lively island of Koh Samui.

Dive operators
Chaweng Beach
Samui International Diving School, PO Box 40, Koh Samui, Surat Thani, 84140 Thailand, tel/fax (077) 231242, email: planet@mozart.inet.co.th PADI 5 STAR IDC Centre. This is the largest and most established operator in the area. Daily dive trips are scheduled to the local sites and Koh Tao and overnight diving excursions to Koh Tao. All trips are aboard one of the centre's own dive boats which all carry oxygen and radios. The largest boat also features a fresh water shower. The complete range of PADI courses are available in English, French, German, Italian, Swedish and Thai. Courses are scheduled all year round. Instructor courses are run four times a year. The centre has an extensive retail service. **The Dive Shop**, 167/25 Chaweng Beach Road, PO Box 67, Nathon, Koh Samui, Surat Thani, tel/fax (077) 230232, email: diveshop@samart.co.th PADI 5-star IDC Centre, IANTD Facility. Professionally run dive center offering daily and overnight dive trips to all the top sites. The center also operates the only live-aboard boat on Koh Samui. The full range of PADI and IANTD courses is available in a selection of languages. Good retail outlet.
Chang Divers is located on Chaweng beach in front of Lotus resort. PADI courses are taught in English. One-day local trips and

overnight excursions to Koh Tao. Divers leave aboard rented boats. No retail outlet.

Lamai Beach
Easy Divers, tel (077) 231190. PADI 5-star Centre. Located on the road between Lamai and Chaweng. PADI courses are available in English, French and German. Daily and overnight excursions are offered onboard rented boats. The shop has a retail outlet.

Big Buddha Beach
Asian Divers Den; tel (077) 425346/fax (077) 425384. There are two offices, one on Big Buddha beach and the other on Chaweng. PADI courses are available in English and French. Daily and overnight excursions to Koh Tao are offered on rented boats. There is no retail service.

FILM PROCESSING

Every beach, town and main street on Koh Samui is littered with photographic services.

HOSPITALS AND RECOMPRESSION CHAMBERS

There are two hospitals are on Koh Samui: **Koh Samui Provincial Hospital**; tel (077) 421399, 421230-2 is located just outside Nathon on the way to Lamai beach. There is always an English speaking member of staff in reception to greet you, usually with an inquiry as to if you have medical insurance as treatment is very expensive.
Bandon International Hospital; tel (077) 425382-3/fax (077) 425342 is located on the main road between Bophut and Ban Chaweng.

The nearest **recompression chamber** is at The Department of Underwater and Aviation Medicine in Bangkok, which can be reached in around four hours from call-out to chamber. Victims of, or suspected victims of, DCS are evacuated via helicopter from the boat or the island depending on the situation, then flown at low altitude to the department.
The Department of Underwater and Aviation Medicine; Office hours tel (02) 468 6100, 24 hours; tel (02) 460 0000 ext. 341. **Tourist Police** in Nathon Town; tel (077) 421281.

LOCAL HIGHLIGHTS

The largest and most famous temple on the island is **Wat Phra Yai (Big Buddha Temple)** on the small islet of Koh Fan at the northern end of **Big Buddha Beach**. A 12m (40 feet) Golden Buddha image statue sits with its hands in the 'Touching Earth' position looking out over the long Beach. **Wat Khunaram** is an old wooden monastery, built in the south of the island.

On the right hand side of the inner entrance to the monastery is a glass cabinet containing the mummified remains of the **Monk Loung Pordeang**, laid to rest in the classic meditating position. **Na Muang fall** is one of the most impressive waterfalls on the island and is well worth a visit. **Hin Lat waterfall** is another interesting waterfall worth visiting. Nathon Town has the largest selection of shops on Koh Samui, or any of the surrounding islands. All Thailand's main banks have branches here. **Chaweng Beach** is without doubt the most popular beach on Koh Samui, the relatively quiet 7 km (4.3 miles) east coast beach has many resorts and restaurants located amongst fringing coconut trees. Due to its size the silvery white sandy beach never seems to be overcrowded. **Lamai Beach** is another popular beach with lots of water sports. There are also a number of organised daily excursions available on the island which can be booked at virtually every resort or travel shop. Trips leave for **Ang Thong Marine National Park, Koh Phangan**, or to one of the attractions on the island, such as one of the Temples, the Butterfly garden, monkey theatre, go-kart track, family zoo or one of the islands many beauty spots.

Car and Motorbike Rental
Jeeps and motorbikes can be rented on a daily basis but take care as the roads here are sprinkled with loose chippings and, in the beach areas, loose sand.

USEFUL WORDS	
Sawadee	Hello
Kop Khun Kaa	Thank you (f)
Kop Khun Krap	Thank you (m)
Mai Chi	No
Hu Kow	Hungry
Pett	Spicy
Gai	Chicken
Mai Kow Ji	Don't understand
Hu Nam	Thirsty
Aroy	Delicious
Neuh	Beef
Moo	Pork
Prik	Chilli
Kai	Egg
Kow	Rice
Cafe Yen	Iced coffee
Cafe Rawn	Hot coffee
Nam Kem	Ice
Nom	Milk
Nam Cha	Tea
Nam Tan	Sugar
Chop	Like
Sanuk	Enjoy

PATTAYA

Some 145km (90 miles) southeast of Bangkok the bustling metropolis that is Pattaya city has shot up during the past 35 years, being built up primarily as a vast recreational complex catering for the US Armed Forces during the Vietnam War. Growing demands for accommodation were met by the construction of guesthouses, which quickly grew into hotels and then resort complexes. Local fishermen sold fish to the numerous new restaurants, and increased their income by offering fishing trips to tourists. In due course, international tourism kicked in and during the 1970s development soared. Pattaya became the massive entertainment centre it is today: quite literally, whatever people want, by day or night, they can get it in Pattaya.

DIVING AROUND PATTAYA

During the week there is little diving on offer in Pattaya – a waste, since the sites in this area offer all year-round diving, with the best conditions being between November and March. Weekends are another matter as large groups of divers descend from Bangkok to escape the capital's high levels of air pollution.

The local diving centres on two groups of islands, described very simply as the Near and Far Islands.

THE NEAR ISLANDS

Diving around the Near Islands is very poor: there is a lot of silt in the waters and the reefs have suffered dynamite, trawling and, worst of all, tourist-related damage. Pollution is the biggest problem; it is most severe around Koh Lan. This island, 7 sq km (5 sq miles) in area, has been established as a recreation centre in an attempt to reduce the heavy boat traffic around Pattaya Bay. These sparse coral reefs are a highlight of tourist trips in glass-bottomed boats, although the turbid waters allow little enough to be seen through those glass bottoms. Local diving operators use the Near Islands for training and, more significantly, for night-diving.

Opposite: *Regimented speedboats await those wishing to enjoy watersports available on Koh Lan.*
Above: *An Indian lionfish (Pterois volitans) spreads its feathery pectoral fins as a warning sign.*

THE FAR ISLANDS

The Far Island sites have conditions similar to those of the Chumphon area and afford better diving. The corals are healthier here and more abundant as they are less affected by high levels of tourism and freshwater runoff from the mainland. It takes about $1^1/2$–2hr to get to the Far Island sites, and this is done aboard larger boats; the sites are too distant to be reached safely by Longtail boats. Sites generally have to be accessed direct from the boat.

Pattaya also offers wreck diving, with a choice of two wrecks (Sites 10 and 11). Unfortunately, both are in deep water and susceptible to strong currents, so are well beyond the capability of most novice divers. For more experienced divers, training courses in wreck diving are available at the better dive centres.

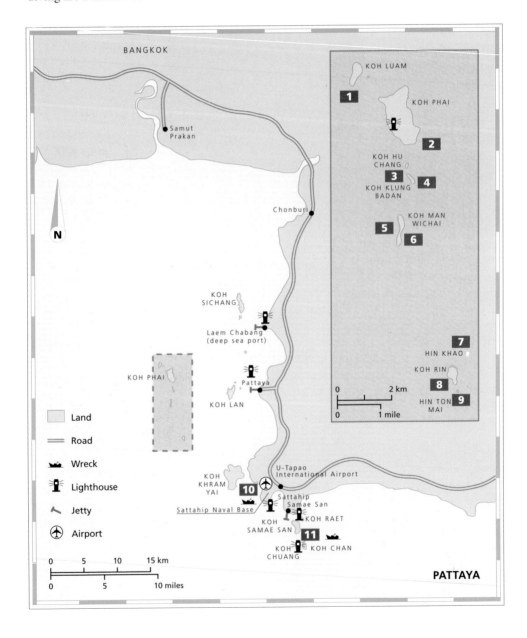

1 KOH LUAM
★★☆☆

Location: Around the southern headland of Koh Luam, the northernmost of the Far Island chain.
Access: Just under 2hr by boat from Pattaya Beach. The site is unbuoyed.
Conditions: Southerly winds increase visibility from the customary 5m (16ft) to 10m (33ft). The currents around this sheltered end of the island will also be weaker at this time. These conditions allow snorkelling.
Average depth: 10m (33ft)
Maximum depth: 18m (60ft)

The lower reef-slope is highlighted by many soft corals; these are neither as radiant nor as large as they could be, having been restricted by excessive siltation in the water, although much of the silt is redistributed by the currents present during northerly winds and spring tides.

The reef is fairly typical of the area. It is frequently punctuated by sponge-encrusted rocks and large mounds of lesser and greater star corals, occasionally split by clusters of smaller, less hardy corals. The hard corals tend to dominate the shallower waters: coral laminates form terraces that descend to deeper-water areas where long, spiralling sea whips are embedded among larger rocks.

The marine life is fair. Familiar reef inhabitants – parrotfish, wrasse and pufferfish – are always present. Away from the reef, juvenile snappers, jacks and fusiliers repeatedly pass by.

2 KOH PHAI
★★☆☆

Location: The second northernmost island in the Far Island chain; about 2km (1 n. mile) southeast of Koh Luam (Site 1).
Access: About 2hr by boat from Pattaya Beach. There is no mooring buoy. The usual entry point is 30m (100ft) off this small island's southeast coast.
Conditions: Currents are generally weak to moderate; stronger currents, though fairly rare, make this a good drift-diving site. Visibility averages 4m (13ft).
Average depth: 6m (20ft)
Maximum depth: 10m (33ft)

Descend directly from the boat and follow the fringing reef southeast. Countless brown and white featherstar worms burrow deeply into the many boulders of star coral that dominate the coral flats in the shallower waters. The reef itself is not particularly impressive. The few coral heads present – mainly brain, staghorn, and a small selection of foliaceous corals.

Following the reef down to the sandy sea-bed, you

REEF CLEAN-UP AND TREASURE HUNT

Every two months the Bangkok-based operator Planet Scuba organises a reef clean-up at Pattaya, with divers descending with plastic crates to remove rubbish they find underwater. The locally based dive operator Aquanauts does likewise. These operators also organise an annual underwater treasure hunt in appreciation of divers' hard work. Small objects are concealed at one of the dive sites, and prizes donated by local companies are awarded for their retrieval. The event is followed by an evening barbecue. For more information contact either Planet Scuba or Aquanauts direct or get in touch with Divelink Thailand (see page 21).

---

find many colourful blue and yellow blennies darting in and out of small holes in the cratered sand. Black Sea Cucumbers, Long-spined Sea Urchins and lots of fallen Zigzag Oysters share this area. Just above the sand-line, a multitude of colourful nudibranchs are slightly obscured by fallen rubble.

The marine life, as one would expect from the paucity of corals, is fairly limited.

3 KOH KLUNG BADEN (WEST REEF)
★★☆☆

Location: In the Far Island chain, about 5km (2.7 n. miles) south of Koh Hu Chang.
Access: About 1hr 40min by boat from Pattaya Beach. There is no mooring buoy. The dive follows the reef north around the headland. Alternatively, the site can be reached by a short surface swim from the beach.
Conditions: Currents are generally weak to moderate, allowing snorkelling – particularly during northerly winds, when the site is in the lee of the island. On the infrequent occasions when strong currents flow, this is a good site for drift-diving. Visibility averages 5m (16ft).
Average depth: 6m (20ft)
Maximum depth: 12m (40ft)

Entry to the site is in about 4m (13ft) of water. Beneath the boat are numerous mounds and heads of coral,

---

SAFETY BATS

No one, no matter how experienced, can accurately predict the pattern of currents. It is possible to estimate them but there will always be the odd occasions when they will catch you unaware. Most sites are susceptible to strong currents which can either build up gradually or appear immediately.

One particular example of this occurred at this site when the current suddenly picked up and carried two divers to Koh Klung Baden. The divers had listened to the advice given to them by master instructor Dave Wright, to carry safety bats (also known as 'safety sausages') which fortunately enabled them to be located immediately.

notably staghorn, as well as coral laminates. This is a very good location for snorkelling.

To the northwest the reef becomes a relatively shallow fringing reef whose flat and slope consist mainly of rocks and sponges. Compressed barrel sponges shelter small crustaceans and invertebrates.

The fish life at this site is not abundant, though there are reasonable numbers and varieties of chromis, basslet, blenny, gobies and bannerfish, plus a few resident Bicolour Parrotfish and wrasse.

4 KOH KLUNG BADEN (EAST REEF)
★★★☆

Location: In the Far Island chain, about 5km (2.7 n. miles) south of Koh Hu Chang.
Access: About 1hr 40min by boat from Pattaya Beach. As at the western site (Site 5), there is no mooring buoy.
Conditions: The conditions are similar to those off the west coast.
Average depth: 8m (26ft)
Maximum depth: 18m (60ft)
The small bay midway along the eastern coast is shallow – about 5m (20ft) – and suitable for snorkelling. The water gets deeper towards the southern headland. Two large coral mounds of lesser star coral stand away from the southernmost point; these have completely engulfed big rocks. Past the mounds, the sandy bottom slopes from 15m (50ft) to the site's maximum depth. This area is, alas, littered with broken bottles and other rubbish; uncharacteristically, the octopuses have taken up residence in them. Other residents of this otherwise sandy area are rays and pufferfish.

5 KOH MAN WICHAI (WEST REEF)
★★

Location: In the Far Island chain, just over 2km (1 n. mile) south of Koh Klung Baden. The site follows the western coast southward from its midpoint.
Access: About 1hr 40min by boat from Pattaya Beach. There is no mooring buoy; boats moor 30m (100ft) off the southwest coast.
Conditions: During northerly winds this is a good site for novices. Visibility ranges between 5m (16ft) and 15m (50ft).
Average depth: 7m (23ft)
Maximum depth: 15m (50ft)
Though not one of the area's stronger sites, this is worth an occasional visit when conditions are favourable. A steeply sloping reef consists of corals settled between many fallen rocks; most are foliaceous, with a good representation of lettuce, vase and carnation. The

shallower portions of the reef-flats have small clusters of staghorn and cauliflower corals. Towards the island's southern tip, and here Honeycomb Groupers rest among sponge-encrusted rocks and beside particular areas of Carpet Anemones.

Away from the reef there are the familiar mounds of lesser star corals highlighted by colourful plumeworms. Large Red Snappers and schools of Yellowtail Fusiliers are regular visitors.

6 KOH MAN WICHAI (EAST REEF)
★★★☆

Location: In the Far Island chain, about 2km (1 n. mile) south of Koh Klung Baden. The site begins off the southeastern coast and encompasses the southern headland.
Access: Just over 1hr 40min by boat from Pattaya Beach. There is one mooring buoy, just off the southeast coast.
Conditions: Visibility ranges between 5m (16ft) and 15m (50ft). Currents are generally weak to moderate.
Average depth: 12m (40ft)
Maximum depth: 15m (50ft)
One of the more enjoyable sites off Pattaya. Descent is directly from the boat, where the sea-bed is littered with numerous clumps and mounds of smooth porite corals. The water at this point is shallow – 4m (13ft) – and ideal for snorkelling. Snorkellers continue their swim towards the island; divers head off south, slightly away from the headland.

Most of the corals are not in the form of fringing reefs, as with most of this area's sites, but in large patches. As you go south for about 30m (100ft), the water deepens; an elongated plateau continues for a further 400m (440yd) in a depth of 13m (43ft), rising to 10m (33ft) – and beyond this are two more of similar size! The plateaux are covered in gardens of sea anemones, plus their abundant symbiotes: Three-spot Dascyllus and Pink Anemonefish.

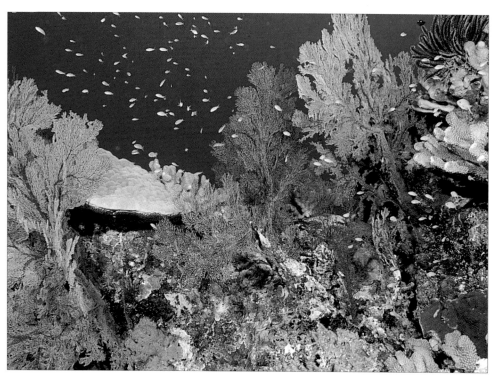

Above: *Scenes like this can still be enjoyed around the Far Islands.*
Below: *Orange tube coral with polyps open for feeding.*

7 HIN KHAO
★

Location: A small rocky outcrop 8km (4 n. miles) south of Koh Man Wichai (Sites 6 and 7). The dive circumnavigates the outcrop.

Access: Just under 2hr by boat from Pattaya Beach.

Conditions: Strong currents and limited visibility restrict this site to experienced divers only.

Average depth: 6m (20ft)

Maximum depth: 15m (60ft)

This is not one of the area's better sites. The corals, mainly patch corals, being subject to strong currents from both directions, show only restricted growth and succour only limited marine life, although there is a small shallow reef of coral laminates. In deeper waters, away from the rocks, there are a few areas of sea whips, to which cling featherstars; below these, in the rubble, are colourful nudibranchs. Reasonable sightings of pelagics – Barracuda, jacks, trevallies and the occasional school of tuna – are fairly regular, so the site is not entirely without attractions.

8 KOH RIN
★★★★★

Location: Starting at the northern end of the bay on the southwest coast of Koh Rin – the large islet at the bottom of the Far Island chain, about 1km (1/2 n. mile) southwest of Hin Khao – and continuing northwards.

Access: About 2hr by boat from Pattaya Beach.

Conditions: Between November and March this site has very favourable conditions, when a year-round visibility of 5m (16ft) increases to 15m (50ft), and when very mild currents can be expected. During northerly winds the sheltered bay is calm enough to snorkel in.

Average depth: 7m (23ft)

Maximum depth: 14m (46ft)

A steadily sloping reef falls more dramatically as it heads north; it consists of fallen rocks covered with a few foliaceous corals. However, it does improve as it steepens towards the western headland, and a higher percentage of corals slowly begin to dominate the rocks to a depth of 12m (40ft), where you find sea whips and black coral bushes. The diversity of marine life around the reef is above average for the area, with many examples of Harlequin Sweetlips, snappers, squirrelfish and lionfish. Communities of Magnificent Anemones, Three-spot Dascyllus, basslets and chromis are restricted to the rocky ledges. Neptune Barrel Sponges lodge among the crevices or are inhabited by moray eels and a range of invertebrates.

The shallow bay is absolutely perfect for snorkelling,

---

many coral mounds that are heavily pitted by bivalves and plumeworms, with, between the mounds, Black Sea Urchins and small cowrie shells.

9 HIN TON MAI
★★

Location: Around the eastern perimeter of low-lying rocky outcrops at the extreme south of the Far Island chain, about 1km (1/2 n. mile) south of Koh Rin (Site 9).

Access: About 2 1/2hr by boat from Pattaya Beach. There is one mooring buoy.

Conditions: During northerly winds this site is quite suitable for novice divers. Southerly winds, however, make it suitable for experienced divers only. Visibility ranges between 5m (16ft) and 15m (50ft).

Average depth: 6m (20ft)

Maximum depth: 14m (46ft)

You enter the water and follow the mooring line. The coral formations are in two major categories: fringing reef and patch. The section of reef around the entry point is fairly barren, but as you go south the seascape changes into a more coral-rich, undulating terrain. Soft corals are plentiful in the shallower waters; elkhorns and foliaceous corals lay claim to the midwaters, and sea whips, gorgonian seafans and many bushes of stinging hydroids on dead coral heads are prominent at the base of the reef. There are lots of barrel and encrusting sponges everywhere, the latter having claimed small areas from the corals. Marine life is plentiful and varied.

10 PETCHBURY BREMEN WRECK
★★★

Location: About 30km (16 n. miles) from Pattaya Beach, in the channel between Koh Khram Yai and Sattahip on the mainland.

Access: About 3hr by diveboat from Pattaya Pier. Finding the site requires a skilled captain.

Conditions: There are strong currents and low visibility. To enjoy this wreck, you need to plan your dive around the slack tides.
Average depth: 19m (63ft)
Maximum depth: 24m (80ft)
The *Petchbury Bremen* sank during the 1930s when a fire broke out in the midships engine room; the resultant explosion buckled the hull and allowed water to gush in.

This 60m (200ft) steel freighter has settled upright on the sandy sea-bed; its highest point is just under 17m (56ft) below the surface. Since sinking, it has received further damage to the bow and hull, courtesy of the Royal Thai Navy, who many years ago used it for bombing practice.

In addition to the structural dangers, the large numbers of stinging hydroids and urchins present should inspire caution, especially in the low visibility.

Almost totally encrusted with a diversity of marine growth, this wreck has now become an extremely impressive artificial reef. Soft corals add a colourful frame around the eroding structures and portholes. You can still see, around the wreck, the forms of multiple pulley systems and broken parts of heavy machinery – there's even a bathtub!

11 HARDEEP WRECK
★★★

Location: 14km (7½ n. miles) southeast of Sattahip Pier. The wreck lies in about 30m (100ft) of water off the southern headland of Koh Samae San, in the narrow channel between it and Koh Chuang.
Access: 30min by diveboat from the pier in Samaesan. Weekend wreck expeditions are regularly scheduled from Pattaya.
Conditions: Extreme currents – occasionally visible on the surface – flow through this narrow strait. The wreck can be successfully dived only during slack tides. Visibility ranges between 2m (6½ft) and 15m (50ft).
Average depth: 28m (93ft)
Maximum depth: 32m (106ft)
This wreck is believed to be of an Indonesian freighter requisitioned by the Japanese during World War II and sunk by Allied bombing in 1942.

The recommended (and often only) way to dive the *Hardeep* is to descend down the mooring line directly onto the structure; free descents are not advised. When currents are stronger you might limit exploration to the wreck's leeward side. The ship's structures are radiantly coloured by a multitude of soft corals, encrusting sponges, sea whips and white bushes of stinging hydroids.

Associated reef inhabitants are also plentiful. As you arrive, Moorish Idols, fusiliers and snappers often shy away into the darker recesses. This wreck can be penetrated, although a number of snagged nets restrict some passageways and caution is required. Many of the steel plates, doors and portholes remain in place, and the engine is intact.

Settings such as this take many years to develop so dive carefully.

How to Get There

Pattaya is easiest to access by road. It can also be reached by rail and air but there is no straightforward transfer at the Pattaya end and it therefore becomes more time-consuming than travelling directly.

By bus: Buses (air-conditioned) leave every thirty minutes from Bangkok's eastern bus terminal in Sukhumvit Road at the junction of Soi Ekamai (Soi 63). The journey to Pattaya takes around three hours. The journey from the bus terminal to the city centre continues onboard one of the local taxi-buses which wait at the terminal. Fares are paid at the destinations and the buses are stopped by ringing a bell. The return journey to the bus terminal is, oddly, double the price as the outward trip. For further information regarding buses contact Bangkok eastern bus terminal; tel (02) 391 4900, 2504.

By train: Trains leave from Bangkok's Hua Lumphong railway station on an irregular basis. For further information about any of the train services contact Hua Lumphong railway station, Bangkok; tel (02) 223 7010.

By air: Pattaya is served by U-Tapao International Airport. As yet there is only a rather unorganised skeleton service running between Bangkok and U-Tapao International airport, with only four flights a week. These cannot be termed as scheduled flights as there is no fixed timetable; there are however, plans to increase this service in the future. Duration of flights from domestic airport are 45 mins, leaving passengers to transfer by local taxi-bus for the remaining one hour, 40 km, journey to Pattaya. For updated information and flight prices contact Bangkok Airways; tel (02) 253 4014-6

By taxi: It is possible to access Pattaya by limousine, which is the equivalent of a taxi. This is an expensive way of travelling but it does avoid awkward transfers at either end of the journey.

By road: It is advisable to access Pattaya by bus and rent your transport on arrival. The Sukhumvit Road can be treacherous and unless visitors are familiar with Thai driving techniques it is best avoided. However, cars can be hired through all the major hotels in Bangkok.

For any additional information on Pattaya contact the **Tourism Authority of Thailand**; tel (038) 427 667/fax (038) 429 113.

Where to Stay

There are literally thousands of places to stay in Pattaya catering for all budgets.

Below are three which I think are particularly good. The quieter accommodation is to be found around the northern end of the beach but you can choose from a very comprehensive list of accommodation available from the TAT Office in Beach Road.

High Five; tel (038) 427115/fax (038) 427119. This hotel is very clean and the rooms are spacious, all with private bathroom, h/c water, satellite TV and fridge. The hotel has a good restaurant and coffee shop. There is also a rooftop swimming pool. **Flipper Lodge Hotel**; tel (038) 426401/fax (038) 426403. All rooms have air-conditioning, fridge and satellite TV. Other facilities include two swimming pools, a good international restaurant, a small selection of shops and an on-site hairdresser. **Jomtien Beach**. This 4 km (2.5 miles) beach is located 3km (2 miles) south of Pattaya, it takes ten minutes to access on board one of the many local taxi buses. During the day the beach offers an enormous selection of water sports including windsurfing. It is easy to imagine this quiet area becoming an extension of the Pattaya scene but for now it provides a somewhat quieter alternative to lively Pattaya City.

Where to Eat

Although the majority of hotels have good restaurants the general trend is to eat out. Locals claim that it is possible to eat in a different restaurant every night of the year and still miss some! **Lobster Pot**, opposite Soi 14, south Pattaya. Located on the old fisherman's wharf, this is possibly the best seafood restaurant in Pattaya, and definitely the most popular. They serve a fine selection of seafood dishes as well as steaks and local food, all at reasonable prices.

Dive Facilities

Please take the following advice very seriously indeed. Pattaya has a wide selection of diving operators to choose from and it is imperative that you are 100% happy about which operator you choose. For those wishing to learn to dive, check the instructor's credentials, make sure that the instructor is both qualified and currently registered to teach, that you feel safe in their care and above all that you trust them. The same goes for dive trips. Do not feel embarrassed about making enquiries or be intimidated - remember that safe operators will always check every diver's certification.

Dive trips

Dive trips are run on a daily basis, with a number of operators renting fishing boats for use as dive boats. Dive trips vary greatly in price and in the services provided and therefore cannot be generalised, as they can in other areas around the Gulf of Thailand.

Dive courses

Both PADI and NAUI courses are run in the Pattaya area, both carry world-wide recognition, and are perfectly acceptable. NAUI courses generally last slightly longer. Prices vary greatly between agencies and individual operators. Courses are available in English, French, German, Swedish and Thai.

Dive Operators

Mermaid's Dive School, PADI 5 Star Facility; tel (038) 232220/fax (038) 232221. Daily dive trips are scheduled to both the inner and far islands on a purpose-fitted 18m (60 ft) boat, complete with oxygen, radio, and depth finder. The boat has a shaded area, sun deck and fresh water shower. Dive trips include transfer to and from either of the two dive shops, a meal and drinking water.

Seafari Sports Centre Co. Ltd, PADI 5 Star Facility; tel (038) 429060/fax (038) 424708. The facility covers two levels, the lower contains a welcoming area, an enormous servicing workshop, retail outlet, offices, and an equipment store with separate maintenance area. Upstairs there are two air conditioned classrooms, library and consultation area. Daily dive trips to the Inner and Far islands on rented boats. Included in the price are transfers to and from the shop, a meal and soft drinks. Snorkellers, families and friends are also welcome to join the trips.

Scuba Tek Dive Centre; tel (038) 361616/fax (038) 361616, email: scubatek@loxinfo.co.th PADI courses available in English. Friendly dive centre with a small retail outlet, offering the full range of PADI courses in English, French German and Thai. Dive trips to the Far Islands sites, as well as overnight excursions on own dive boat.

Aquanauts, tel (038) 361724, fax (038) 412097, email: aquanaut@loxinfo.co.th New PADI dive centre, already setting high standards for others to follow. All PADI dive courses are on offer, in a variety of languages. Day trips to the Far Islands and overnight ventures to Koh Chang (see next section). Also available are overnight trips to a tanker which lies vertically in a secret location!

FILM PROCESSING

Print and slide films are on general sale everywhere. There are a number of photographic shops along the southern ends of Beach and Pattaya second roads.

HOSPITALS AND COMPRESSION CHAMBERS

There are three main hospitals that serve Pattaya city: **Pattaya Memorial Hospital**; tel (038) 422741-2, 429422-4. **Pattaya International Hospital**; tel (038) 428374-5, 422774/fax (038) 422773 **Bangkok - Pattaya Hospital**; tel (038) 427751-5. The nearest **recompression chamber** is 50 km (31 miles) south, at the Naval Base in the town of Sattahip. Patients are evacuated from Pattaya and transferred by road. The journey takes around two hours from the beach. **Sattahip Naval Base**, Sattahip - direct line to chamber; tel (038) 437171, Operator tel; (038) 438457 ext. 0684549. **Tourist Police**; tel (038) 429371, Pattaya Police station ; tel (038) 428223, 428967, **Pattaya Sea Rescue**; tel (038) 423752.

LOCAL HIGHLIGHTS

Pattaya is notorious for its nightlife but there are a variety of other entertainments and pastimes, suitable for the entire family, which are often overlooked. There are a number of really good excursions in the area aimed towards the tourist.

Every Wednesday there is an interesting **scheduled tour of the** **eastern seaboard** which visits Buddhist Temples, Thai silk factories, an orchid farm, Ang Sila stone masonry, a cave full of giant bats and a village that still maintains the ancient art of brick carving. **Khao Khiao Open Zoo** in the town of Chonburi and is reputed to be one of the largest open zoos in South East Asia, covering 1,200 acres of forest. At Elephant Village, exhibitions depict the role of elephants in everyday working life, with examples of round-ups, training, riding and feeding.

The Institute of Marine Science, Burapha University is located on the road that leads to Bangsaen Villa Resort Hotel. There are three separate departments: a museum, an aquarium and science laboratories. The main feature is the impressive aquarium which has over forty five indoor display tanks with over one hundred and fifty species.

Pattaya is famed for its **shops** and there are plenty of them. Popular bargains include souvenirs, cheap swim-wear, leather goods, gemstones, inexpensive silk suits, copies of designer western clothes, videos and audio cassettes. On the whole all shops will take credit cards but the majority will employ a surcharge for their use. There is the usual range of high street **banks**, the ones listed all provide a currency exchange service. Bangkok Bank; tel (038) 422801, Krung Thai; tel (038) 429275-6, Siam Commercial; tel (038) 428700, Thai Farmers; tel (038) 422335-6.

Just about every **sports** activity is available in the city with tennis courts, golf courses, game fishing tours, go-kart tracks, horse riding stables, shooting ranges and a bungee jump. Indoor facilities include darts, ten pin bowling alleys, badminton courts, table tennis and snooker tables. There is also a large selection of health clubs and gyms.

All of Pattaya's highlights and facilities are listed, along with several other informative articles, in a number of regular tourist periodicals which can be picked up literally anywhere in the city. The noticeable ones are *Explore Pattaya and the east coast, What's on Pattaya, Guide to the east* and the *Pattaya pocket guide*. Pattaya also has it's own radio station broadcasting in English on 107.5 FM which announces forthcoming attractions, special events and new services.

Car and Motobike rental
There are many car rental agencies in Pattaya - an International driving license will be required and in some cases the renting agency will require a passport as deposit. Pre-rental vehicle checks should be undertaken as hirers will be charged for any damage that was not present when the vehicle was taken. Two of the better agencies are Pattaya Vehicle Rental Service; tel (038) 425700 and Prapat; tel (038) 429854. Most visitors rent motor bikes, of which there is an enormous selection.

The small fishing port at Samaesan is the favoured take-off point to dive the Hardeep wreck.

KOH CHANG MARINE NATIONAL PARK

Situated in the country's easternmost province, Trat, Koh Chang Marine National Park comprises 52 islands scattered along the coastline close to the Kampuchean border. Established in 1982, it is one of the least visited of Thailand's National Parks, and covers just over 650 sq km (250 sq miles).

Koh Chang is the second largest island in Thailand, covering some 240 sq km (93 sq miles). Tourism is only just beginning, with the majority of the small-scale resorts – most fairly basic wooden or bamboo huts. Blanketed in almost impenetrable virgin rainforest, the hilly interior rises to a peak at Khao Jom Prasat (744m; 2440ft) in the centre of the island. Wildlife is sparse, although wild boar are found here, and hornbills, parrots and sunbirds can be seen in the forest. Most of the island's inhabitants make their living from fishing. A single dirt track runs around the island, and transport is limited to motorcycle taxis or mountain bikes.

Alternatively, to explore these sites you can stay on some of the other islands nearby; Koh Mak, for instance, has a small resort on a good beach on its northwest coast. Camping is permitted on any island within the Park.

Several endemic strains of malaria exist in the area, so precautions should be taken.

DIVING AROUND KOH CHANG

While it could never be classified as one of Thailand's prime diving areas, Koh Chang Marine National Park does have some healthy fringing reefs, an interesting wreck, and several snorkelling sites. In general, visibility is low (averaging 5–10m; 16–33ft). Freshwater runoff from the mainland, swirling currents carrying silt as well as tailings from the extensive gem-mining operations on the Trat coastline all limit visibility. Marine life is far less prolific than elsewhere, and dynamite fishing has taken its toll on the reefs.

However, on the plus side there are numerous Giant Clams and plenty of colourful reef-dwellers, and there is always the chance of spotting pelagics. Diving here has an exploratory feel to it. The season here is November to May.

Opposite: *Sunsets like this can be enjoyed from White Sand Beach, Koh Chang.*
Above: *The striking Clown triggerfish (Balistoides conspicillum).*

1 KOH CHANG WRECK
★

Location: About 200m (220yd) from the mouth of the river running off the southeastern headland of Koh Chang. Locating the wreck is difficult, but helped by a large round scar in the cliff face; this was the result of mortar fire during the first attempt to sink the warship. Operators without an electronic fish-finder start at the mouth of the river and head directly away from the island, trawling behind them a weighted line to snag the wreck.

Access: About 90min by diveboat from the small pier on Khlong Phrao Beach. The wreck is unbuoyed.

Conditions: Heavy silting and mud severely restrict the visibility around and above the wreck to 1m (40in). Currents are generally moderate to strong.

Average depth: 13m (43ft)

Maximum depth: 15m (50ft)

The wreck is an old Thai warship, the Thonburi, which was sunk during the conflict between Thailand and France in 1941. It now sits in one piece on its side; the dislodged figurehead has never been recovered, remaining somewhere in the muddy bottom. The wreck now acts as an artificial reef

2 HIN LUK BAT
★★

Location: A rocky outcrop, 5m (16ft) in diameter and projecting 1m (40in) above the water, about 3km (1.6 n. miles) southwest of Koh Chang.

Access: Just over 1hr by diveboat from the small pier on Khlong Phrao Beach. There is no mooring buoy. Boats drop off divers about 30m (33yd) from the rock's leeward side. The boats then anchor away from the rock to await the divers' return.

Conditions: Visibility is poor, generally below 10m (33ft) and with 4m (13ft) being the average. Current runs weak to moderate.

Average depth: 11m (36ft)

Maximum depth: 18m (60ft)

The dive is around an elevated plateau that reaches to 10m (33ft) below the surface. The plankton-enriched waters afford a good diversity of marine life. The steeply sloping walls feature numerous barrel sponges and shelves of relatively healthy soft corals down to the sandy bottom. Fusiliers, barracuda and many other pelagics frequently visit. In the deeper waters are Crown-of-Thorns Starfish, bushy black corals, sea whips and small gorgonian seafans.

Above: *The Mantis shrimp (Odontodactylus scyllarus) has powerful claws for crushing molluscs.*
Below: *A healthy head of mixed stony coral with lettuce coral predominating.*

3 HIN RAP

★★☆

Location: This site is marked by a row of several small outcrops about 30m (100ft) from end to end. The site is 5km (2.6 n. miles) south of Koh Chang.

Access: About 2hr by diveboat from the small pier on Khlong Phrao Beach. There is no mooring buoy. Access is by 'live-boat' dive.

Conditions: Often good visibility, between 10m and 15m (33–50ft). Beware of strong currents, which can sweep divers away from the small site.

Average depth: 10m (33ft)

Maximum depth: 18m (60ft)

The reef fringes the outcrops. There are many staghorns, barrel sponges and soft corals in the shallow waters, which can provide reasonable snorkelling when conditions are calm. There are also small submerged rocks around the pinnacles' perimeter. Most of the reef-fish are small compared with those at other local sites. All the site's best features are above 12m (40ft); below this the terrain is fairly barren and shows evidence of dynamite damage, the main survivors of which are mounds of brain coral and sea whips. Dynamite fishing here is happily a thing of the past, and the corals are slowly begining to flourish once more.

4 KOH WAI

★★☆

Location: Immediately east of Koh Khlum. The reef follows along the island's northwestern bay.

Access: Just over 2hr by diveboat from the small pier on Khlong Phrao Beach. There is no mooring buoy.

Conditions: Visibility is about 10m (33ft). The long parabolic bay generally experiences mild conditions with gentle currents, but you should be aware that strong currents can occur and can carry divers away from the island. In such conditions the site should be attempted only by experienced divers, and even they must stay fairly close to the reef.

Average depth: 9m (30ft)

Maximum depth: 20m (66ft)

This is a nice shallow fringing reef, consisting of mainly hard corals; there are soft corals along the deeper part of the reef-slope, but the best features are all at depths shallower than 12m (40ft). The only real attraction of the deeper waters is that you might be lucky enough to spot a Leopard Shark or a ray on the sandy bottom. The shallower parts of the reef are characterized by a good range of reef-fish, in plentiful numbers, and invertebrates. Being reasonably sheltered, this is a fine site for a night-dive.

5 KOH GRA

★★☆

Location: Koh Gra is the series of islands running east–west about 1km (1/2 n. mile) off the northeast shore of Koh Rang Yai and the same distance due east of Koh Mapring.

Access: 2 1/2hr by diveboat from the small pier on Khlong Phrao Beach. Boats can access the site from any direction. There is no mooring buoy; divers generally surface swim from the diveboat, which anchors away from the rocks.

Conditions: Visibility averages 7m (23ft). Currents can be strong. In calm conditions with good visibility this site is more suitable for snorkelling.

Average depth: 4m (13ft)

Maximum depth: 6m (20ft)

Although snorkelling is the major appeal here, there is no reason why the site should not be dived as well. The reef is gently sloping and is made up of hard corals, with gardens of staghorns running from 3m (10ft) down to 6m (20ft). Many colourful little reef-fish are in evidence, as are bivalves and invertebrates; you can see Plume Worms on the many small mounds of lesser star corals. Further down, on the sandy bottom, you should be able to spot a ray or two idling.

6 KOH RANG PINNACLES

★★★☆

Location: Around the Pinnacle, which is at the island's northwest and rises to form a sharp point, 1m (40in) clear of the surface in low water. There are several smaller pinnacles to its immediate north.

Access: About 2hr by diveboat from the small pier on Khlong Phrao Beach. There is no mooring buoy.

Conditions: Visibility ranges from 5m to an impressive 30m (16–100ft). Currents are weak to moderate. There is generally quite a severe thermocline at around 15m (50ft).

Average depth: 12m (40ft)

Maximum depth: 30m (100ft)

This is a great multi-level site. Of the two main pinnacles, one is at 12m (40ft) and the other at 5m (16ft); the seabed between them is at 21m (70ft). There is a good shelf of coral on the deeper pinnacle, at about 15m (50ft).

The western side of the site consists of coral dropoffs. Parrotfish are plentiful and reef sharks are frequently spotted. Smaller stingrays are on view at about 12m (40ft). Pelagics often intrude into the surrounding waters; most are barracuda, but there are also large Cobias (Kingfish).

Above: *A stunning reef scene of mixed corals and sponges.*
Below: *Numerous Zig zag oysters (Pycnodonta hyotis) cling to a small wall at Koh Man Wachai.*

HOW TO GET THERE

A three stage journey is required to reach Koh Chang:

By bus: Air-conditioned, daily buses from Bangkok leave every hour on the hour between 07.00hrs and midnight from Bangkok's eastern bus terminal in Sukhumvit Road at the junction of Soi Ekamai (Soi 63). The journey to Trat Town takes around five hours. On arrival in Trat Town passengers transfer to the pier at Laem Ngop. For further information regarding buses ring Bangkok eastern bus terminal; tel (02) 391 2504.

By mini-bus: to Laem Ngop pier. This second section of the journey is by mini bus and takes 30 minutes.

By ferry: The next stage is a fifty minute ferry crossing to the island. There are two ferries daily at 12.00hrs and 15.00hrs. Boats land at Ban Dan Mai and Tha Than Mayom on the island.

By boat: It is also possible to access Koh Mak directly from the Laem Ngop pier. This is via a private boat run by Koh Mak Resort and needs to be booked in advance. For further information regarding boats to Koh Mak contact Koh Mak Resort; tel 01 327 0220. Once on the island transport is either by Longtail boat or motorbike taxis.

For any additional information on Koh Chang or Koh Mak contact **Tourism Authority of Thailand**; tel (038) 427 667/fax (038) 429 113.

WHERE TO STAY

Trat Town

Amenities for tourists in Trat Town remain fairly basic, but there is a range of hotels to choose from - such as the two listed below - serving as either stopping off points en route to the islands or as a base whilst visiting the local attractions:

Muang Trat Hotel, Trat Town; tel (039) 511091. This is the largest hotel with a total of 140 fan-cooled and air-conditioned rooms. **Muang Trat Ok**, Trat Town; tel (039) 512657. A total of 60 fan-cooled and air-conditioned rooms which, along with its own restaurant, provide a cheaper alternative than the above.

Koh Chang

Accommodation is scattered along the coast with resorts ranging from the very basic to the luxurious. It is possible to pitch tents on the island with permission from the Royal Forestry Department. Contact National Parks Division of the Royal Forestry Department, Bangkok; tel (02) 579 0529/579 4842.

Khlong Phrao Beach

Koh Chang Resort; tel (039) 597028. This 3km white sandy beach is located halfway down the western coast.

Kai Bae Beach

Seaview Resort; tel (039) 597143. This resort comprises bungalows, a small hotel and a restaurant.

Ao Sapparot

Magic Bungalows; tel 01 329 0408. There are around 20 fan-cooled bungalows in the bay. There is a good restaurant, and an associated dive operation.

On Koh Mak

Koh Mak Resort and Cabana; tel 01 327 0220. Fan-cooled bungalows spread out in a landscaped garden area. There is a good restaurant.

WHERE TO EAT

There are a number of independent restaurants in Trat Town, most of which serve Thai food. The resorts listed have their own eating facilities. Most feature menus with a good choice of local seafood dishes and a small European menu selection.

DIVE FACILITIES

There is one operator on Koh Chang. Occasionally trips are chartered from Pattaya City, but there is no regular scheduled service; trips are arranged on demand.

Dive Courses

PADI courses are available in English and German. Full equipment, and certification is included in all the courses. Courses available are Non-certification Discover Scuba experience programme, PADI Open Water Dive Course, PADI Advanced Open Water Diver Course, PADI Rescue Diver and PADI Speciality Courses.

Dive operators

Koh Chang Divers, PO Box 48, Trat, 23000 Thailand. Located on White Sand beach in Had Sai Khao Bungalow Resort. Dive trips to all the local sites. Full range of PADI courses on offer.

Aquanauts, see Pattaya for details, page 149.

FILM PROCESSING

The nearest convenient services are in Pattaya, see page 149.

HOSPITALS AND RECOMPRESSION CHAMBERS

There are no hospitals on either of the islands. The nearest is in Trat. **Trat Hospital**, 3 Sukjumvit Road, Trat Town; tel (039) 520214. The nearest **recompression chamber** is over 160km (100 miles) away, at the Naval Base in the northern coastal town of Sattahip. Patients are evacuated from the islands by boat, and then transfered via road. The total journey can take around four hours. **Sattahip Naval Base**, Sattahip; Direct line to chamber tel (038) 437171, Operator tel (038) 438457 ext 0684549; Mobile tel (01) 922 5889.

LOCAL HIGHLIGHTS

On the Mainland

Wat Buppharam is located 2km west of the town at the end of the canal. Built in 1652 it dates back to the Ayutthaya period. This temple is noted for relics of the Buddha, and its large wooden praying hall and bell tower. **Wat Muang Kao Saan Tum** has a number of large brown stones which, when tapped, resonate in varying tones. This temple is located around 35 kms (22 miles) north west of Khao Saming Town, which along with Bo Rai has been developed as a centre for the region's famed gem mining industry. The latter was where the World famous 'Tap Tim Siam' or King Ruby was excavated, and there is an interesting early morning gem market here.

On Koh Chang

The island is particularly noted for its beautiful long white sandy beaches, most of which are along the west coast. These are relatively deserted, and strolling along the shore can make you feel as though you are the only person on the island.

There are a number of delightful waterfalls on the island, in particular **Than Mayom** waterfall located 1km (0.5 miles) from the boat pier and National Park Office. There is a footpath which follows the falls. **Klong Plu** waterfall is located 3km (2 miles) from Ao Klong Prao.

The two most popular and picturesque beaches on the island are **White Sand** beach and **Sai Khao** beach. The latter, on the northwest coast, is the longest beach on the island and is bordered by coconut groves and forest. Heading south is the steep Klong Phrao beach. It is possible to swim here but care must be taken regarding undertows during the rougher sea conditions.

Another popular seaside destination is **Ao Sapparot** or Pineapple Bay on the northeast coast. Daily Excursions are available in the town from the majority of the hotels. On the island excursions are arranged throught the resorts. Daily excursions are fairly limited, on land they involve the temples and gem markets whilst on the island they are to the waterfalls and island-hopping snorkelling and swimming trips.

Please note, the southern island of Koh Rang has a birds nest concession; landing on any of the Rang islands should never be attempted.

Trat Town has the range of high street banks; there are no banks as such on the island but foreign currency can be exchanged at the majority of beach resorts.

Car and Motorbike rental
There are no facilities for renting cars on the island, however the island can be explored on motorbikes or mountain bikes available from the larger resorts.

Relaxing and comparing notes after a hard day's diving at Koh Chang Beach Resort.

The Marine Environment

SOUTHEAST ASIAN REEFS AND REEF LIFE

Most of the reefs around Southeast Asia are – at least in geological terms – quite young. Towards the end of the last ice age, sea levels were as much as 100m (330ft) lower than they are today, and much of the area between the large islands of Borneo, Sumatra and Java was dry land. Since then the sea has reasserted itself, so that now this area is flooded with warm, shallow water dotted with islands and reefs.

THE NATURE OF CORALS AND REEFS

Tropical reefs are built mainly from corals, primitive animals closely related to sea anemones. Most of the coral types that contribute to reef construction are colonial; that is, numerous individuals – polyps – come together to create what is essentially a single compound organism. The polyps produce calcareous skeletons; when thousands of millions of them are present in a single colony they form large, stony (in fact, limestone) structures which build up as reefs.

What happens is that, when corals die, some of the skeleton remains intact, thus adding to the reef. Cracks and holes then fill with sand and the calcareous remains of other reef plants and animals, and gradually the whole becomes consolidated, with new corals growing on the surface of the mass. Thus only the outermost layer of the growing reef is alive.

There are about 450 species of reef-building coral in the seas around Southeast Asia. Corals grow slowly, adding about 1–10cm (0.4–4in) growth in a year. Once over a certain age they start being able to reproduce, releasing tiny forms that float freely among the plankton for a few weeks until settling to continue the growth of the reef. The forms corals create as they grow vary enormously according to the species and to the place on the reef where it is growing.

Colonies range in size from a few centimetres in diameter to giants several metres across and many hundreds of years old. Some are branched or bushy, others tree-like, others in the form of plates, tables or delicate leafy fronds, and yet others are encrusting, lobed, rounded or massive.

Microscopic plants called zooxanthellae are of great importance to the growth and health of corals. These are packed in their millions into the living tissues of most reef-building corals (and of various other reef animals, such as Giant Clams). Although reef corals capture planktonic organisms from the water, a significant amount of their food comes directly from the zooxanthellae. It is for this reason that the most prolific coral growths are in the shallow, well lit waters that the zooxanthellae prefer.

The presence of coral communities does not, in fact, necessarily lead to the development of thick deposits of reef limestone; for example, the Krakatoa Islands off the southern tip of Sumatra consist mainly of slabs of volcanic rock with a patchy veneer of corals.

Types of Reef

In most regions with plentiful coral communities, the calcareous skeletons have built up to form a variety of different types of reef:

- fringing reefs
- patch reefs, banks and shoals
- barrier reefs
- atolls

Fringing Reefs

Fringing reefs occur in shallow water near to land. Typically they extend to depths of 15m–45m (50–150ft), depending on factors such as the profile and depth of the seabed and the clarity of the water. Islands that stand in deep water, like Pulau Sipadan, have precipitous fringing reefs that descend hundreds of metres, but these are exceptions rather than the rule.

Many mainland coastlines in Southeast Asia are too close to river estuaries for reefs to develop, and instead support stands of mangroves – another marine ecosystem of enormous importance in the region. But the offshore islands, away from the influence of freshwater runoff, are often surrounded by reefs. In Malaysia and Thailand a large proportion of reefs are of this type.

Patch Reefs, Banks and Shoals

In theory, reefs can develop anywhere that the underlying rock has at some time been close enough to the surface for corals to become established and grow. Sea levels may have risen considerably since then, or other geological changes may have occurred to lower the depth of the bed beneath the surface; either way, there are many places where reefs exist as isolated mounds or hillocks on the seabed. Such patch reefs are widespread throughout the Southeast Asian region in relatively shallow waters surrounding the islands and on the continental shelves. They vary in size from tens to thousands of metres in diameter, usually with their tops coming to within a few metres of the surface – indeed, some emerge above the surface and are topped by sand cays. Patch reefs further offshore, lying in waters hundreds of metres deep and with even their tops 20m (66ft) or more below the surface, are usually referred to as banks or shoals. Some of the most extensive lie in the South China Sea.

Opposite: *At open water sites like this one, divers can enjoy the marine characteristics of the reef.*

Barrier Reefs

Barrier reefs occur along the edges of island or continental shelves, and are substantial structures. The major difference, apart from size, between them and fringing reefs is that they are separated from the shore by a wide, deep lagoon. The outer edge of the barrier drops away steeply to the ocean floor beyond. Initially these reefs formed in shallow waters; then, as sea levels increased, they built progressively upwards so that their living topmost parts were still near the surface of the water.

There are a few barrier reefs in the Philippines and Indonesia, but the best-developed are to be found around Papua New Guinea – for example, the 180km (110-mile) barrier running along the outside of the Louisiade Archipelago off the southern tip of the mainland.

Atolls

These are formations of ancient origin – millions of years ago – and take the form of ring-shaped reefs enclosing a shallow lagoon and dropping away to deep water on their outsides. Atolls begun life as fringing reefs around volcanic islands and kept growing as the underlying base gradually subsided beneath the water level.

Most of the world's atolls are in the Indian and Pacific oceans, but there are a number to explore in Southeast Asian waters, particularly around Papua New Guinea and the eastern provinces of Indonesia; what is reputedly the third largest atoll in the world, Taka Bone Rate atoll, is off the southern coastline of Sulawesi.

REEF LIFE

The reef ecologies of Southeast Asia – and those off northern Australia – harbour a greater range of species than anywhere else in the Indo-Pacific: they are packed with all manner of bizarre and beautiful plants and exotic animals.

It is likely the region became established as a centre of evolutionary diversification millions of years ago; it has remained so, despite changes in sea levels and in the fortunes of individual reefs, right up until the present day.

On most reefs your attention is likely to be held initially by the fish life: in a single dive's casual observation you might see well over 50 different species, while a more concentrated effort would reveal hundreds. Even that is only part of the story.

The reefs and associated marine habitats of most Southeast Asian countries support well over 1000 species, but many are hidden from view within the complex framework of the reef – gobies, for example, usually in fact the most numerous of all the fish species on a reef, are seldom noticed.

Reef Zones and Habitats

Reefs can be divided into a number of zones reflecting differences in such features as depth, profile, distance from the shore, amount of wave action, and type of seabed. Associated with each zone are characteristic types of marine life.

The Back Reef and Lagoon

The back reef and lagoon fill the area between the shore and the seaward reef. Here the seabed is usually a mixture of sand, coral rubble, limestone slabs and living coral colonies. The water depth varies from a few metres to 50m (165ft) or more, and the size of the lagoon can be anywhere from a few hundred to thousands of square metres. The largest and deepest lagoons are those associated with barrier reefs and atolls, and may be dotted with islands and smaller reefs.

Sites within lagoons are obviously more sheltered than those on the seaward reef, and are also more affected by sedimentation. Here you will find many attractive seaweeds; most of the corals are delicate, branching types. Large sand-dwelling anemones are often found, and in places soft corals and 'false corals' are likely to form mats over the seabed. Especially where there is a current you may encounter extensive beds of seagrasses, the only flowering plants to occur in the sea. Among the many species of animals that make these pastures their home are the longest Sea Cucumbers you will find anywhere around the reef.

Although some typical reef fishes are absent from this environment, there is no shortage of interesting species. On the one hand there are roving predators – snappers, wrasse, triggerfish, emperors and others – on the lookout for worms, crustaceans, gastropods, sea urchins and small fish. Then there are the bottom-dwelling fishes that burrow into the sand until completely hidden, emerging only when they need to feed.

Most entertaining to watch – if you spot them – are the small gobies that live in association with Pistol Shrimps. In this partnership the shrimp is the digger and the goby, stationed at the entrance to the burrow, is the sentry. The small fish remains ever on the alert, ready to retreat hurriedly into the burrow at the first sign of disturbance. The shrimp has very poor eyesight; it keeps its antennae in close touch with the goby so that it can pick up the danger signal and, likewise, retire swiftly to the safety of the burrow.

The Reef Flat

Reef flats are formed as their associated reefs push steadily seaward, leaving behind limestone areas that are eroded and planed almost flat by the action of the sea. The reef flat is essentially an intertidal area, but at high tide it can provide interesting snorkelling.

The inner part of the reef flat is the area most sheltered from the waves, and here you may find beautiful pools full of corals and small fish. Among the common sights are 'micro-atolls' of the coral genus Porites; their distinctive doughnut (toroidal) shape, with a ring of coral surrounding a small, sandy-bottomed pool, occurs as a result of low water level and hot sun inhibiting the upward growth of the coral. In deeper water, as on the reef rim, the same coral forms huge rounded colonies.

Towards the outer edge of the reef flat, where wave action is much more significant, surfaces are often encrusted with calcareous red algae, and elsewhere you will usually find a fine mat of filamentous algae that serves as grazing pasture for fish, sea urchins, gastropods, molluscs and other animals. Some fish are permanent inhabitants of the reef-flat area, retreating to pools if necessary at low tide; but others, like parrotfish and surgeonfish, spend a great deal of their time in deeper water, crowding over onto the reef flat with the rising tide.

The Seaward Reef Front

Most divers ignore the shoreward zones of the reef and head straight for sites on the reef front, on the basis that here they are most likely to see spectacular features and impressive displays of marine life. Brightly lit, clean, plankton-rich water provides ideal growing conditions for corals, and the colonies they form help create habitats of considerable complexity. There is infinite variety, from shallow gardens of delicate branching corals to walls festooned with soft corals and sea fans.

The top 20m (66ft) or so of the seaward reef is especially full of life. Here small, brilliantly coloured damselfish and anthias swarm around the coral, darting into open water to feed on plankton. Butterflyfish show their dazzling arrays of spots, stripes and intricate patterns as they probe into crevices or pick at coral polyps – many have elongated snouts especially adapted for this delicate task. By contrast, you can see parrotfish biting and scraping at the coral, over time leaving characteristic white scars.

Open-water species like fusiliers, snappers and sharks cover quite large areas when feeding, and wrasse often forage far and wide over the reef. But many species are more localized and can be highly territorial, on occasion even being prepared to take on a trespassing diver. Clownfishes (*Amphiprion spp*) and *Premnas biaculeatus* are among the boldest, dashing out from the safety of anemone tentacles to give chase.

Fish-watching can give you endless pleasure, but there is much else to see. Any bare spaces created on the reef are soon colonized, and in some places the surface is covered with large organisms that may be tens or even hundreds of years old. These sedentary reef-dwellers primarily rely on, aside from the omnipresent algae, water-borne food. Corals and their close relatives – anemones, sea fans and black corals – capture planktonic organisms using their tiny stinging cells. Sea squirts and sponges strain the plankton as seawater passes through special canals in their body-walls. Other organisms have rather different techniques: the Christmas-tree Worm, for example, filters out food with the aid of its beautiful feathery 'crown' of tentacles.

Apart from the fishes and the sedentary organisms there is a huge array of other lifeforms for you to observe on the reef. Tiny crabs live among the coral branches and larger ones wedge themselves into appropriate nooks and crannies, often emerging to feed at night. Spiny lobsters hide in caverns, coming out to hunt under cover of darkness. Gastropod molluscs are another type of marine creature seldom seen during the day, but they are in fact present in very large numbers, especially on the shallower parts of the reef; many of them are small, but on occasion you might come across one of the larger species, like the Giant Triton (*Charonia tritonis*).

Some of the most easily spotted of the mobile invertebrates are the echinoderms, well represented on Southeast Asian reefs. Most primitive of these are the feather stars, sporting long delicate arms in all colours from bright yellow to green, red and black. The best-known of their relatives, the sea urchins, is the black, spiny variety that lives in shallow reef areas and is a potential hazard to anyone walking onto the reef.

Many of the small, brightly coloured starfish that wander over the reef face feed on the surface film of detritus and micro-organisms. Others are carnivorous, browsing on sponges and sea mats, and a few feed on living coral polyps. The damage they cause depends on their size, their appetite and, collectively, their population density. Potentially the most damaging of all is the large predator *Acanthaster planci*, the Crown-of-Thorns Starfish; fortunately populations of this creature have so far reached plague proportions on relatively few of the Southeast Asian reefs, and so extensive damage caused by it is not yet commonplace.

Whether brilliantly attractive or frankly plain, whether swiftly darting or sessile, all the life forms you find on the reef are part of the reef's finely balanced ecosystem. You are not: you are an intruder, albeit a friendly one. It is your obligation to cause as little disturbance and destruction among these creatures as possible.

MARINE CONSERVATION

Reefs in the Southeast Asian region are among the most biologically diverse in the world; they are also valuable to the local people as fishing grounds and as sources of other important natural products including shells. Unfortunately, in the past few decades they have come under increasing pressure from human activities, and as a result they are, in places, showing signs of wear and tear.

Corals are slow-growing: if damaged or removed they may require years to recover or be replaced. In the natural course of events, storm-driven waves from time to time create havoc on coral reefs, especially in the typhoon belt. But some human activities are similarly destructive, especially blast fishing and the indiscriminate collection of corals to sell as marine curios.

Overfishing is a further deadly hazard to reef environments, and has already led to perilously declining populations of target species in some areas. Another way overfishing can cause grave damage is through altering the balance of local ecosystems; for example, decreasing the populations of herbivorous fish can lead to an explosive increase in the algae on which those species feed, so the corals of the reef may be overgrown and suffer.

Some areas are being damaged by pollution, especially where reefs occur close to large centres of human population. Corals and other reef creatures are sensitive to dirty, sediment-laden water, and are at risk of being smothered when silt settles on the bottom. Sewage, nutrients from agricultural fertilizers and other organic materials washed into the sea encourage the growth of algae, sometimes to the extent that – again – corals become overgrown.

One final point affects us divers directly. Although, like other visitors to the reef, we wish simply to enjoy ourselves, and although most of us are conscious of conservation issues and take steps to reduce any deleterious effects of our presence, tourism and development in general have created many problems for the reefs. Harbours, jetties and sea walls are on occasion built so close to reefs – sometimes even on top of them! – that the environment is drastically altered and populations of reef organisms plummet. Visiting boats often damage the corals through inadvertent grounding or careless or insouciant anchoring. And divers themselves, once they get in the water, may, unintentionally cause damage as they move about on the reef.

Growing awareness of environmental issues has given rise to 'ecotourism'. The main underlying principle is often summarized as 'take nothing but photographs, leave nothing but footprints', but even footprints – indeed, any form of touching – can be a problem in fragile environments, particularly among corals. A better way to think of ecotourism is in terms of managing tourism and the tourists themselves in such a way as to make the industry ecologically sustainable. The necessary capital investment is minimal, and thereafter much-needed employment becomes available for the local population. In the long term the profits would exceed those from logging or overfishing.

Although divers, as well as many dive operators and resorts, have been at the forefront in protecting reefs and marine ecosystems, we all need somewhere to eat and sleep. If a small resort is built without a waste-treatment system, the nearby reefs may not be irreparably damaged; but if those same reefs start to attract increasing numbers of divers and spawn further resorts, strict controls become necessary.

In such discussions of ecotourism we are looking at the larger scale. It is too easy to forget that 'tourists' and 'divers' are not amorphous groups but collections of individuals, with individual responsibilities and capable of making individual decisions. Keeping reefs ecologically sustainable depends as much on each of us as it does on the dive and resort operators. Here are just some of the ways in which you, as a diver, can help preserve the reefs that have given you so much:

- Try not to touch living marine organisms with either your body or your diving equipment. Be particularly careful to control your fins, since their size and the force of kicking can damage large areas of coral. Don't use deep fin-strokes next to the reef, since the surge of water can disturb delicate organisms.
- Learn the skills of good buoyancy control – too much damage is caused by divers descending too rapidly or crashing into corals while trying to adjust their buoyancy. Make sure you are properly weighted and learn to achieve neutral buoyancy. If you haven't dived for a while, practise your skills somewhere you won't cause any damage.
- Avoid kicking up sand. Clouds of sand settling on the reef can smother corals. Snorkellers should be careful not to kick up sand when treading water in shallow reef areas.
- Never stand on corals, however robust they may seem. Living polyps are easily damaged by the slightest touch. Never pose for pictures or stand inside giant basket or barrel sponges.
- If you are out of control and about to collide with the reef, steady yourself with your fingertips on a part of the reef that is already dead or covered in algae. If you need to adjust your diving equipment or mask, try to do so in a sandy area well away from the reef.
- Don't collect or buy shells, corals, starfish or any other marine souvenirs.
- On any excursion, whether with an operator or privately organized, make sure you take your garbage back for proper disposal on land.
- Take great care in underwater caverns and caves. Avoid lots of people crowding into the cave, and don't stay too long: your air bubbles collect in pockets on the roof of the cave, and delicate creatures living there can 'drown in air'.
- If booking a live-aboard dive trip, ask about the company's environmental policy – particularly on the discharge of sewage and anchoring. Avoid boats that cause unnecessary anchor damage, have bad oil leaks, or discharge untreated sewage near reefs.
- Don't participate in spearfishing for sport – it is anyway now banned in many countries. If you are living on a boat and relying on spearfishing for food, make sure you are familiar with all local fish and game regulations and obtain any necessary licensing.
- Don't feed fish. It may seem harmless but it can upset their normal feeding patterns and provoke aggressive behaviour – and be unhealthy for them if you give them food that is not part of their normal diet.
- Don't move marine organisms around to photograph or play with them. In particular, don't hitch rides on turtles: it causes them considerable stress.

COMMON FISH

Angelfish (family Pomacanthidae)
These beautiful fish, with their minute, brushlike teeth, browse on sponges, algae and corals. Their vibrant colouring varies according to the species, like those of the butterflyfish (q.v.) and were once thought part of the same family. However, they are distinguishable by a short spike extending from the gill cover. Angelfish are territorial in habit and tend to occupy the same caves or ledges for a period of time.

Three spot angelfish (*Apolemichthys trimaculatus*). Up to 26cm.

Butterflyfish (family Chaetodontidae)
Among the most colourful of reef inhabitants, butterfly-fish have flat, thin bodies, usually with a stripe through the eye and sometimes with a dark blotch near the tail: this serves as camouflage and confuses predators, who lunge for the wrong end of the fish. Butterflyfish can also swim backwards to escape danger. Many species live as mated pairs and have territories while others school in large numbers.

Head-band butterflyfish (*Chaetodon collare*). Up to 14cm.

Damselfish and Clownfish (family Pomacentridae)
These pugnacious little fish often farm their own patch of algae, aggressively driving away other herbivores. Found almost everywhere on the reef, they also sometimes form large aggregations to feed on plankton. Clownfishes (Amphiprion spp) and *Premnas Biaculeatus*, which live among the stinging tentacles of sea anemones, are also members of this family.Of the 27 clownfish species known from the Indo-Pacific, 15 are found on the reefs of Southeast Asia.

Red saddle-back anemonefish (*Amphiprion ephippium*).
Up to 12cm.

Grouper (family Serranidae)
Groupers range from just a few centimetres long to the massive Giant Grouper, 3.5m (12ft) long. They vary enormously in colour; grey with darker spots is the most common. Movement is slow except when attacking prey with remarkable speed. All groupers are carnivorous, feeding on invertebrates and other fish. Like wrasse and parrotfish, some start out as females and become males later while others are hermaphroditic.

Coral grouper (*Cephalopholis miniata*). Up to 40cm.

Goby (family Gobiidae)
The Goby is a 'bottom dweller' with the ability to remain stationary and undetected on the sea bed for long periods of time. They have large protrud-ing eyes which are raised above the level of the head and powerful jaws which enable them to snatch prey and dart back to safety. Gobies are among the most successful reef families, with liter-ally hundreds of species. In fact new species of these small, secretive fish are being discovered all the time.

Purple flame goby (*Nemateleotris decora*). Up to 75cm.

Moray Eel (family Muraenidae)
This ancient species of fish have gained their undeserved reputation for ferocity largely because, as they breathe, they open and close the mouth to reveal their numerous sharp teeth. They do not have fins or scales. Moray Eels anchor the rear portion of their bodies in a selected coral crevice and stay hidden during the day. They emerge at night to feed on shrimp, octopuses and mussels.

Honeycomb moray (*Gymnothorax favagineus*). Up to 2m.

Moorish Idol (family Zanclidae)
This graceful and flamboyant fish reaches a maximum size of 20cm. It is easily distinguished by its long dorsal fin, thick protuding lips and pointed snout. It probes for food (mostly algae and invertebrates) in nooks and crannies. Moorish Idols are usually seen individually, but may sometimes form large aggregations prior to spawning. Moorish Idols are related to surgeonfish even though their body shape is different.

Moorish idols (*Zanclus canescens*). Up to 20cm.

Parrotfish (family Scaridae)
So-called because of their sharp, parrot-like beaks and bright colours, the parrotfishes are among the most important herbivores on the reef. Many change colour and sex as they grow, the terminal-phase males developing striking coloration by comparison with the drabness of the initial-phase males and females. Many build transparent cocoons of mucus to sleep in at night, the mucus acting as a scent barrier against predators.

Ember parrotfish (*Scarus rubroviolaceus*). Up to 55cm.

Pufferfish (family Tetraodontidae)
These small to medium-size omnivores feed on algae, worms, molluscs and crustaceans. Pufferfish are found all the way down the reef to depths of around 30m (100ft). They are slow moving but when threatened, they inflate themselves into big, round balls by sucking water into the abdomen, so that it becomes almost an impossible task for predators to swallow them.

Masked pufferfish (*Arothron nigigripunctatus*). Up to 30cm.

Triggerfish (family Balistidae)
Medium to large fish with flattened bodies and often striking markings (e.g., the Picasso Triggerfish [*Rhinecanthus aculeatus*]), these have powerful teeth and feed on crustaceans and echinoderms on the mid-reef. When a triggerfish is threatened it squeezes itself into a crevice and erects its first dorsal spine, locking it into place with a second, smaller spine: this stays wedged until the 'trigger' is released.

Clown triggerfish (*Balistoides conspicillum*). Up to 35cm.

UNDERWATER PHOTOGRAPHY

Photography has become one of the most popular underwater pastimes. Being able to capture on film some of the amazing creatures we see underwater is highly rewarding, but can also prove incredibly frustrating, as the real difficulties of underwater photography – backscatter, fish that refuse to stay still, flooded camera housings and so on – become apparent. You need a lot of perseverance – and luck – to get really good results, but if you're prepared to persist you'll find you've developed a passion that will last for a lifetime of diving.

Shallow-Water Cameras

There are several cameras on the market that are suitable for snorkelling. Kodak and Fuji both offer cheap, single-use cameras that are waterproof down to about 2m (6$^{1}/_{2}$ft) and work well enough in clear, sunlit waters. If you object to disposables, Minolta and Canon make slightly more expensive cameras that can be used down to depths of about 5m (16ft).

Submersible Cameras and Housings

You have essentially two main options for serious underwater photography. The first is to lash out on a purpose-built waterproof camera; the second is to buy a waterproof housing for your normal SLR land camera. Each system has its pros and cons.

The submersible camera used by most professionals is the Nikonos, a 35mm non-reflex camera with TTL (through-the-lens) automatic exposure system and dedicated flashguns. (A popular alternative is the Sea & Sea Motor Marine II.) The specially designed Nikonos lenses give sharper results underwater than any housed lenses, but the lack of reflex focusing makes it difficult to compose pictures, and you can easily cut off part of a subject. They range from 15mm to 80mm in focal length, but must be changed in air. Underwater, the 35mm lens is of much use only with extension tubes or close-up outfits, though it can be used in air. The 28mm lens should be considered the standard.

Other companies supply accessories for the Nikonos: lenses, lens converters, extension tubes and housings to accommodate fish-eye and superwide land-camera lenses. Lens converters are convenient: they can be changed underwater. The Motor Marine II makes good use of these, with converters for wide-angle and macro. The Nikonos close-up kit can also be changed underwater.

Nikonos have recently introduced the RS-AF, a fully waterproof reflex camera with autofocus and dedicated lenses and flashgun, but it is extremely heavy and expensive. It is a poor buy by comparison with land cameras like Nikon's 801, F90 and F4 in housings; these are more versatile, weigh less, and can be used also on land.

Land cameras can be used underwater in specialist metal or plexiglass housings. Housings without controls, as used for fully automatic cameras, require fast films to obtain reasonable shutter speeds and lens apertures in the low ambient light underwater. Housings are available for all top-grade reflex cameras, but there are advantages and disadvantages to each system:

- Metal housings are strong, reliable, work well at depth and last a long time if properly maintained; they are heavier to carry, but are buoyant in water. Their higher cost is justified if your camera is expensive and deserves the extra protection.

- Plexiglass housings are fragile and need careful handling both in and out of the water; they are available for a wide range of cameras. They are lightweight, which is convenient on land, but in water are often too buoyant, so that you have to attach extra weights to them. Some models compress at depth, so the control rods miss the camera controls … but, if you adjust the rods to work at depths they do not function properly near the surface! However, as most underwater photographs are taken near the surface, in practice this drawback is not usually serious.

E6 PUSH/PULL PROCESSING

If you have been on holiday or on a longer trip, there is always a possibility that, unknown to you, your cameras, flashguns or meters may not have been performing correctly. The exposures may be wrong: while colour negative films allow an exposure latitude of four f-stops (black-and-white films even more), colour transparency films are sensitive to within a quarter of an f-stop. Your problems do not stop there: the processor himself can suffer from power cuts or machinery failures.

In light of these considerations, professional photographers never have all their exposed film processed at the same time. Instead, they have it done in small batches.

This way you can review the results of the film processed so far. If all is not right, the processing of an E6 film can be adjusted by a professional laboratory so that, in effect, the exposure is made faster by up to two f-stops or slower by up to one f-stop. Some changes in colour and contrast result, but they are not significant.

Kodachrome films can likewise be adjusted in the processing, although not to the same extent. This can be done by various laboratories in the USA or, in the UK, by the Kodak Professional Laboratory at Wimbledon.

If you suspect a particular film, have a clip test done. This involves the initial few frames being cut off and processed first so that you can have a look at the results.

'O' Rings

Underwater cameras, housings, flashguns and cables have 'O' ring seals. These and their mating surfaces or grooves must be kept scrupulously clean. 'O' rings should be lightly greased with silicone grease to prevent flooding; too much grease will attract grit and hairs. Silicone spray should not be used, as the cooling can crack the 'O' ring.

Removable 'O' rings should be stored off the unit to stop them becoming flat, and the unit itself should be sealed in a plastic bag to keep out moisture. User-removable 'O' rings on Nikonos cameras and flash-synchronization cables are best replaced every 12 months; non-removable 'O' rings should be serviced every 12–18 months. The 'O' rings on housings usually last the life of the housing.

Lighting

Sunlight can give spectacular effects underwater, especially in silhouette shots. When the sun is at a low angle, or in choppy seas, much of the light fails to penetrate surface. To get the best of it, photograph two hours either side of the sun's highest point. Generally you should have the sun behind you and on your subject.

Water acts as a cyan (blue–green) filter, cutting back red, so photographs taken with colour film have a blue–green cast. Different filters can correct this in either cold or tropical waters, but they reduce the already limited amount of light available. The answer is flash, which will put back the colour and increase apparent sharpness.

Modern flashguns have TTL automatic-exposure systems. Underwater, large flashguns give good wide-angle performance up to 1.5m (5ft). Smaller flashguns have a narrower angle and work up to only 1m (40in); diffusers widen the angle of cover, but you lose at least one f-stop in output. Some land flashguns can be housed for underwater use.

Flashguns used on or near the camera make suspended particles in the water light up like white stars in a black sky (backscatter); the closer these are to the camera, the larger they appear. The solution is to keep the flash as far as possible above and to one side of the camera. Two narrow-angle flashguns, one each side of the camera, often produce a better result than a single wide-angle flashgun. In a multiple-flash set-up the prime flashgun will meter by TTL (if available); any other flashgun connected will give its pre-programmed output, so should be set low to achieve modelling light.

When photographing divers, remember the eyes within the mask must be lit. Flashguns with a colour temperature of 4500K give more accurate skin tones and colour.

Fish scales reflect light in different ways depending on the angle of the fish to the camera. Silver fish reflect more light than coloured fish, and black fish almost none at all, so to make sure you get a good result you should bracket exposures. If using an automatic flashgun, do this by altering the film-speed setting. At distances under

---

1m (40in) most automatic flashguns tend to overexpose, so allow for this. The easiest way to balance flash with available light is to use TTL flash with a camera set on aperture-priority metering. Take a reading of the mid-water background that agrees with your chosen flash-synchronization speed, and set the aperture one number higher to give a deeper blue. Set your flash to TTL and it will correctly light your subject.

Once you have learnt the correct exposures for different situations you can begin experimenting aesthetically with manual exposure.

Film

For b/w photography, fast 400 ISO film is best. For beginners wishing to use colour, negative print film is best as it has plenty of exposure latitude. (Reversal film is better for reproduction, but requires very accurate exposure.) Kodachrome films are ideal for close work but can give mid-water shots a blue–green water background; although this is in fact accurate, people are conditioned to a 'blue' sea. Ektachrome and Fujichrome produce blue water backgrounds; 50–100 ISO films present the best compromise between exposure and grain, and pale yellow filters can be used to cut down the blue.

Subjects

What you photograph depends on your personal interests. Macro photography, with extension tubes and fixed frames, is easiest to get right: the lens-to-subject and flash-to-subject distances are fixed, and the effects of silting in the water are minimized. Expose a test film at a variety of exposures with a fixed set-up; the best result tells you the exposure to use in future for this particular setting and film. Some fish are strongly territorial. Surgeonfish, triggerfish and sharks may make mock attacks; you can get strong pictures if you are brave enough to stand your ground. Manta rays are curious and will keep coming back if you react quietly and do not chase them. Angelfish and Butterflyfish swim off when you first enter their territory, but if you remain quiet they will usually return and allow you to photograph them.

Diver and wreck photography are the most difficult. Even with apparently clear water and wide-angle lenses there will be backscatter, and you need to use flash if you are going to get a diver's mask lit up.

Underwater night photography introduces you to another world. Many creatures appear only at night, and some fish are more approachable because half-asleep. However, focusing quickly in dim light is difficult, and many subjects disappear as soon as they are lit up, so you need to preset the controls.

On the Shoot – Tips

- Underwater photography starts before you enter the water. If you have a clear idea of what you wish to photograph, you are likely to get better results. And, remember, you can't change films or prime lenses underwater.
- Autofocus systems that work on contrast (not infrared) are good underwater but only for high-contrast subjects.
- When you are balancing flash with daylight, cameras with faster flash-synchronization speeds – 1/125sec or 1/250sec – give sharper results with fast-moving fish. The lens aperture will be smaller, so you must be accurate in your focusing.
- Masks keep your eyes distant from the viewfinder. Buy the smallest-volume mask you can wear.
- Cameras fitted with optical action finders or eyepiece magnifiers are useful in housings but not so important with autofocus systems.
- Coloured filters can give surrealistic results, as do starburst filters when photographing divers with shiny equipment, lit torches or flashguns set to slave.
- Entering the water overweight makes it easier to steady yourself. Wearing an adjustable buoyancy lifejacket enables you maintain neutral buoyancy.
- Remember not to touch coral and do not wear fins over sandy bottoms – they stir up the sand.

- Wear a wetsuit for warmth.
- Refraction through your mask and the camera lens makes objects appear one-third closer and larger than in air. Reflex focusing and visual estimates of distances are unaffected but, if you measure a distance, compensate by reducing the resultant figure by one-third when setting the lens focus.
- When there is a flat port (window) in front of the lens, the focal length is increased and the image sharpness decreased due to differential refraction. Most pronounced with wide-angle lenses, this should be compensated using a convex dome port. Dome ports need lenses that can focus on a virtual image at about 30cm (12in), so you may have to fit supplementary +1 or +2 dioptre lenses.

A major problem for travelling photographers and videographers is battery charging. Most mainland towns have stockists for AA or D cell batteries, though they may be old or have been badly stored – if the weight does not preclude this, it is best to carry your own spares. Despite their memory problems, rechargeable nickel–cadmium batteries have advantages in cold weather, recharge flashguns much more quickly and, even if flooded, can usually be used again. Make sure you carry spares and that your chargers are of the appropriate voltage for your destination. Quick chargers are useful so long as the electric current available is strong enough. Most video cameras and many flashguns have dedicated battery packs, so carry at least one spare and keep it charged.

Video

Underwater video photography is easier. Macro subjects require extra lighting but other shots can be taken using available light with, if necessary, electronic improvement afterwards. Backscatter is much less of a problem. You can play the results back on site and, if unhappy, have another try – or, at the very least, use the tape again somewhere else.

Health and Safety for Divers

The information in this section is intended as a guide only, it is no substitute for thorough training or professional medical advice. The information is based on currently accepted health and safety information but it is certainly not meant to be a substitute for a comprehensive manual on the subject. We strongly advise that the reader obtains a recognised manual on diving safety and medicine before embarking on a trip.

- Divers who have suffered any injury or symptom of an injury, no matter how minor, related to diving, should consult a doctor, preferably a specialist in diving medicine, as soon as possible after the symptom or injury occurs.

- No matter how confident you are in formulating your own diagnosis remember that you remain an amateur diver and an amateur doctor.
- If you yourself are the victim of a diving injury do not be shy to reveal your symptoms at the expense of ridicule. Mild symptoms can later develop into a major illness with life threatening consequences. It is better to be honest with yourself and live to dive another day.
- Always err on the conservative side when considering your ailment, if you discover you only have a minor illness both you and the doctor will be relieved.

GENERAL PRINCIPLES OF FIRST AID

The basic principles of first aid are:
- doing no harm
- sustaining life
- preventing deterioration
- promoting recovery

In the event of any illness or injury a simple sequence of patient assessment and management can be followed. The sequence first involves assessment and definition of any life threatening conditions followed by management of the problems found.

The first thing to do is to ensure both the patient's and your own safety by removing yourselves from the threatening environment (the water). Make sure that whatever your actions, they in no way further endanger the patient or yourself.

Then the first things to check are:
- A : for AIRWAY (with care of the neck)
- B : for BREATHING
- C : for CIRCULATION
- D : for DECREASED level of consciousness
- E : for EXPOSURE (the patient must be adequately exposed in order to examine them properly)

- **Airway (with attention to the neck):** - is there a neck injury? Is the mouth and nose free of obstruction? Noisy breathing is a sign of airway obstruction.
- **Breathing:** Look at the chest to see if it is rising and falling. Listen for air movement at the nose and mouth. Feel for the movement of air against your cheek.
- **Circulation:** Feel for a pulse next to the wind pipe (carotid artery)
- **Decreased level of consciousness:** Does the patient respond in any of the following ways:
  - A - Awake, Aware, Spontaneous speech
  - V - Verbal Stimuli, does he answer to 'Wake up!'
  - P - Painful Stimuli, does he respond to a pinch
  - U - Unresponsive
- **Exposure:** Preserve the dignity of the patient as far as possible but remove clothes as necessary to adequately effect your treatment.

Now, send for help
If you think the condition of the patient is serious following your assessment, you need to send or call for help from the emergency services (ambulance, paramedics). Whoever you send for help must come back and tell you that help is on its way.

Recovery Position
If the patient is unconscious but breathing normally there is a risk of vomiting and subsequent choking on their own vomit. It is therefore critical that the patient be turned onto his side in the recovery position. If you suspect a spinal or neck injury, be sure to immobilize the patient in a straight line before you turn him on his side.

Cardiopulmonary Resuscitation (CPR)
Cardiopulmonary Resuscitation is required when the patient is found to have no pulse. It consists of techniques to:
- ventilate the patient's lungs - expired air resuscitation
- pump the patient's heart - external cardiac compression.

Once you have checked the ABC's you need to do the following:

Airway
Open the airway by gently extending the head (head tilt) and lifting the chin with two fingers (chin lift). This will life the tongue away from the back of the throat and open the airway. If you suspect a foreign body in the airway sweep your finger across the back of the tongue from one side to the other. If one is found, remove it. Do not attempt this is in a conscious or semi-conscious patient as they will either bite your finger off or vomit.

Breathing
- If the patient is not breathing you need to give expired air resuscitation, in other words you need to breath air into their lungs.
- Pinch the patient's nose closed
- Place your mouth, open, fully over the patient's mouth, making as good a seal as possible.
- Exhale into the patient's mouth hard enough to cause the patient's chest to rise and fall.
- If the patient's chest fails to rise you need to adjust the position of the airway.
- The 16% of oxygen in your expired air is adequate to sustain life.
- Initially you need to give two full slow breaths.
- If the patient is found to have a pulse, in the next step continue breathing for the patient once every five seconds, checking for a pulse after every ten breaths.
- If the patient begins breathing on his own you can turn him/her into the recovery position.

Circulation
After giving the two breaths as above you now need to give external cardiac compression.
- Kneel next to the patient's chest
- Measure two finger breadths above the notch where the ribs meet the lower end of the breast bone.
- Place the heel of your left hand just above your two fingers in the centre of the breast bone
- Place the heel of your right hand on your left hand
- Straighten your elbows

- Place your shoulders perpendicularly above the patient's breast bone
- Compress the breast bone 4 to 5cm to a rhythm of 'one, two, three . . .'
- Give fifteen compressions

Continue giving cycles of two breaths and fifteen compressions checking for a pulse after every five cycles. The aim of CPR is to keep the patient alive until more sophisticated help arrives in the form of paramedics or a doctor with the necessary equipment. Make sure that you and your buddy are trained in CPR. It could mean the difference between life and death.

TRAVELLING MEDICINE

Many doctors decline to issue drugs, particularly antibiotics, to people who want them 'just in case'; but a diving holiday can be ruined by an otherwise trivial ear or sinus infection, especially in a remote area or on a live-aboard boat where the nearest doctor or pharmacy is a long and difficult journey away.

Many travelling divers therefore carry with them medical kits that could lead the uninitiated to think they were hypochondriacs! Nasal sprays, eardrops, antihistamine creams, anti-diarrhoea medicines, antibiotics, sea-sickness remedies ... Forearmed, such divers can take immediate action as soon as they realize something is wrong. At the very least, this may minimize their loss of diving time.

Remember that most decongestants and sea-sickness remedies can make you drowsy and therefore should not be taken before diving.

DIVING DISEASES AND ILLNESS

Acute Decompression Illness

Acute decompression illness means any illness arising out of the decompression of a diver, in other words, by the diver moving from an area of high ambient pressure to an area of low pressure. It is divided into two groups:
- Decompression Sickness
- Barotrauma with Arterial Gas Embolism

It is not important for the diver or first aider to differentiate between the two conditions because both are serious and both require the same emergency treatment. The important thing is to recognise Acute Decompression Illness and to initiate emergency treatment. For reasons of recognition and completeness a brief discussion on each condition follows:

Decompression Sickness

Decompression sickness or 'the bends' arises following inadequate decompression by the diver. Exposure to higher ambient pressure underwater causes nitrogen to dissolve in increasing amounts in the body tissues. If this pressure is released gradually during correct and adequate decompression procedures the nitrogen escapes naturally into the blood and is exhaled through the lungs. If this release of pressure is too rapid the nitrogen cannot escape quickly enough and physical nitrogen bubbles form in the tissues.

The symptoms and signs of the disease are related to the tissues in which these bubbles form and the disease is described by the tissues affected, e.g. joint bend.

Symptoms and signs of decompression sickness include:
- Nausea and vomiting
- Dizziness
- Malaise
- Weakness
- Joint pains
- Paralysis
- Numbness
- Itching of skin
- Incontinence

Barotrauma with Arterial Gas Embolism

Barotrauma refers to the damage that occurs when the tissue surrounding a gaseous space is injured followed a change in the volume or air in that space. An arterial gas embolism refers to a gas bubble that moves in a blood vessel usually leading to obstruction of that blood vessel or a vessel further downstream.

Barotrauma can therefore occur to any tissue that surrounds a gas filled space, most commonly the:
- Ears • middle ear squeeze • burst/ear drum
- Sinuses • sinus squeeze • sinus pain, nose bleeds
- Lungs • lung squeeze • burst lung
- Face • mask squeeze • swollen, bloodshot eyes
- Teeth • tooth squeeze • toothache

Burst lung is the most serious of these and can result in arterial gas embolism. It occurs following a rapid ascent during which the diver does not exhale adequately. The rising pressure of expanding air in the lungs bursts the delicate alveoli of lung sacs and forces air into the blood vessels that carry blood back to the heart and ultimately the brain. In the brain these bubbles of air block blood vessels and obstruct the supply of blood and oxygen to the brain, resulting in brain damage.

The symptoms and signs of lung barotrauma and arterial gas embolism include:
Shortness of breath, chest pain and unconsciousness

Treatment of Acute Decompression Illness
- ABC's and CPR as necessary
- Position the patient in the recovery position with no tilt or raising of the legs
- Administer 100% Oxygen by mask (or demand valve)
- Keep the patient warm
- Remove to the nearest hospital as soon a possible
- The hospital or emergency services will arrange the recompression treatment required

Carbon Dioxide or Monoxide Poisoning Carbon dioxide poisoning can occur as a result of skip breathing

ROUGH AND READY NONSPECIALIST TESTS FOR THE BENDS

A Does the diver know:
who he or she is?
where he or she is?
what the time is?

B Can the diver see and count the number of fingers you hold up?
Place your hand 50cm (20in) in front of the diver's face and ask him/her to follow your hand with his/her eyes as you move it from side to side and up and down. Be sure that both eyes follow in each direction, and look out for any rapid oscillation or jerky movements of the eyeballs.

C Ask the diver to smile, and check that both sides of the face bear the same expression. Run the back of a finger across each side of the diver's forehead, cheeks and chin, and confirm that the diver feels it.

D Check that the diver can hear you whisper when his/her eyes are closed.

E Ask the diver to shrug his/her shoulders. Both sides should move equally.

F Ask the diver to swallow. Check the Adam's apple moves up and down.

G Ask the diver to stick out the tongue at the centre of the mouth — deviation to either side indicates a problem.

H Check there is equal muscle strength on both sides of the body. You do this by pulling/pushing each of the diver's arms and legs away from and back towards the body, asking him/her to resist you.

I Run your finger lightly across the diver's shoulders, down the back, across the chest and abdomen, and along the arms and legs, both upper and lower and inside and out, and check the diver can feel this all the time.

J On firm ground (not on a boat) check the diver can walk in a straight line and, with eyes closed, stand upright with his/her feet together and arms outstretched.

If the results of any of these checks do not appear normal, the diver may be suffering from the bends, so take appropriate action (see previous page).

(diver holds his breath on SCUBA); heavy exercise on SCUBA or malfunctioning rebreather systems.Carbon monoxide poisoning occurs as a result of: exhaust gases being pumped into cylinders; hookah systems; air intake too close to exhaust fumes. Symptoms and signs would be: Blue colour of the skin; shortness of breath; loss of consciousness.
Treatment: Safety, ABC's as necessary; CPR if required;100% oxygen through a mask or demand valve; remove to nearest hospital

Head Injury All head injuries should be regarded as potentially serious.
Treatment: The diver should come to the surface, and wound should be disinfected, and there should be no more diving until a doctor has been consulted. If the diver is unconscious, of course the emergency services should be contacted; if breathing and/or pulse has stopped, CPR (page 168) should be administered. If the diver is breathing and has a pulse, check for bleeding and other injuries and treat for shock; if wounds permit, put sufferer into recovery position and administer 100% oxygen (if possible). Keep him or her warm and comfortable, and monitor pulse and respiration constantly. **DO NOT** administer fluids to unconscious or semi-conscious divers.

Hyperthermia (increased body temperature) A rise in body temperature results form a combination of overheating, normally due to exercise, and inadequate fluid intake. The diver will progress through heat exhaustion to heat stroke with eventual collapse. Heat stroke is an emergency and if the diver is not cooled and rehydrated he will die.
Treatment: Remove the diver from the hot environment and remove all clothes. Sponge with a damp cloth and fan either manually or with an electric fan. Conscious divers can be given oral fluids. If unconscious, place the patient in the recovery position and monitor the ABC's. Always seek advanced medical help.

Hypothermia Normal internal body temperature is just under 37°C (98.4°F). If for any reason it is pushed much below this – usually, in diving, through inadequate protective clothing – progressively more serious symptoms may occur, with death as the ultimate endpoint. A drop of 1C° (2F°) leads to shivering and discomfort. A 2C° (3°F) drop induces the body's self-heating mechanisms to react: blood flow to the peripheries is reduced and shivering becomes extreme. A 3C° (5°F) drop leads to amnesia, confusion, disorientation, heartbeat and breathing irregularities, and possibly rigor.
Treatment: Take the sufferer to sheltered warmth or otherwise prevent further heat-loss: use an exposure bag, surround the diver with buddies' bodies, and cover the diver's head and neck with a woolly hat, warm towels or anything else suitable. In sheltered warmth, re-dress the diver in warm, dry clothing and then put him/her in an exposure bag; in the open the diver is best left in existing garments. If the diver is conscious and coherent, a warm shower or bath and a warm, sweet drink should be enough; otherwise call the emergency services and meanwhile treat for shock, while deploying the other warming measures noted.

Near Drowning Near drowning refers to a situation where the diver has inhaled some water. He or she may be conscious or unconscious. Water in the lungs interferes with the normal transport of oxygen from the lungs into the blood.
Treatment: Remove the diver from the water and check the ABC's. Depending on your findings commence EAR or CPR where appropriate. If possible, administer oxygen by mask or demand valve. All near drowning victims may later develop secondary drowning, a condition where fluid oozes into the lungs causing the diver to drown in his own secretions, therefore all near drowning victims should be observed for 24 hours in a hospital.

Nitrogen Narcosis The air we breathe is about 80% nitrogen; breathing the standard mixture under compression, as divers do, can lead to symptoms very much like those of drunkenness - the condition is popularly called 'rapture of the deep'. Some divers experience nitrogen narcosis at depths of 30-40m (100-130ft). Up to a depth of about 60m (200ft) - that is, beyond the legal maximum depth for sport diving in both the UK and USA - the symptoms need not (but may) be serious; beyond about 80m (260ft) the diver may become unconscious. The onset of symptoms can be sudden and unheralded. The condition itself is not actually harmful: dangers arise through secondary effects, notably the diver doing something foolish.
Treatment: The sole treatment required is to return immediately to a shallower depth.

Shock Shock refers not to the emotional trauma of a frightening experience but to a physiological state in the body resulting from poor blood and oxygen delivery to the tissues. As a result of oxygen and blood deprivation the tissues cannot perform their functions. There are many causes of shock, the most common being the loss of blood.
Treatment: Treatment is directed as restoring blood and oxygen delivery to the tissues, therefore maintain the ABC's and administer 100% oxygen. Control all external bleeding by direct pressure, pressure on pressure points and elevation of the affected limb. Tourniquet should only be used as a last resort and only then on the arms and legs. Conscious victims should be laid on their backs with their legs raised and head to one side. Unconscious, shocked victims should be placed on their left side in the recovery position.

GENERAL MARINE RELATED AILMENTS
Apart from the specific diving related illnesses, the commonest divers' ailments include sunburn, coral cuts, fire-coral stings, swimmers' ear, sea sickness and various biting insects.

Cuts and Abrasions
Divers should wear appropriate abrasive protection for the environment. Hands, knees, elbows and feet are the commonest areas affected. The danger with abrasions is that they become infected so all wounds should be thoroughly rinsed with water and an antiseptic as soon as possible. Infection may progress to a stage where antibiotics are necessary. Spreading inflamed areas should prompt the diver to seek medical advice.

Swimmer's Ear
Swimmer's ear is an infection of the external ear canal resulting from constantly wet ears. The infection is often a combination of a fungal and bacterial one. To prevent this condition, always dry the ears thoroughly after diving and, if you are susceptible to the condition, insert drops after diving as follows:

- 5% acetic acid in isopropyl alcohol *or*
- aluminium acetate/acetic acid solution

Once infected, the best possible treatment is to stop diving or swimming for a few days and apply ear drops.

Sea or Motion Sickness
Motion sickness can be an annoying complication on a diving holiday involving boat dives. If you are susceptible to motion sickness, get medical advice prior to boarding the boat. A cautionary note must be made that the antihistamine in some preventative drugs may make you drowsy and impair your ability to think while diving.

Biting Insects
Some areas are notorious for biting insects. Take a good insect repellent and some antihistamine cream to relieve the effects.

Sunburn
Take precautions against sunburn and use high protection factor creams.

Tropical diseases
Visit the doctor before your trip and make sure you have the appropriate vaccinations for the specific countries you are visiting.

Fish that Bite
- **Barracuda**
  Barracuda are usually seen in large safe shoals of several hundred fish, each up to 80cm (30in) long. Lone individuals about twice this size have attacked divers, usually in turbid or murky shallow water, where sunlight flashing on a knife blade, camera lens or jewellery has confused the fish into thinking they are attacking their normal prey, such as sardines.
  Treatment: Thoroughly clean the wounds and use antiseptic or antibiotic cream. Bad bites will also need antibiotic and anti-tetanus treatment.

- **Moray Eels**
  Probably more divers are bitten by morays than by all other sea creatures added together – usually through putting their hands into holes to collect shells or lobsters, remove anchors or hide baitfish. Often a moray refuses to let go, so, unless you can persuade it to do so with your knife, you can make the wound worse by tearing your flesh as you pull the eel off.
  Treatment: Thorough cleaning and usually stitching. The bites always go septic, so have antibiotics and anti-tetanus available.

- **Sharks**
  Sharks rarely attack divers, but should always be treated with respect. Attacks are usually connected with speared or hooked fish, fish or

meat set up as bait, lobsters rattling when picked up, or certain types of vibration such as that produced by helicopters. The decomposition products of dead fish (even several days old) seem much more attractive to most sharks than fresh blood. The main exception is the Great White Shark, whose normal prey is sea lion or seal and which may mistake a diver for one of these. You are very unlikely to see a Great White when diving in Southeast Asian waters, but you might encounter another dangerous species, the Tiger Shark, which sometimes comes into shallow water to feed at night. Grey Reef Sharks can be territorial; they often warn of an attack by arching their backs and pointing their pectoral fins downwards. Other sharks often give warning by bumping into you first. If you are frightened, a shark will detect this from the vibrations given off by your body. Calmly back up to the reef or boat and get out of the water.

Treatment: Victims usually have severe injuries and shock. Where possible, stop the bleeding with tourniquets or pressure bandages and stabilize the sufferer with blood or plasma transfusions before transporting to hospital. Even minor wounds are likely to become infected, requiring antibiotic and antitetanus treatment.

- **Triggerfish** Large triggerfish – usually males guarding eggs in 'nests' – are particularly aggressive, and will attack divers who get too close. Their teeth are very strong, and can go

through rubber fins and draw blood through a 4mm (1/6 in) wetsuit.

Treatment: Clean the wound and treat it with antiseptic cream.

Venomous Sea Creatures

Many venomous sea creatures are bottom-dwellers, hiding among coral or resting on or burrowing into sand. If you need to move along the sea bottom, do so in a shuffle, so that you push such creatures out of the way and minimize your risk of stepping directly onto sharp venomous spines, many of which can pierce rubber fins. Antivenins require specialist medical supervision, do not work for all species and need refrigerated storage, so they are rarely available when required. Most of the venoms are high-molecular-weight proteins that break down under heat. Apply a broad ligature between the limb and the body — remember to release it every 15 minutes. Immerse the limb in hot water (e.g., the cooling water from an outboard motor, if no other supply is available) at 50°C (120°F) for 2 hours, until the pain stops. Several injections around the wound of local anaesthetic (e.g., procaine hydrochloride), if available, will ease the pain. Younger or weaker victims may need CPR (page 168). Remember that venoms may still be active in fish that have been dead for 48 hours.

- **Cone Shells** Live cone shells should never be handledwitout gloves: the animal has a mobil tube-likeorgan that shoots a poison dart. The resultis initial numbness followed by local muscular paralysis, which may extend to respiratory paralysis and heart failure. *You should not be collecting shells anyway!*
  Treatment: Apply a broad ligature between the wound and the body. CPR may be necessary.
- **Crown-of-Thorns Starfish** The Crown-of Thorns Starfish has spines that can pierce gloves and break off under the skin, causing pain and sometimes nausea lasting several days.
  Treatment: The hot-water treatment (30min) helps the pain. Septic wounds require antibotics.
- **Fire Coral** Fire corals (*Millepora* spp) are not true corals but members of the class Hydrozoa – i.e., they are more closely related to the stinging hydroids. Many people react violently from the slightest brush with them, and the resulting blisters may be 15cm (6in) across.
  Treatment: As for stinging hydroids .
- **Jellyfish** Most jellyfish sting, but few are dangerous. As a general rule, those with the longest tentacles tend to have the most painful stings. The Box Jellyfish or Sea Wasp (*Chironex fleckeri*) of Northern Australia is the most venomous creature known, having caused twice as many fatalities in those waters as have sharks; it has yet to be found in Asian waters but its appearance one day cannot be precluded. Its occurrence is seasonal, and in calmer weather it invades shallow-water

beaches; it is difficult to see in murky water. It sticks to the skin by its many tentacles, causing extreme pain and leaving lasting scars. The victim often stops breathing, and young children may even die.

Treatment: Whenever the conditions are favourable for the Box Jellyfish, wear protection such as a wetsuit, lycra bodysuit, old clothes or a leotard and tights. In the event of a sting, there is an antivenin, but it needs to be injected within three minutes. The recommended treatment is to pour acetic acid (vinegar) over animal and wounds alike and then to remove the animal with forceps or gloves. CPR (page 168) may be required.

- **Lionfish/Turkeyfish** These are slow-moving except when swallowing prey. They hang around on reefs and wrecks and pack a heavy sting in their beautiful spines.
Treatment: As for stonefish.

- **Rabbitfish** These have venomous spines in their fins, and should on no account be handled.
Treatment: Use the hot-water treatment.

- **Scorpionfish** Other scorpionfish are less camouflaged and less dangerous than the stonefish, but are common and quite dangerous enough.
Treatment: As for stonefish.

- **Sea Snakes** Sea snakes have venom 10 times more powerful than a cobra's, but luckily they are rarely aggressive and their short fangs usually cannot pierce a wetsuit.
Treatment: Apply a broad ligature between the injury and the body and wash the wound. CPR may be necessary. Antivenins are available but need skilled medical supervision.

- **Sea Urchins** The spines of sea urchins can be poisonous. Even if not, they can puncture the skin – even through gloves – and break off, leaving painful wounds that often go septic.
Treatment: For bad cases give the hot-water treatment; this also softens the spines, helping the body reject them. Soothing creams or a magnesium-sulphate compress will help reduce the pain, as will the application of wine or the flesh of papaya fruit. Septic wounds need antibiotics.

- **Stinging Hydroids** Stinging hydroids often go unnoticed on wrecks, old anchor ropes and chains until you put your hand on them, when their nematocysts are fired into your skin. The wounds are not serious but are very painful, and large blisters can be raised on sensitive skin.
Treatment: Bathe the affected part in methylated spirit or vinegar (acetic acid). Local anaesthetic may be required to ease the pain, though antihistamine cream is usually enough.

- **Stinging Plankton** You cannot see stinging plankton, and so cannot take evasive measures. If there are reports of any in the area keep as much of your body covered as possible.

Treatment: As for stinging hydroids.

- **Sting Rays** Sting rays vary from a few centimetres to several metres across. The sting consists of one or more spines on top of the tail; though these point backwards they can sting in any direction. The rays thrash out and sting when trodden on or caught. Wounds may be large and severely lacerated.
Treatment: Clean the wound and remove any spines. Give the hot-water treatment and local anaesthetic if available; follow up with antibiotics and anti-tetanus.

- **Stonefish** Stonefish are the most feared, best camouflaged and most dangerous of the scorpionfish family. The venom is contained in the spines of the dorsal fin, which is raised when the fish is agitated.
Treatment: There is usually intense pain and swelling. Clean the wound, give the hot-water treatment and follow up with antibiotic and anti-tetanus.

- **Others** Venoms occur also in soft corals, the anemones associated with Clownfish and the nudibranchs that feed on stinging hydroids; if you have sensitive skin, do not touch any of them. Electric (torpedo) rays can give a severe electric shock (200–2000 volts); the main problem here is that the victim may be knocked unconscious in the water and drown.

Cuts

Underwater cuts and scrapes – especially from coral, barnacles or sharp metal – will usually, if not cleaned out and treated quickly, go septic; absorption of the resulting poisons into the body can cause bigger problems. After every dive, clean and disinfect any wounds, no matter how small. Larger wounds will often refuse to heal unless you stay out of seawater for a couple of days. Surgeonfish have sharp fins on each side of the caudal peduncle; they use these against other fish, lashing out with a sweep of the tail, and occasionally may likewise when defending territory against a trespassing diver. These 'scalpels' are often covered in toxic mucus, so wounds should be cleaned and treated with antibiotic cream.As a preventative measure against cuts in general, the golden rule is do not touch! Learn good buoyancy control so that you can avoid touching anything unnecessarily - remember, anyway, that every area of the coral you touch will be killed.

Fish-feeding

You should definitely not feed fish: you can harm them and their ecosystem. Not only that, it is dangerous to you, too. Sharks' feeding frenzies are uncontrollable, and sharks often bite light-coloured fins. Triggerfish can come at you very fast, and groupers and moray eels have nasty teeth. Napoleon Wrasse have strong mouth suction and can bite. Even little Sergeant Majors can give your fingers or hair a nasty nip.

Allen, Gerald R. and Steene, Roger: Indo Pacific Coral Reef Field Guide, Tropical Reef Research

Allen, Gerald R. and Steene, Roger: Reef Fishes of the Indian Ocean, Western Australian Museum

Auerbach, Paul S: A Medical Guide to Hazardous Marine Life, Progressive Printing Co. Inc

Debelius, Helmut and Kuiter, Rudie: South East Asia - Tropical Fish Guide, Ikan

Debelius, Helmut: Armoured Knights of the Sea, Aquaprint Verlags GmbH

Debelius, Helmut: Indian Ocean - Tropical Fish Guide, Aquaprint Verlags GmbH

Fautin, Daphne G. and Allen, Gerlad R: A Field Guide to Anemonefishes and their host Sea Anemones, Western Australian Museum

Graham, Mark and Piprell, Collin and Gray, Dennis: National Parks of Thailand, Communications Resources (Thailand) Ltd

Gremli, Margaret S and Newman, E: Marine Life in the South China Sea, Insight Guide Underwater

Hanna, Nick and Wells, Sue: The Greenpeace book of Coral Reefs, Blandford Press

Lekagul, Boonsong and Round, Philip: A Guide to the Birds of Thailand, Saha Karn Bhaet Co. Ltd

Lieske, Edwald and Myers, Robert: Coral Reef Fishes - Indo-Pacific and Caribbean, HarperCollins

Majchacheep, Surin: Marine Animals of Thailand, Prae Pittaya Publishers

Ming, Chou Loke and Alino, Porfirio M: Underwater Guide to the South China Sea, Times Editions

Piprell, Colin and Boyd, Ashley J: Thailand's Coral Reefs, White Lotus

Piprell, Collin: Thailand: The Kingdom Beneath the Sea, Art Asia Press

Ryan, Paddy: The Snorkeller's Guide to the Coral Reef, Crawford House Press

Index